Visualizing Atrocity

CRITICAL CULTURAL COMMUNICATION

General Editors: Sarah Banet-Weiser and Kent A. Ono

Visualizing Atrocity

Arendt, Evil, and the Optics of Thoughtlessness

Valerie Hartouni

NEW YORK UNIVERSITY PRESS

New York and London

NEW YORK UNIVERSITY PRESS
New York and London
www.nyupress.org

References to Internet Websites (URLs) were accurate at the time of writing.
Neither the author nor New York University Press is responsible for URLs that
may have expired or changed since the manuscript was prepared.

Library of Congress Cataloging-in-Publication Data
Hartouni, Valerie.
Visualizing atrocity : Arendt, evil, and the optics of thoughtlessness
/ Valerie Hartouni.
p. cm. — (Critical cultural communication)
Includes bibliographical references and index.
ISBN 978-0-8147-3849-8 (cloth : acid-free paper)
ISBN 978-0-8147-6976-8 (pbk. : acid-free paper)
ISBN 978-0-8147-7183-9 (ebook)
ISBN 978-0-8147-3899-3 (ebook)
1. Arendt, Hannah, 1906–1975. Eichmann in Jerusalem.   2. Arendt, Hannah,
1906–1975—Criticism and interpretation.   3. Arendt, Hannah, 1906–1975—
Political and social views.   4. Eichmann, Adolf, 1906–1962—Trials, litigation,
etc.   5. War crime trials—Jerusalem—History—20th century.   6. Holocaust,
Jewish (1939–1945)   7. World War, 1939–1945—Atrocities Germany.   8. Genocide—Germany—History—20th century.   9. Good and evil—Political aspects.
10. Good and evil—Social aspects.   I. Title.
DD247.E5A734   2012
940.53′18092—dc23   2011051503

New York University Press books are printed on acid-free paper, and their binding
materials are chosen for strength and durability. We strive to use environmentally
responsible suppliers and materials to the greatest extent possible in publishing our
books.

Manufactured in the United States of America

c 10 9 8 7 6 5 4 3 2 1
p 10 9 8 7 6 5 4 3 2 1

Contents

Acknowledgments

At the University of California, San Diego, I am especially fortunate to share a world with a remarkable group of individuals, deeply committed to teaching and the rich pleasures of intellectual exchange. Members of this seriously eclectic community to whom I am hugely indebted for their insights and steadfast support as well as good humor include Carol Padden, Mike Cole, David Serlin, Patrick Anderson, Dan Halin, Nitin Govil, Michael Schudson, Tom Humphries, Chandra Mukerji, and especially Robert Horwitz. For nearly two decades, Robert has been a trusted friend and colleague, available to talk and willing to challenge, encourage, and, during the middle stages of this book, comment extensively on drafts I am quite sure by the nth iteration he was sick of reading. He kindly never complained.

Other friends and colleagues who read, thought about, and offered critical comments and suggestions include Chris Littleton, Wendy Brown, Donna Haraway, Peter Dimock, Etienne Pelaprat, Dan Scripture, Lucyann Carlton, and Lisa Cartwright, with whom I also shared a bus ride to Theresienstadt on a cold, rainy, late November afternoon in 2005 and a train ride to Nuremberg shortly after in heavy snowfall. It was an instructive and sobering moment, sitting in the Nuremberg courtroom listening to German high school students rehearse the history of the postwar trials and puzzle over what it meant that the country that had led the prosecution at those trials was itself at that moment wreaking havoc across the globe, flagrantly disavowing the human rights norms it helped put in place.

Judith Butler and two anonymous reviewers read the original version of the manuscript for NYU Press and together offered many detailed, valuable suggestions for sharpening arguments. Eric Zinner and Ciara McLaughlin of NYU Press along with series editors Kent Ono and Sarah Banet-Weiser were enthusiastic and gracious interlocutors: for their direction at each stage of this book's production, I extend my deepest appreciation. Financial and institutional support for portions of this project were provided by the Department of Communication, UC San Diego; Media and Gender Studies at Ruhr University, Bochum, Germany; the photo archive departments at Yad Vashem, Jerusalem, Israel, and the United States Holocaust Memorial Museum, Washington, D.C.; and Academic Senate Research Grants and sabbatical release time from UC San Diego.

Introduction

As the twentieth century draws to a close, it is difficult to avoid being overwhelmed by moral nausea. There are well-known numbers: ten million dead
in the First World War, a war fought over virtually nothing; roughly forty million in the Second World War, including the six million Jews killed in the Nazi
concentration and extermination camps; twenty million or more in the Soviet
gulag; thirty million dead as a result of the debacle of Mao's "Great Leap Forward"; plus the millions from a host of less spectacular but no less horrific
massacres. Any conception of human dignity that hinges upon the presump-
tion of the moral progress of the species has been shattered by these events.
—Dana Villa, *Politics, Philosophy, Terror*

I.

Rare is the case that the end we imagined at the beginning of a project is the
end that we find or that finds us once all is at least provisionally said and done.
It might be life or the world, each with its often unpredictable, surprising, and
sometimes shocking turns; the work or critical interventions of like-minded
(or not) scholars; it might be the unanticipated but unavoidable demands of
narratives internal to the text itself that upset the particular trajectory one
had thought one would or needed to traverse to turn a set of curiosities into
questions and questions into themes and themes into arguments whose development might then shepherd an imagined audience, ideally, through the contained world we call a book. Such has been the story with this collection of
loosely related chapters that orbit thematically around issues raised by Hannah
Arendt in her 1963 report on the Adolf Eichmann trial in Jerusalem.

A reading of Arendt's *Eichmann in Jerusalem* in the context of a graduate
seminar I co-taught some years ago led me to begin thinking about Nazi atrocity and its continuously invoked presence in popular discourse and debate.[1] I
had no intention at that time—which now turns out to be this project's particular moment of conception—of taking up Arendt or of using her oft-cited
and controversial characterization of evil as banal as a point of entry for thinking about or linking contemporary moral discourses, contemporary preoccupations with the Holocaust, and contemporary political life refigured and
disfigured domestically and abroad in the wake of 9/11. Yet Arendt's study of
Adolf Eichmann—a midlevel bureaucrat in the Gestapo's Department of Jewish Affairs who facilitated the death of millions, murdered no one, and claimed
only to have been a "transportation officer"—was both provocative and timely

in its effort to show how a world, ostensibly nested in modernity, could fracture in fundamentally irreparable ways. "The tradition is broken and the Ariadne thread is lost," Arendt wrote. "If the series of crises in which we have lived since the beginning of the [twentieth] century can teach us anything at all, it is, I think, the simple fact that there are no general standards to determine our judgments unfailingly, no general rules under which to subsume the particular cases with any degree of certainty."[2]

Arendt's study of Eichmann led me in a variety of directions but first, not surprisingly, to thinking about genocide. And of particular interest to me were the ways in which the specter of genocide—and here the dehistorized, decontextualized death world of Auschwitz tends to be treated as the sole, paradigmatic model—was invoked by skeptics of "postmodernism" to underscore the limitations *and* dangers of an indiscriminately grouped ensemble of critical practices that appear, in the view of some detractors, stylishly hostile to notions of truth, value, progress, and rationality or those features typically regarded as hallmarks of modernity.[3] By rejecting all foundationalism, or so the argument goes, the postmodern turn proffers precious few resources for confronting or countering genocide when it appears on the political landscape; and it may well foster genocide's very condition of possibility. If meaning and truth are social technologies, culturally shaped and contingent, indeed, if the distinction between what is called "fact" and "fiction" or "history" and "parable" is established and maintained (both discursively and materially) "only" through particular relations and practices of power, by what standards or principles are we then to identify, judge, or condemn (state-sanctioned) acts of genocide and those who perpetrate them?[4]

II.

These are not unreasonable questions. And over the course of the past decade they have assumed additional practical urgency as the more immediate specter of terrorism has joined genocide in ostensibly exposing the bankruptcy of a particular contemporary turn in thinking. Readers might recall that in the confused weeks following the Al Qaeda–linked assault on the World Trade Center and on the eve of fighting a newly declared war in Afghanistan, commentary appeared in the *New York Times* as well as *Time* magazine, among other prominent and popular news venues, that sought to highlight the pernicious character of ideas promoting what some referred to as "a pseudosophisticated relativism." These ideas, or so it was said, had managed to work their way into all corners of life over the course of several decades only to weaken the nation's resolve, obscure its judgment, and render it blind to its now obvious responsibility as a leading world power (and perhaps the only world power able) to use force in a benign and prudent fashion, always already for good.[5] Thus Edward Rothstein saw in the collapse of the Twin Towers—or perhaps heard better describes it— what he insists was an unmistakable "cry . . . for a transcendent ethical perspective." Rothstein elaborates:

> The rejection of universal values and ideals leave[s] little room for unqualified condemnations of a terrorist attack, particularly one against the West. . . . One can only hope that finally, as the ramifications sink in, as it becomes clear how close the attack came to undermining the political, military, and financial authority of the United States, the Western relativism of pomo [postmodernism] and the obsessive focus of poco [postcolonialism] will be widely seen as ethically perverse. Rigidly applied, they require a form of guilty passivity in the face of ruthless and unyielding opposition.[6]

In this same vein, Roger Rosenblatt offered commentary in *Time* that echoed Rothstein's sentiments; Rosenblatt similarly saw in the collapse of the Twin Towers a clarion call for moral realignment:

> One good thing could come from this horror: it could spell the end of the age of irony. For some 30 years—roughly as long as the Twin Towers were upright—the good folks in charge of America's intellectual life have insisted that nothing was to be believed in or taken seriously. Nothing was real. . . . The ironists, seeing through everything, made it difficult for anyone to see anything. The consequence of thinking that nothing is real—apart from prancing around in an air of vain stupidity—is that one will not know the difference between a joke and a menace. No more. . . . Are you looking for something to take seriously? Begin with evil. The fact before our eyes is that a group of savage zealots took the sweet and various lives of those ordinarily traveling from place to place, ordinarily starting a day of work or—extraordinarily—coming to help and rescue others. Freedom? That real enough for you? Everything we cling to in our free and sauntering country was imperiled by the terrorists.[7]

To be sure, such charges did not go unanswered. Writing in response to these accusations and other anxious declarations, also in the pages of the *New York Times*, Stanley Fish questioned whether marshaling universal absolutes— a transcendent ethical perspective however defined—was necessarily the best or most effective strategy in defense of democratic ideals, particularly since it was precisely in terms of such absolutes that our adversaries claimed to be acting. Indeed, as Arendt cautioned in the context of thinking about an altogether different moment of political crisis, "The absolute . . . spells doom to everyone when it is introduced into the political realm." And it "spells doom" for a number of reasons not least of these being that with absolutes there is no need for thought and there can be no ground for disagreement.[8] Moreover, there is the additional, obvious issue of whose absolute gets to be absolute. This has tended, historically at least, to become a matter of fire power, bloodshed, and body counts. Fish also questioned whether "postmodernism"—"a rarified form of academic talk," as he described it—while the apparent target of commentary was actually the issue. Speaking specifically to this issue in an article for the *New York Review of Books*, Joan Didion suggested that it clearly was not the issue, that critics had merely been opportunistic and seized the confused, destabilized moment "to stake new ground in old domestic wars."⁹ But on this front, Fish went further than Didion, noting that what, in his words, "seemed to be bothering people" was the idea that the "how" and "why" of 9/11, its precipitating conditions, might not be transparent and were certainly not questions answerable in the utterly reductive manner adopted by the administration and in most cases early on simply parroted by the press. These were not just "evildoers," and this was not just a matter of a "freedom loving country" being set upon by "savage zealots." Answering the question of how or why, he urged, required an understanding of a complicated history, logic, and set of motives; and acquiring such understanding was not, in turn, about endorsing or condoning the attack. This latter point may seem obvious, but it required repeated restatement as the field of public discourse constricted. Fish explains:

> How many times have we heard these new mantras: "We have seen the face of evil"; "these are irrational madmen"; "we are at war with international terrorism." Each is at once inaccurate and unhelpful. We have not seen the face of evil; we have seen the face of an enemy who comes at us with a full roster of grievances, goals, and strategies. If we reduce the enemy to "evil," we conjure up a shape-shifting demon, a wild-card moral anarchist beyond our comprehension and therefore beyond the reach of any counter-strategies. . . . The same reduction occurs when we imagine the enemy as "irrational." . . . The better course is to think of these men as bearers of a rationality we reject because its goal is our destruction. If we take the trouble to understand that rationality, we might have a better chance of figuring out what its adherents will do next and preventing it. . . . Is this the end of relativism? . . . [I]f by relativism one means the practice of putting yourself in your adversaries' shoes, not in order to wear them as your own but in order to have some understanding (far short of approval) of why someone else might want to wear them, then relativism will not and should not end, because it is simply another name for serious thought.¹⁰

In the weeks and months following 9/11, there was little patience for drawing out the kinds of histories and connections that Fish and a host of other public intellectuals were insisting might, if nothing else, slow the drumbeat long enough to break the spell of fear and martial inevitability and thereby create an opening for reflection and debate. But a sense of emergency worked against both, indeed rendered the call for either reflection or debate a sign of weakness and disloyalty. An otherwise alarmed public was encouraged in the impulse to confuse righteous anger with moral clarity and moral clarity with a reawakened sense of unity, purpose, and national ardor. Former secretary of education under Ronald Reagan, William Bennett, saw in this reawakening "all that is instinctually grand about the American character"— a goodness that defeated Hitler and was matched by none, a "new realism" that marked the end of decades of guilty passivity.[11] It was good against evil, indeed, us against them. But as the months advanced and rumor of a coming war now with Iraq entered the news cycle with some regularity, the much celebrated "new realism," discursively linked to a rediscovered sense of moral purpose, anchored no less to a midcentury struggle against tyranny; this new realism displayed a chilling disregard for the reality, the worldly conditions, that had initially called it forth. But for being part of a larger ideologically driven strategy, what, after all, did Iraq have to do with the attack of 9/11?

That the answer to this question was treated for the most part as a public relations problem is something former members of the Bush White House have since confirmed.[12] But the sense in which it mattered hardly at all at the time is underscored by a now oft-cited account the journalist Ron Suskind gives of a conversation he had with an unnamed member of the Bush administration— widely believed to have been Karl Rove—in summer 2002. In this conversation, it was spelled out for Suskind precisely what the prerogatives of power were with respect to the real in the new world order that had been ushered in with the collapse of the Twin Towers. Suskind elaborates:

> After I had written an article in *Esquire* that the White House didn't like . . . I had a meeting with a senior advisor to Bush. He expressed the White House's displeasure, and then told me something that at the time I didn't fully comprehend. . . . The aide said that guys like me were "in what we call the reality-based community," which he defined as people who "believe that solutions emerge from your judicious study of discernable reality." I nodded and murmured something about enlightenment principles and empiricism. He cut me off. "That's not the way the world really works anymore," he continued. "We're an empire now, and when we act, we create our own reality. And while you're studying that reality—judiciously, as you will—we'll act again, creating other, new realities, which you can study too, and that's how things will sort out. We're history's actors . . . and you, all of you, will be left to just study what we do."[13]

What are we to make of these claims, the cynical dismissal of enlightenment principles and empiricism that after all form the basis of the Constitution and democratic political formation this senior advisor had sworn to protect? Moreover, how are we to understand the suggestion that reality is just a matter of what the powerful make of it and say it will be? And, finally, what happened to the "transcendent ethical perspective" that was supposed to have anchored this new post-9/11 world in which good and evil were unambiguously clear; indeed, what do "good" and "evil" mean in a context in which, apparently, not merely "truth," but reality itself are regarded as matters of manufacture?

Ironically, or perhaps not, those familiar with Thucydides' account of the Peloponnesian War may hear in these comments resonances of claims repeatedly put forward by the Athenians as they subdued friend and enemy alike through subjection and slaughter in pursuit of empire. Insisting that traditional forms of justification and sanction were no longer necessary or relevant—being equal to none, Athenians were answerable to none—Athens proceeded without discursive or material restraint, appropriating what of the world and its inhabitants suited its sometimes capricious needs and interests while regarding its needs and interests as the sole measure of order and meaning: "right, as the world goes, is only a question between equals in power, while the strong do what they can and the weak suffer what they must."[14] We know how this particular story ends: "the whole Hellenic world convulsed" into civil war, and Athens eventually came to ruin. But more significant still is what happened along the way to precipitate this end: accompanying death in every shape was the collapse of a culture of discourse, of established understandings, shared language, and structures of argument that enabled coexistence even among adversaries. And in this context, according to Thucydides, "words had to change their meaning and take that which was now given them."[15] What followed was a kind of chaos, for as conventional meaning was destabilized so too were the shared forms and practices of life such meaning made possible. "When the language in which the world is constituted falls apart, it becomes impossible, as Thucydides shows us, not only to act rationally within it but to make satisfactory sense of it."[16]

Suskind's conversation with a senior Bush advisor on the eve of what turns out to have been a carefully orchestrated preemptive strike in the Middle East conveys certainly the conceit of power: as we represent the world, so it will be; "We're an empire now and we create our own reality." As political theorist Sheldon Wolin observes, "It would be difficult to find a more faithful representation of the totalitarian credo that true politics is essentially a matter of 'will,' of a determination to master the uses of power and to deploy them to reconstitute reality."[17] We know now, nearly a decade later, that this particular "creation" of reality entailed an elaborate campaign of misinformation and deception on behalf of an ideologically driven vision that was as much about changing structures of authority and governance in the United States as it was about exporting freedom to Iraq.[18] From this campaign, the world and country continue to convulse. But more damaging still is the problem that persists of being unable to clearly discern where precisely the fictions begin and end or what of the real owes itself to the lie: this erodes and is designed to erode a sense of bearing and a basis for taking one's bearing.[19] Perhaps not surprisingly, these challenges return us to Arendt and an observation she proffered regarding the nature of what she called "the modern lie" in the context of an early effort to make sense of totalitarian techniques and their lasting legacy:

> If Western philosophy has maintained that reality is truth—for this is of course the ontological basis of the *aequatio rei et intellectus*—than totalitarianism has concluded from this that we can fabricate truth insofar as we can fabricate reality; that we do not have to wait until reality unveils itself and shows us its true face, but can bring into being a reality whose structures will be known to us from the beginning because the whole thing is our product. In other words, it is the underlying conviction of any totalitarian transformation of ideology into reality that it will become true whether it is true or not. Because of this totalitarian relationship to reality, the very concept of truth has lost its meaning. The lies of totalitarian movements, invented for the moment, as well as the forgeries committed by totalitarian regimes, are secondary to this fundamental attitude that excludes the very distinction between truth and falsehood. It is for this end, that is, for the consistency of a lying world order, rather than for the sake of power . . . that totalitarianism requires total domination and global rule and is prepared to commit crimes which are unprecedented.[20]

III.

If terrorism is a recent example invoked to demonstrate what a lack of fidelity to conventional notions of truth, value, progress, and rationality may foster, genocide remains the more commonly cited practice that challenges the postmodern turn in thinking: genocide demands an unambiguous response critics maintain cannot be given if the status of Truth, values, facts, and rationality is in doubt. If conventional knowledge-producing practices are discredited; if there is no universal or universally recognized ground for value;[21] if there is no domain of meaning, judgment, or law that escapes indeterminancy, by what standards or principles are we to identify, judge, or condemn acts of genocide and those who perpetrate them? These are important questions as I noted earlier, but we might ask as well or instead what standards or principles have been invoked to judge and condemn or thwart such acts since World War II? And we find that even with a world organized by a particular regime of truth in which conventional notions of objectivity, evidence, value, progress, and rationality are constitutive elements (or effects), genocide's reappearance has hardly been thwarted, indeed, has hardly been recognized as such except perhaps after the fact.

In a comprehensive study, aptly titled *A Problem from Hell*, Samantha Power notes that there have been at least four major genocides since World War II— Pol Pot in Cambodia, Saddam Hussein in northern Iraq, the Hutus' mass murder of Tutsi in Rwanda, and Serbian efforts to "ethnically cleanse" Bosnia. And were Power writing today, one imagines that she would surely add the continuing debacle in Darfur, with its displaced (2.5 million as of this writing) and its dead (200,000), to this list. These genocides have for the most part gone unacknowledged and/or unchallenged as they unfolded by both the international community and the United States, even while, in Power's words, policy makers "knew a great deal about the crimes being perpetuated . . . [and had] countless opportunities to mitigate and prevent slaughter."[22] What was happening on the ground in each of these regions, in other words, was not in question, nor were any of the many facts of each matter. Indeed, the "not on our watch" principles and convictions of the first world were recited repeatedly by leaders and their representatives in other places and contexts along with the vow, true to the spirit of Nuremberg, to "never again" assume a passive, disinterested posture when confronted with "the terrible crime of genocide." And yet, while ignoring, dismissing, or explaining away the seriousness of the slaughter, first world members of the international community often went to great lengths to avoid (and prevent others from) invoking the UN Convention (on the Prevention and Punishment of the Crime of Genocide). The critical question was not whether lethal violence was being employed (in each case successfully) to decimate marked populations; the critical question for policy makers was what significance to attach to it. And in each instance, determinations were shaped by particular geopolitical interests and worked to shore up the strategic imperative to look away.[23] In the context of contemporary mass murders, in other words, fidelity to conventional notions of truth, value, progress, and rationality saved no one.

What, then, of the dense dissonance that emerges when real-time atrocities across the globe are set alongside contemporary preoccupations with memorializing so as never to forget the mass murder of European Jewry? What of ongoing efforts to institutionalize the "lessons" of that genocide? Do contemporary "real-time" atrocities constitute genocide but for the international implications (and inconveniences) of addressing them as such? I mentioned the study of Samantha Power earlier. Consider the disconnect Power notes at a State Department press conference detailing the status of U.S. personnel and nationals in Rwanda. At this press conference, Acting Assistant Secretary for African Affairs Prudence Bushnell announced the department's decision to temporarily close the embassy amid mounting violence that she described, despite reports from UN Peacekeepers, as yet another ethnic "flare-up." After Bushnell left the podium, Power writes,

Michael McCurry, the [State] department spokesman, took her place and criticized foreign governments for preventing the screening of the Steven Spielberg film *Schindler's List*. "This film movingly portrays . . . the twentieth century's most horrible catastrophe," McCurry said. "And it shows that even in the midst of genocide, one individual can make a difference." McCurry urged that the film be shown worldwide. "The most effective way to avoid the recurrence of genocidal tragedy," he declared, "is to ensure that past acts of genocide are never forgotten." No one made any connection between Bushnell's remarks and McCurry's. Neither journalists nor officials in the United States were focused on the Tutsi.[24]

Power casts an especially critical eye at the apparent inconsistencies that pervade U.S. foreign policy with respect to genocide—on the one hand, the rhetorical resolve, domestically, of decision makers across administrations who have rarely seemed reticent to leverage the nation's international position as moral arbiter in matters of human rights and their abuse; and on the other, their practical indifference to "gross ethical barbarities" being executed in some (culturally and geographically remote) region elsewhere. Still, Power concludes that what appears to be a glaring failure to mobilize in a timely manner on behalf of marked populations represents instead the successful pursuit of a twofold objective by leaders from both parties in the United States and the foreign policy establishment more generally. Policy makers in the executive branch (with the passive support of Congress, she notes) have sought to avoid becoming entangled in conflicts perceived to be outside American interests even as they have also sought to avoid appearing morally indifferent to such conflicts. And, as Power sees it, they have "by and large . . . achieved both aims. In order to contain the political fallout, U.S. officials overemphasized the ambiguity of the facts. They played up the likely futility, perversity, and jeopardy of any proposed intervention. They steadfastly avoided use of the word 'genocide,' which they believed carried with it a legal and moral (and thus political) imperative to act. And they took solace in the normal operations of the foreign policy bureaucracy, which permitted an illusion of continual deliberation, complex activity, and intense concern."[25]

I begin with Power's general formulation of the dissonance that emerges when we situate the repetitive injunctions, not to mention fervency, of contemporary holocaust discourse alongside the indifference and (con)strained response of the international community to what have been equally disastrous human catastrophes as they've unfolded since World War II. But moving on now from Power's work and by way of expanding the frame, other thinkers have similarly sought to account for and reframe modern genocide in ways that might demystify the logic of the practice and allow forms of address that include but also go beyond what have become the curiously reassuring polemics and now comfortable impediments of the paradigm offered up by Nazism. And, to be clear, by "reassuring" and "comfortable," I mean only to underscore the routine ways in which Nazi atrocity is treated as both a benchmark and an aberration, an event that is both inside and outside history; an event that marks modernity's culmination or definitive failure; an event that must be understood even while it will forever escape understanding and defy commonplace forms of representation. In each instance, the discursive paths are well worn—but more on this shortly.

Notable among such efforts are the first two volumes of Mark Levine's projected four-volume investigation, *Genocide in the Age of the Nation State*.[26] As the title of this project suggests, Levine rejects the notion that genocide can be construed narrowly as a distinctly twentieth-century aberration, the apogee of particular national imperatives, totalitarian tendencies, or cultural forces peculiar to Germany and possibly the former Soviet Union. He argues, instead, for a view that situates "exterminatory violence" in a broad conceptual and historical frame as part and parcel of modernizing processes that are more or less precipitated by "a handful of European maritime states" during the late fifteenth century;[27] that incubate over the course of several hundred years with the colonial expansion of "the West" and the gradual emergence of an international system of rules and conventions as well as global markets; and that culminate in the (geographically, politically, and economically) uneven (re)organization and transformation of territory, populations, policies, and practices into what comes to be known as the "nation-state."[28] And it is, in Levine's view, the consolidation and imperial advance of this modern state formation, for all its liberal and liberating constitutional and democratic features (and perhaps because of these features), that brings with it as a constituent component the universal potential for genocide. To be clear: Levine's point is *not* that the nation-state per se is inherently genocidal but rather that its full emergence by the late nineteenth century fundamentally disrupts the structure and operation of older, ethnically heterogeneous, culturally diverse, politically decentralized world empires—Romanov Russia, Ottoman Turkey, Habsburg Austria-Hungary, and Qing (Manchu) China. In order to survive within an emergent global system of nation-states and remain economically, politically, and militarily competitive, even if only marginally so, these waning empires are driven "towards some form of national, territorially grounded coherence."[29] And at least one of the means some adopt to achieve this coherence is ethnic consolidation through ethnic cleansing, or what is also called "genocide":

> Align late Habsburg and Romanov ethnic policies with the increasingly catastrophic Chinese and Ottoman behavior towards their subject peoples, in this period [1870–1914], and one cannot but come to the conclusion that what each

was doing was not simply responding to a series of unrelated internal exigencies but a single, relentless wave of *external* pressure which was threatening to engulf them all. . . . What was happening, of course, was a fundamental and apparently irreversible geo-political and economic shift in favor of the West. . . . The Western-led global political economy had arrived. . . . It is not simply a question of whether the new empires were perpetrators of genocidal action against the native peoples they directly encountered. There is also the question of the degree to which their political, economic as well as cultural penetration of the residual empires—puncturing in the process the latter's sense of a discrete universal self-sufficiency, and forcing them into an entirely unequal interaction with the West—was bound to have indirect yet serious repercussions on these empires' own relationships with their subject peoples.[30]

Levine provides an expanded historical and geopolitical framework for understanding the conditions that conditioned genocide's emergence and that function as its contemporary wellspring. In his view, genocide is inextricably linked to modern state formations, specifically, Western liberal capitalism and its particular forms of appropriating and regulating populations, resources, wealth, and power domestically and across the second and third worlds; of creating, distributing, and legitimizing concentrations of wealth and suffering; of generating and naturalizing new regimes of truth; of fostering, perpetuating, destabilizing, or undermining regimes abroad that guarantee, obstruct, or reject Western global dominance.[31] And to the extent that he situates and accounts for genocide in a considerably expanded geopolitical and historical frame, he proffers a significant shift in perspective. Power advances a view, both conventional and widely shared, that regards genocide as something that happens in socially, culturally, politically, and fiscally distinct worlds, an object "out there" or for the most part outside the purview of the interests and actions of first world nations—and thus something to which the first world may or may not opt to react or, even less likely, respond. Levine by contrast insists that there is no outside to these interests, and actions and genocide or at least its condition of possibility is precisely one of their effects.[32]

> Whether the verdict is one of distorted ideological (read usually communist or "totalitarian") formation, ethnic conflict, the vestiges of some benighted or god-forsaken strata of pre-modernity, the toxicity is nearly always taken to be a product of mad, bad, or sad polities, societies, structures or predispositions outside or entirely beyond the universe of the ordered, civilized, legally constituted, democratically elected West. . . . The possibility that the emergence of an international political-economic system dominated, controlled and regulated by the West might be intrinsic to the causation, persistence, and prevalence of genocide in the modern world . . . remains an entirely marginal notion.[33]

In its insistence, therefore, that the global economic interdependence of and competition between politically sovereign states has and can have often devastating implications for populations that are or are made marginal, indeed superfluous, to use Arendt's language, by the shifting needs and effects of capital, Levine's analysis compels us to think from and beyond the paradigmatic claims of Auschwitz to reassess what it is we think we know about genocide. His analysis, moreover, throws into sharp relief the ways in which conventional accounts of genocide draw too narrow an analytic frame. Such accounts obscure precisely the broader histories of economic exchange, interest, and interdependencies that not only contribute to genocide's possibility, but make it make a decidedly different kind of sense—a component of global arrangements and the flow of capital, the regulation of goods, and the distribution of suffering, differentially borne among those "who have arrived late at the partition of the world," rather than a regrettable spectacle that happens within discrete borders elsewhere, precipitated by ethnic or tribal rivalries, class conflict or religious wars, deeply rooted "exterminatory" impulses or politically expedient ideologies that gain social momentum and institutional sanction.

Similarly challenged by Levine's analysis are conventional notions of state sovereignty and the right of noninterference. Both have been central in explaining the reluctance of formal bodies to interfere in the domestic operations of states suspected of or known to be pursuing or sanctioning genocidal activities. Indeed, even at Nuremberg, the war crimes trials that followed Allied victory in Europe, the reach of the atrocity charge was largely restricted to acts committed against civilian populations *after* the outbreak of war in 1939, in effect placing prewar atrocities against the Jews and other marked populations within Germany beyond the Tribunal's jurisdiction. As Supreme Court justice and chief prosecutor at Nuremberg, Robert Jackson, explained, "We do not consider that the acts of a government against its own citizens warrant our interference."[34] However, through the analytic lens that Levine provides in which geopolitical interdependence is the given, what counts as interference and noninterference is hardly self-evident (and perhaps utterly irrelevant when considered in light of the claims of Suskind's unidentified White House official). In either case, understanding and rethinking the impact and implications of the ways in which this distinction is drawn, policed, and protected is imperative, a critical if preliminary first step in demystifying and addressing the institutionalized mechanisms and the all too familiar structural disparities and displacements that allow atrocity to emerge and, at the same time, remain utterly unrecognizable as such.[35]

IV.

If the notion that genocide happens "elsewhere," outside the frame of first world interests, activities, and direct responsibilities, in socially, culturally, politically, and fiscally distinct worlds; if this notion for the most part dominates how genocide's appearance in the late twentieth century has been configured and addressed, an oddly similar mode of construction and address can be discerned in contemporary and especially popular representations of World War II's Holocaust. These representations work principally from the assumption of radical discontinuity and historical rupture. And perhaps the most obvious example in this genre of writing are the densely structured discursive regimes that produce and police the Holocaust as a uniquely evil and unknowable event, otherworldly and without parallel in history. As such, and in some essential sense, it is beyond the limits and for some the possibility of representation. As David Caroll formulates it, the Shoah exists as "the limit case of knowledge and feeling, in terms of which all . . . systems of belief and thought, all forms of literary and artistic expression, seem irrelevant or even criminal";[36] and as Terrence Des Pres has instructed on behalf of the disciplinary formation that is Holocaust studies, "The Holocaust shall be represented, in its totality, as a unique event, as a special case, and kingdom of its own, above or below or apart from history. . . . The Holocaust shall be approached as a solemn or even sacred event, with a seriousness admitting no response that might obscure its enormity or dishonor its dead."[37]

Atrocity images from the period, especially the now iconic images of the liberation of the concentration camps, contribute to and reinforce viscerally what these scholars assert as a matter of fact—that the Holocaust is at the limit of knowledge and feeling. And this sense of being transported to some strange other land of inhumanity works in turn to obscure the larger historical frames and continuities that need to be brought to bear to explain the lethal conjunction of processes and practices that together allowed genocide to emerge as more than an abstract possibility; indeed, that directly facilitated the reorganization of bodies of law around laws of the body and worked to produce systematic mass murder as a highly rationalized and medicalized vehicle for reconfiguring social worlds and political territories. For example, however critical to understanding the formative conditions of genocide in Europe, rarely are the colonial projects of European states in Africa and Asia and the racial-imperial hierarchies that developed through them directly linked to the genocide of the Jews in Europe;[38] rarely are the continental imperialism and tribal nationalism of central and eastern European states regarded as an iteration of these colonial projects; and rarely do we encounter the images from the liberation of the concentration camps, or images from Poland's ghettos, or images from army records along with the now more widely published "photographic souvenirs" of *Wehrmacht* veterans and think, "this is what the building of an empire entails; this is what imperialism looks like."[39]

A wide-angle historical lens permits the highlighting of critical links and continuities, and these in turn go a significant distance in actually situating Germany's genocide and demystifying it. But no less important for understanding this genocide are the ways in which conventional regimes of knowledge production and collection principally in the domains of science, law, economics, anthropology, and demography worked together to set the stage for the mass murder of marked populations. And here too one finds a pervasive impulse in the literature to rescue these domains from a contaminating association with the program and practices of Nazism. And while this impulse takes a variety of forms, it is expressed most clearly in the insistence that these and other disciplinary arenas were colonized by a political agenda and ideology, much as Europe itself was colonized, and are thus at best aberrant expressions of methods and practices of inquiry that are otherwise disinterested, in the sense of having no binding relation to power, and value-free.

Consider, by way of example, Nazi science and medicine: both are typically bracketed as perversions of "real" science and medical practices, tainted by racially informed policies, irrationally driven by an obsession with identifying pathological alterity, and dangerously devoted to expanding an array of lethal programs aimed at expunging the racial subaltern on behalf of the health of the individual and national body.[40] Likewise, Nazi law is similarly implicated as having subverted "real" law. As the International Military Tribunal at Nuremberg presented it, Nazi law was a superficial guise, a vehicle and grand alibi, for a criminal conspiracy against the existing international and political order. Indeed, as chief prosecutor throughout the course of the secondary series of twelve trials at Nuremberg, Telford Taylor, notes, Nuremberg itself was selected as the site of the International Tribunal precisely because it represented "the physical geographical manifestation of all that was wrong with Nazi law";[41] how much more dramatic and evocative would the Allies' performance of real law appear, by contrast. And finally, still by way of example of postwar efforts to bracket knowledge-producing fields and practices under the Nazis, consider economics, demography, and statistics. Each of these fields and practices was crucial to rationalizing the regime's management, mobilization, and destruction of populations across occupied Europe. And the efficiency and expansion of each field and practice during this period was largely beholden to IBM and its custom designed and maintained punch card machine and card sorting system:[42] this machine and system allowed administrators to more easily name, distinguish, and track laboring bodies, reproductive bodies, racially marked bodies, bodies deemed genetically productive or pernicious; in short, to manage what the regime regarded as raw materials in ways that could be mobilized, disciplined, resettled, exploited, and discarded by offices and functionaries as needed.

Regarding the Holocaust as a "kingdom of its own" and the Nazi period as a period of rupture writes radical discontinuity into the record and in effect places the period under quarantine. This works most obviously to stabilize and preserve what Mario Biagioli refers to as a "symbiotic relationship" between knowledge production and "the values of modernity as expressed in the culture of Western democracy."[43] But pathologizing and quarantining the Nazi period works less obviously to obscure or, at best, render vague the continuities in what are conventional techniques and practices or components of modern statecraft, deployed to map the social and enable both order and governance. Systems of classification and objectification, regulatory regimes, juridical apparatuses, administrative technologies, organizations of knowledge, and their overlapping infrastructures designed to both capture and facilitate life—these were hardly unique to Hitler's Germany; and they were elaborated in Germany as elsewhere in the context of social modernization efforts to "make the world better." These systems, regimes, technologies, and techniques have as their object the care and security of populations; and in this respect they are the constitutive components of what organizes the project of modernity. But the point is also that they combined as well to make a death world, or combined to create the conditions under which genocide could appear as an administratively plausible and practical "necessity," as part of "the price one pays for progress." These systems, regimes, technologies, and techniques have, in other words, a murderous potential—but a potential that is neither inevitable nor anomalous. The care of life, the distribution of suffering, the administration of death: this is the triangulated relationship on which the German genocide casts an especially bright light, and it is but one, significant, manifestation of the relationship that promised, as others continue to do, a more "perfect" society. To quarantine the period as an aberration, to insist that it poses an enigma in the developmental trajectory of modernity, mystifies to master. It leaves in the end uninterrogated the all too familiar mechanisms and processes by which more deadly worlds are born. As historian Raul Hilberg observes with respect to the German Holocaust, it all began innocuously with a change in definition: do we today recognize the radical potential of such changes?

V.

Toward the end of an account of the forces that congealed to create totalitarianism's condition of possibility, Arendt noted that the particular techniques of terror and mechanisms of population management were likely to be marshaled again in a world where greater numbers of increasingly isolated strangers would be living in closer proximity, competing for ever shrinking resources; a world in which more people in more parts of the globe could expect to be expelled, to potentially catastrophic effect, by political as well as economic systems that found no place or use for them. "Totalitarian solutions," she wrote, "may well survive the fall of totalitarian regimes in the form of strong temptations which will come up whenever it seems impossible to alleviate political, social, or economic misery in a manner worthy of man."[44] That these potential solutions would take new and even unexpected forms went without saying.

What could not be undone in Arendt's view, what was original to the Nazi project and thus subsequently changed the conditions of the lifeworld or the living-together of people after the regime's defeat, were efforts "to make human beings as human beings superfluous." These efforts were evidence of what she called "radical evil"—radical because they represented crimes that were beyond the parameters of extant juridical and moral systems (and here she pointed specifically to the Ten Commandments) and thus could be neither punished nor forgiven; evil because they aimed to kill all that was, in Arendt's view, specifically human in the individual. The concentration and death camps were initially the sites at which this project of remaking was most fully implemented: these were sites where individuals were killed en masse and degraded, to be sure; but they were also, and more significantly for Arendt, sites of experiment for the production of "living corpses" where the capacity for spontaneity, freedom, and solidarity and therefore identity in-relation was crushed.[45] Moreover, a related, integral component of the project of remaking human beings also entailed a shift in the self-understanding of perpetrators. For even as they colonized the world as Nature's chosen, they were also Nature's instruments and as such schooled in their own potential superfluousness, according to its changing needs and demands.[46] As Detlev Peukert notes, to ensure the survival, strength, and triumph of the race, expressed in and through the body of the people, not only were designated enemies of the *Volk* or "pathogens" to be identified and killed; the *Volk* itself would need to be culled: "possibly more than twenty percent of the Aryan population were genetically unfit and [would be] slated for elimination through euthanasia or sterilization."[47] And within this scheme, terror operated in the service of Nature, fixing and stabilizing human beings so that it might then advance unimpeded.

With the trial of Adolf Eichmann, Arendt was led to reconsider her assessment of the Nazi project and in particular her understanding of the character of evil it represented. She stepped away from the spurious grandeur and mythifying effects of an account that saw in the regime's crimes and the criminals that perpetrated them an expression of "radical evil" and moved toward an understanding of evil as "thoughtless" and thought-defying. "It is my opinion now," she wrote, "that evil is never radical"; neither was it, moreover, nor was it necessarily a reflection of evil motives or an expression of natural depravity. The evil she encountered in the figure of Eichmann was better understood, she argued, as the outcome of a certain *thoughtlessness* or inability to think from another's point of view. "One cannot extract any diabolical or demonic profundity from Eichmann," she claimed, "He *merely*, to put the matter colloquially, *never realized what he was doing.* It was sheer thoughtlessness—by no means identical with stupidity—that predisposed him to become one of the greatest criminals of that period. . . . [S]uch thoughtlessness can wreak more havoc than all the evil instincts taken together . . . —that was, in fact, the lesson one could learn in Jerusalem."[48]

It is with Arendt's account of the Eichmann trial, her report on the "banality of evil," and the "lesson" with respect to thoughtlessness she insisted the proceedings boldly featured that this study begins. The war crimes trial of Adolf Eichmann in 1961 was an especially important event for a number of reasons. First, as Jeffrey Shandler notes, it was televised and presented as a major news story in the United States; more significant still, it was during these broadcasts that "American television audiences [were] most likely to have first heard the word *Holocaust* used to describe the Nazi persecution of European Jewry."[49] Second, the trial shed an entirely new light on a dimension of World War II that many insist had been ignored, misnamed, or downplayed at Nuremberg, to wit: that Hitler's war had been driven by a virulent anti-Semitism and waged in large measure against the Jews of Europe for whom a "Final Solution" had been imagined and partially implemented. For fear of alienating public sentiment at home—anti-Semitism was still very much a component of American life—and seeking to avoid charges of staging a show trial organized around the emotionally charged spectacle of obviously biased and fallible victim testimony, chief prosecutor Robert Jackson had opted to build a case against the Nazi leadership on documents gathered by Allied forces in the months following the regime's surrender. Indeed, Jackson refused all but a handful of survivors who sought to testify against the Nazi leadership and in effect rendered their stories for them within the narrative frame of Nuremberg's indictments as crimes against the peace. It was, therefore, in the context of the Eichmann trial that Europe's Jews were given a voice and emerged to bear witness to events that the Nazis had never meant for them to survive. Against all odds, finally, to quote Soshana Felman, the victims were authorized to speak—to create a living record and "writ[e] their own history."[50] In the words of Gideon Hausner, Israeli attorney general at the time and chief architect of the case against Eichmann:

> It was beyond human powers . . . to present the calamity in a way that would do justice to six million personal tragedies. The only way to concretize it was to call surviving witnesses, as many as the framework of the trial would allow, and to ask each of them to tell a tiny fragment of what he had seen and experienced. . . . Put together, the various narratives of different people about diverse experiences would be concrete enough to be apprehended. In this way I hoped to superimpose on a phantom a dimension of reality.[51]

Third and finally, the Eichmann trial is especially important because it begins to organize the Holocaust in large measure as we know and understand it today, as a discrete and coherent event with a distinct narrative structure and set of moral incitements. As Felman notes, "Prior to the Eichmann trial, what we call the Holocaust did not exist as a collective . . . [or] semantically authoritative story."[52] And while the pathos and affect of that story have been inflected and situated in the popular imaginary of different nations in distinctly different ways, the definitive message across national boundaries was that the Holocaust, while past, could never be just history: it was and would remain a "permanent scar on the face of humanity." Hausner again:

> When I stand before you here, Judges of Israel, to lead the prosecution of Adolf Eichmann, I am not standing alone. With me here are six million accusers. But they cannot rise to their feet and point an accusing finger towards him who sits in the dock and cry "I accuse." For their ashes are piled up on the hills of Auschwitz and the fields of Treblinka, and strewn in the forests of Poland. Their graves are scattered throughout the length and breadth of Europe. Their blood cries out, but their voice is not heard. Therefore, I will be their spokesman and in their name will I unfold the terrible indictment.[53]

Arendt rejected the terms in which Hausner opened and framed the case against Eichmann and insisted that, however guilty the defendant was—and about his guilt she had no doubt—the prosecution had fundamentally failed to understand both the unprecedented nature of the crime it had called upon the court to judge and the novel nature of the criminal. Chapter 1 of this study, then, takes the Eichmann trial as its point of departure and examines Arendt's assessment of the proceedings—in particular her assertion that in the figure of Adolf Eichmann she encountered "the banality of evil." The chapter also takes up the vitriolic debate that her assessment inspired and continues to inspire both in Israel and in the United States.

With chapter 2, I turn to consider the Nazi genocide directly. In describing what opportunities the Eichmann trial missed, Arendt suggested that by building its case entirely around the unimaginable atrocities committed against Europe's Jewish population, the prosecution succeeded in establishing the "who" of genocide but failed utterly to grasp the "how"; to grasp, in other words, how administrative murder became part of the rational functioning of an orderly society. Drawing on the research of several contemporary German historians, most centrally Götz Aly, chapter 2 shifts the focus away from the trial and from the mesmerizing centers of destruction to examine the infrastructure of genocide. Aly maintains that it was the pursuit and repeated failure, between 1939 and 1941, of economic and utilitarian goals drafted by demographers, space planners, sociologists, economists, and anthropologists in the context of social modernization efforts that created the conditions for mass murder to emerge as an administratively plausible and practical course of action.

Although controversial in his effort to piece together the logic of mass murder—he assumes what some consider the suspect task of reconstructing the perspective of the perpetrators—Aly proffers a provocative set of arguments that move to the foreground the material effects of otherwise innocuous, easily ignored, and on the face of it utterly banal systems of classification and registration, of knowledge collection and production. These proliferating systems of classification, regimes of knowledge, and ever more refined matrixes of measurement along with the expanding state apparatuses they engendered were conventional, ostensibly unexceptional (because "scientific") components of twentieth-century statecraft. Under the direction of then–President Woodrow Wilson, for example, they were deployed to racially organize and rationally partition the continent after World War I so as to better serve a lasting peace.[54] *And* these regimes of truth, modes of order, and mechanisms of governance were similarly deployed by the Nazi state—essential to the spread of terror during World War II and to the formulation of ever more radical solutions that culminated in systematic mass murder. To be sure, state racism and the technocratic, managerial logic animating it were not always and everywhere expressed, understood, or practiced in identical ways.[55] But the critical if often understated or ignored point of some consequence is that they nevertheless constituted (and constitute) a structural feature of nearly all modern states.[56]

If chapter 2 attempts to make some sense of how the unprecedented might emerge from a deadly conjunction of otherwise "mundane" state policy and practice, chapter 3 returns to Arendt's encounter with Eichmann to restage the *how* of genocide on the historically more familiar terrain of individual responsibility and judgment. The centerpiece of this chapter is Arendt's claim that in the figure of Eichmann she encountered evil in the form of thoughtlessness rather than diabolical monstrosity. Such *thoughtlessness* she described as an inability to think from the standpoint of another; and this inability she regarded as potentially more destructive "than all the evil instincts taken together." Part of my effort in this chapter is to draw out Arendt's position while also situating it alongside what is a relatively common, certainly instructive, but nevertheless mistaken rendering that sees in thoughtlessness "merely" an absence of empathy.[57] This interpretive move—equating "thinking from the standpoint of somebody else" with empathetic identification—marks a significant shift in registers in the context of Arendt's argument. It perhaps understandably follows from the constitutive (though not uncontested) place empathy occupies in contemporary accounts of moral development as well as conventional understandings of what anchors moral sensibility. But there are a number of problems, I argue, with reading Arendt's Eichmann through the optics of empathy. Perhaps the most consequential is that such a reading renders what she claimed was fundamentally a political failure (a question of solidarity) primarily a moral one (a question of sentiment). A move, then, by many commentators to clarify Arendt's position ultimately ends up undermining it.

To follow this thread I turn at the end of chapter 3 to Eyal Sivan and Rony Brauman's 1999 documentary/drama, *The Specialist: Portrait of a Modern Criminal*.[58] Using restored and manipulated (which is to say, extensively edited and remixed) video footage from the Jerusalem proceedings, *The Specialist* follows the narrative arc of Arendt's argument to interrogate anew what was both novel and commonplace about the criminal, Eichmann, and his crime. It presents and scrutinizes for a contemporary audience the panoply of issues that the Jerusalem court, at least in Arendt's view, failed fully to grasp. Of special interest to me is the logic of a particular sequence early in the film which then quite inadvertently hijacks its subsequent argument. In this sequence, the courtroom is darkened and we watch Eichmann watching a screen on which is projected footage, originally shot by the Allied forces as they liberated camps across Europe and subsequently used to facilitate denazification in the months following Germany's defeat. I argue that with this sequence—in which thoughtlessness is staged and clearly enacted or conveyed as a kind of *apathy*—Sivan and Brauman's documentary inadvertently reproduces precisely the problem it seeks to challenge. In other words, despite the film's otherwise quite controversial alliance with Arendt's assessment of the trial—it was referred to as a "forgery" by the former director of the Steven Spielberg Jewish Film Archive in part because of this alliance—and notwithstanding its best critical efforts, the apathetic indifference of Sivan and Braumann's Eichmann reinforces the view that the problem he represents is one of pathology rather than politics, organized by an absence of feeling rather than thought.[59]

In chapter 4 I again step back from Arendt, narratively, to revisit the war crimes trial at Nuremberg whose record the trial of Adolf Eichmann aimed to set straight. I take up what some might regard as a relatively minor or incidental component of the overall legal effort in terms of its bearing on the case, to wit: the use made during the Nuremberg proceedings of the same documentary film footage shown some fifteen years later in Jerusalem (and incorporated in the sequence of *The Specialist*, considered in chapter 3). Introduced at Nuremberg a mere eight days into what was more or less an eight-month trial, the visual texts lent the proceedings a certain visceral immediacy, urgency, and credibility that Justice Jackson's marshaling of documents did not initially inspire. Indeed, at the time the visual texts had everything to do with how (and for what) "the Nazi regime was given official 'criminal status'"; and likewise they have everything to do with Nuremberg's legacy, now, at least as this legacy lives on in popular memory and understanding.[60] Finally, and most significantly in terms of the themes and arguments taken up in earlier chapters, I argue that a certain regime of truth was set in place at Nuremberg with respect to the images that established a set of imperatives (and injunctions) about looking and a powerful set of rules for remembrance and understanding; both we see reiterated in Jerusalem and remain even today more or less in place.[61]

Following an account of the Nuremberg proceedings, I return in the book's final chapter to Arendt and her widely considered but enigmatic characterization of evil as banal: what "this long course of wickedness had taught us," she wrote at the end of her report on the trial of Eichmann, was a lesson about the "word-and-thought-defying *banality of evil*." Many commentators insist that she meant only to portray Eichmann as banal, but about this reading I am skeptical. If evil is, as Arendt came to suggest, "action which destroys the conditions of its own possibility,"[62] our attention is directed well beyond the figure of Eichmann to a lifeworld organized now as then by practices and processes that while designed to sustain life nevertheless work as well to efface it.

In what follows, and to conclude now, readers can expect to find five chapters that are linked thematically by a broad and resonant set of concerns. Because the chapters do not follow a strictly linear trajectory that marches toward or culminates in a set of sweeping recommendations or conclusions, they can be read sequentially or in an order of one's choosing. That said, a critical task of this book is to take apart the serviceable myths that have come to shape and limit our understanding both of the Nazi genocide and of totalitarianism's broader, constitutive, and recurrent features. These myths, I argue throughout, are inextricably tied to and reinforced viscerally by the atrocity imagery that emerged with the liberation of the concentration camps at the war's end and came to play an especially important, evidentiary role in the postwar trials of perpetrators. At Nuremberg, as I noted earlier, particular practices of looking and seeing were first established that have since (and through) the Eichmann trial become simply part of the fabric of fact. They constitute a certain visual rhetoric that now circumscribes the moral and political fields and powerfully assists in contemporary mythmaking about how we know genocide and what counts as such. Arendt's claims about the "banality of evil" disrupt this visual rhetoric and may provide just enough critical leverage to consider how this rhetoric works and on behalf of what; her claims may also go some distance toward explaining the nature of an age that seems content to confuse solidarity and spectacle and is thus inclined to "put up with anything while finding everything intolerable."[63]

1 Arendt and the Trial of Adolf Eichmann

Contextualizing the Debate

Evil in its total banality: this is what Hannah Arendt claimed to have seen in the figure of Adolf Eichmann when she observed him in an Israeli court in 1961. Eichmann was considered a core member of the Nazi leadership and would have undoubtedly been tried at Nuremberg in 1946 alongside Göring, Speer, and Hess among others for war crimes had he not fled Europe following the collapse of Germany's Third Reich. He was living in relative obscurity in Argentina when he was captured by the Israeli Secret Service and clandestinely returned to Jerusalem to stand trial for his central role in the genocide of European Jewry.

Initially, at least, Eichmann was one of only a handful of officials in the Nazi SS whose sole job it was to implement or make operational the regime's various political and physical *solutions* for what it identified as its *Jewish problem*. Among other things, this entailed organizing the forced emigration and so-called resettlement of Jewish communities throughout (eastern) Europe and later, as the war progressed, overseeing their transport first to the ghettos and then to the camps where, as it is known, large numbers were systematically killed. While Eichmann never denied his role in helping *solve* Germany's Jewish problem—he claimed to have been an "expert" in Jewish affairs, a pro-Zionist no less, and an idealist—he stressed repeatedly that he harbored no ill-will towards the Jews and acted not from base motives but out of a sense of responsibility and duty and with an eye towards personal advancement. In his view, the annihilation of the Jews was "one of the greatest crimes in the history of humanity," but a crime in which he did not participate directly. He had served the regime only as a midlevel bureaucrat on the margins of power, someone who sat at his desk and did his work, evacuating and deporting rather than killing. And although his account was not entirely accurate, Eichmann's rendering of his Nazi past was, in Arendt's view, nevertheless somewhere in the general vicinity of truth: "Technically and organizationally, Eichmann's position was not very high; his post turned out to be such an important one only because the Jewish question, for purely ideological reasons, acquired a greater importance with every day and week and month of the war, until in the years of defeat—from 1943 on—it had grown to fantastic proportions."

Not surprisingly, the prosecution in Jerusalem advanced a somewhat different view of Eichmann's position in the Nazi hierarchy and role in the genocide

Figure 1.1. Eichmann in Court, 1961. Courtesy of Yad Vashem Photo Archive, Jerusalem, Israel.

of European Jewry. Indeed, Gideon Hausner, Israel's attorney general at the time and lead prosecutor in the case against Eichmann, maintained that it was Eichmann and Eichmann alone whose business had been the destruction of the Jewish people in its entirety. He had been the architect of Nazi terror against the Jews and, in Hausner's words, "the central pillar of the whole wicked system"—personally selecting the sites of the gas chambers, choosing the kind of poisoned gas that was to be used in these chambers, and specifying the number of people to be killed in them daily.[1] And while Eichmann may have performed his "bloody craft" from the security of his desk in Berlin—in this Hausner echoed Arendt's claim that Eichmann represented a new kind of criminal—in the end, the prosecution settled on constructing a somewhat more predictable, conventional, and politically more useful portrait of the former Nazi official. Sitting in a bulletproof glass enclosure—designed to protect the accused from possible attack while in court—Eichmann emerged from mounds of documents and weeks of oral testimony by survivors as a sadistic, demonic figure even while, it should be said, most of those who testified had no direct dealings with the man and were brought to the stand by the prosecution to humanize the larger historical picture of Nazi atrocity.[2] In the view of the prosecution, he was a consummate liar and "savage sociopath whose abominations made the crimes of Genghis Khan, Attila, or Ivan the Terrible . . . pale in significance."[3] Where Arendt saw in Eichmann a disturbingly average man of middling intelligence who, while implicated in a crime of gigantic proportions, was in the end "simply" a petty, deferential, careerist bureaucrat, someone who was not incited by ideological convictions, driven by base motives, or, based on the evidence presented, psychologically capable of committing the kind of acts of overt violence attributed to him; where Arendt saw, in other words, not Attila the Hun or Ivan the Terrible but the embodiment of something she described as *evil in its total banality*, the prosecution produced and pursued a diabolically wicked, morally monstrous Nazi official whose hatred of the Jews was relentless in its pursuits, deadly in its expression, riddled with sadistic impulse, and far from banal.

I.

Considerable outrage greeted Arendt's report of the trial when it was first published in the *New Yorker* as a series of articles in 1963. And in the four decades since, her claims regarding the meaning of the Final Solution, her arguments regarding the nature of individual responsibility, agency, and culpability under conditions of terror, and her scathing review of Israel's case against the accused continue to incite and confound commentators. Two issues in particular have consistently aroused the ire of some readers and the interest of others, and both go to the heart of the problem I want to take up in this and subsequent chapters. There is, first, Arendt's insistence that great evil is not necessarily a reflection of evil motives or an expression of natural depravity. Such evil, she argued, is better understood as the outcome of a certain *thoughtlessness* or inability to think—that is, an inability to think from another's point of view or, as Elaine Scarry has more plainly put it, "to follow the path of the bullet."[4] To regard Eichmann as a perverted sadist or to see in his actions a straightforward display of demonic intelligence was to fail, utterly, to grasp the criminal character of the accused and the nature of his crime. It was also, significantly, to misidentify the larger problem that he represented and that now confronted the world in the aftermath of Auschwitz. "One cannot extract any diabolical or demonic profundity from Eichmann," Arendt wrote.

> He *merely*, to put the matter colloquially, *never realized what he was doing*. It was sheer thoughtlessness—by no means identical with stupidity—that predisposed

him to become one of the greatest criminals of that period. . . . [S]uch thoughtlessness can wreak more havoc than all the evil instincts taken together . . . —that was,
in fact, the lesson one could learn in Jerusalem.[5]

Arendt would return repeatedly to parsing the implications of this lesson
throughout the rest of her intellectual life in an effort to make sense of and
clearly render the relationship between thoughtlessness and the capacity for
evil. While most of the animating links of this relationship would remain an
impressionistic patchwork of claims and questions, what she seemed to see
clearly and refuse was the all too convenient tendency to equate great evil with
a wicked heart. This refusal led many of her critics on the publication of her
report to charge that she was, in effect, absolving Eichmann and others in the
Nazi leadership of responsibility for their part in building and administering
a machinery of death. Her insistence that one of the most remarkable and, for
the purpose of comprehending great evil, relevant things about Eichmann and
others like him was his—and their—extraordinary shallowness and normality was regarded as an affront to the memory of those murdered.[6] It worked
against the pull of suffering graphically portrayed in the liberation footage of
the camps—shown in Jerusalem as at Nuremberg but, significantly, as evidence
not "just" of war crimes but of the *Holocaust*.[7] It worked against the pull of suffering graphically recounted in the testimony of survivors even while Arendt
went on to argue that this "normality" was, by implication, infinitely more terrible and "terrifying than all the atrocities put together."[8]

If Arendt was thought to have exonerated Eichmann by suggesting that he
was "perfectly incapable of telling right from wrong" and "never realized what
he was doing"—issues to which I return in subsequent chapters—she provoked
an even greater firestorm in challenging the ostensibly self-evident distinction
between the victims of Nazi atrocity and their persecutors. This distinction
was, of course, sharply drawn by the prosecution in Jerusalem and easily assum-
able by all who had encountered the many postwar images of corpses and open
graves. Arendt contended that things were not so clear cut: there was a chapter,
by far "the darkest chapter of the whole dark story" as she described it, that had
been omitted in Jerusalem but was nevertheless essential to understanding the
totality of the moral collapse caused by the Nazis.[9] And this chapter concerned
the cooperation of the Jewish leadership across Europe in working out the
details of SS directives, implementing the policies of Nazi officials, and shoring
up the power of occupying forces. In fact, the cooperation of Jewish authorities constituted a cornerstone of the Nazi's program, and, in Arendt's view, this
cooperation had a great deal to do with its success. As Arendt put it bluntly in
what Lawrence Douglas describes as "the most controversial and vilified statement in her book":[10] "The whole truth was that if the Jewish people had really

been unorganized and leaderless, there would have been chaos and plenty of misery but the total number of victims would hardly have been between four and a half and six million people."[11] If Eichmann bore responsibility for the death of millions—and Arendt was absolutely clear that he did—a significant measure of responsibility for these deaths lay also with the Jewish authorities. Indeed, of the numerous outbursts by spectators in the Jerusalem court that disrupted the proceedings, a significant number "were directed not at Eichmann, but at those Jewish witnesses who had served prominently in the Judenräte."[12] And of all the hard questions Hausner put to the many witnesses he called to testify—*why did you not rebel? resist? or try to escape?*—he did not ask them what for Arendt was the more troubling question, that is, why had they cooperated in their own ruin? As Arendt saw it, Hausner's lapse while grave was not surprising: the omission of this chapter from the prosecution's otherwise meticulously spun story boldly underscored for her the extent to which the trial sought primarily to display a certain truth about Auschwitz rather than decipher its actual horror, in the interest of an emerging Israeli national identity rather than justice.

It is now a matter of public record that Hausner and Prime Minister David Ben-Gurion had sought to use the trial to establish "the correct historical perspective" on what would come to be known, after and in large measure because of the trial, as the Holocaust.[13] Their strategy—of fashioning a "canvas soaked in blood and tears . . . that would reach the hearts of men"—entailed explicitly interweaving two narratives, one having to do with the suffering and destruction of the Jews, not only in the context of the second world war, but across centuries, beginning with the Pharaoh in Egypt and climaxing in an unimaginable martyrdom. "It is not an individual in the dock at this historic trial," wrote Ben-Gurion, "and not the Nazi regime alone, but anti-Semitism throughout history."[14] This narrative of persecution was coupled with another detailing the remarkable passivity of the world at large as a tragedy of gigantic proportions unfolded.[15] And then there was, of course, a lesson to be drawn from the story for which this "correct historical perspective" was required—in fact, several different lessons for different audiences. As Ben-Gurion envisioned it, the trial was to foster a certain consciousness among Jews about their vulnerabilities in a historically hostile world, dramatically rehearsing what it meant to live among non-Jews and emphasizing the obvious conclusion to be drawn from the incontrovertible fact of such vulnerability, that only a Jewish state could guarantee the survival of the Jewish people. For a non-Jewish world, brought into the courtroom by television,[16] the trial was to underscore the extent of the destruction of the Jewish people and the culpability and, thus, responsibility of Western powers for the slaughter of innocents: the free world

Figure 1.2. The prosecutor at the Eichmann trial, Gideon Hausner, 1991. Courtesy of Yad Vashem Photo Archive, Jerusalem, Israel.

had not only failed to act in either a swift or decisive fashion as a nation was led to slaughter, but had happily forgotten about the catastrophe once the war ended.[17] They were to be reminded of their shameful inaction and obligations to the new Jewish state. Finally, for an Israeli audience, the trial was to do a different kind of work, repairing and consolidating an otherwise fractured set of histories through education and "factual enlightenment." Among other things, this would entail rehabilitating the picture held by many of Diaspora Jews as meek, submissive, and hapless victims who went like sheep to the slaughter.[18] What would emerge, therefore, during the trial through witness testimony and in place of this hapless victim was the *survivor*: Israel (primarily Israeli youth) and the world at large would encounter a figure who had heroically resisted, thwarted, and ultimately overcome the Nazis' grand and evil designs and whose survival against all odds symbolized the rebirth of the entire Jewish people. And of the many who perished before liberation? They were now to be seen as having died fighting—"*not* on their bedraggled knees but on their blood soaked

feet."[19] Writing some years after the trial, Hausner described the transformation of individual and collective identity that took place over the course of the
proceedings in terms that clearly vindicated the past while also authorizing the
nation's political future:

> It came as a discovery to many that we are actually a nation of survivors. . . . The
> trial . . . brought home to everyone in Israel the basic facts and lessons of our
> time. But even more significant was the feeling of self-assurance and confidence
> that swept the nation. If Hitler, for all his fiendish powers, enormous resources,
> and unrelenting efforts, did not succeed in wiping out Jewry when he had it at his
> mercy, then the age old belief in the eternity of Israel was reaffirmed before our
> very eyes. The Jews had survived their mightiest enemy. The prophetic assurance
> bequeathed by Isaiah to the Jewish people—"No weapon that is formed against
> thee shall prosper"—was once again proved true. In comparison with Hitler's
> might the present-day anti-Semitics and foes of Jewry and of Israel, formidable
> as they may be, still look less menacing. There can be no complacency in facing
> them, but there is a valid and reasonable hope of overcoming them. . . . [T]he great
> national disaster has . . . been a fountain of new strength, and it holds out new hope
> for a better future.[20]

Nowhere on the ambitious, multivalent agenda that Hausner and Ben-Gurion set for the trial was there room for questions of complicity or collaboration.
And that was precisely their intent. These questions were to the side of their
efforts to refashion a history in which victims and survivors alike "struggled
valiantly to resist their physical, psychic, and religious destruction,"[21] and they
had been raised, in any event, in Israel in the decade preceding the Eichmann
case. In 1950 the Israeli Nazi Collaboration Law—calling for the prosecution of any person suspected of collaborating with the Nazis—was passed at
least in part as a response to the growing agitation and vigilante-style violence
among survivors as they encountered individuals—fellow citizens of the new
state—whom they believed had assisted the Nazis and/or been members of the
Judenräte.[22] And in 1954, the issue of collaboration became the subject of a ran-
corous, widely divisive public debate with the trial of Rezsö Kasztner. A former leader of the Hungarian Jewish community and press spokesman for the
Israeli Ministry of Commerce and Industry at the time of the trial, Kasztner
was accused of having "paved the way for the murder of Hungarian Jewry" by
assisting the Nazis when they arrived in Budapest, organizing the ghettoization of Jews and overseeing their deportation to Auschwitz. More damning still
was an arrangement Kasztner made with Eichmann in late spring, 1944, to ran-
som Jewish lives—$2 million for 100,000 Jews. Although the Nazis took the
money, they originally refused to allow the departure of any Jews from Hungary and eventually permitted only a small fraction of the originally agreed

upon number—1,685, which included a sizable contingent of Kasztner's friends and relatives—to leave by special train for Switzerland. In having entered into such an arrangement, Kasztner was said by the district judge in the case to have made a "pact with the devil"—opting to collaborate with the Nazis rather than organize resistance against them, saving the few while damning the many. On appeal, the Israeli Supreme Court would find that Kasztner had not engaged in treason or treachery and argue that not every act of cooperation could be seen as collaboration. They would also caution against the impulse to evaluate the actions of individuals under occupation in terms of how events eventually played out and, significantly for the Eichmann trial, urged Jews to focus their ire not on each other but on those who had sought to destroy them.[23] And this is precisely what Hausner would attempt—for the most part successfully—to do. When Yitzhak Zuckerman, a leader of the Warsaw ghetto uprising, worried that questions about the Jewish Councils would be raised during the trial, Hausner reassured him that only the truth would be told while also indicating how. "This is a trial of the murderer," he replied, "not of his victims."[24]

II.

If the issue of Jewish cooperation in the Final Solution had been so widely discussed and debated in Israeli society throughout the 1950s, the obvious question, then, is why Arendt's treatment of the subject in 1961 was greeted with such shock and outrage. Indeed, her claim that had it not been for their leaders, more Jews might have survived Hitler's scourge appears to echo what many in Israel were arguing at the time of the Kasztner trial. And certainly by the early 1960s other scholars had begun to take a long critical look at the complicated character of complicity and cooperation in times of political terror—for example, Raul Hilberg, from whose book, *The Destruction of the European Jews*, Arendt drew heavily in her account of the Judenräte. Hilberg subsequently disparaged the use Arendt made of his research—in his opinion, she was a mediocre philosopher trying, unsuccessfully, to write history—and clearly rued the day his name became linked with hers.[25] But Hilberg's criticism, while dismissive, is comparatively tame. Immediately following the publication of her report and for years after, Arendt's work was the subject of a vitriolic debate both at home (New York) and abroad (Israel and Germany). For having questioned the judgment of the Jewish leadership in Europe and thereby raised, for all the world to consider, an issue many apparently believed would "plague Jews for years to come," she was described as soulless, heartless, and lacking in love for her people.[26] For having exonerated the Nazis and excoriated their victims—for this is how she was widely, and inaccurately, read—she was said to have been "a self-hating Jewess" and a "shameless anti-Semite." Her arguments were described as malicious, her tone flippant and sneering, and her scholarship unoriginal and incompetent—"deficient in both factual knowledge and judgment"[27] and prone to "a kind of demagogic will-to-overstatement."[28] Indeed, she had presumed "to pass judgment on a matter far beyond her competence,"[29] and succeeded with her "evil book" only in feeding "a well of poisonous slander."[30]

Commentators typically see fear of a resurgence of anti-Semitism as the impetus for these bitter and at times violent recriminations. But clearly other issues were at stake as well. Political theorist Jennifer Ring, for example, argues—as Arendt herself never would—that gender played a pivotal role in the reception of the report. Adding a decidedly important and otherwise ignored dimension to the debate, Ring contends that the particular way in which Arendt was taken to task, the passionate denunciation of her authority and discrediting of her claims, had, in large measure, to do with Arendt being a woman and more specifically the only woman at the time to question, publicly, the judgments of a primarily male leadership in Europe and postwar Jerusalem. Ring elaborates:

> It is my hunch that Arendt's most strident critics, the *Partisan Review* crowd in
> New York, and Ben Gurion and the Mapai [Socialist Zionist party] in Israel,
> felt not only guilty and powerless about their responses to the Holocaust, but
> "unmanned" by the power of the Nazis and what appeared to be the collu-
> sion of most of the Western world in the face of the slaughter of the European
> Jews. . . . On their own merit, Arendt's arguments undoubtedly would have drawn
> criticism, even if a man had written them. But the same controversy initiated by
> a man wouldn't have been so one-sided. . . . [T]here would have been two volatile
> sides to the issue, just as there had been to the major Jewish issues of the previ-
> ous two decades: negotiate with the Nazis or not? Armed resistance or survival
> tactics? Those battles were fierce and hard fought, but there was a "critical mass"
> of opinion on both sides. That Arendt was the *only* woman to criticize the entirely
> male leadership of both European and Israeli Judaism, and that she drew so much
> universally severe criticism from men who had disagreed with each other on other
> important issues, points to a role for gender in catalyzing their rage.[31]

Although some scholars may regard the interpretive lens of gender that Ring brings to bear to be itself controversial and even trivializing, one cannot read the numerous memoirs written by those who participated in the Eichmann trial or, for that matter, the original war crimes trial at Nuremberg without appreciating the extent to which issues of gender and identity, and, specifically, masculinity, were very much at play in both contexts.[32] At Nuremberg, for example, these issues constituted a notable subtext with Germany's cultural corruption and eventual defeat loosely linked to the deviant, failed masculinity of its leaders.[33] Defendants were feminized by (the primarily American staff) members of the prosecution and described as weak, soft, and cowardly, in every respect mere caricatures of the hard-bodied, virile *Übermensch* of Nazi (and clearly Allied) fantasy. Much was made of Hermann Göring's corpulence, drug addiction, and alleged habit of wearing women's clothing, jewelry, and makeup when not in uniform; they were said to evidence a criminal psyche and corrupt nature. And when Göring was weaned off drugs in the months prior to the trial, the chief prison officer claimed to have finally "made a man of him."[34] Hans Frank, former governor general of Occupied Poland (i.e., the part of German-occupied Poland not annexed to the Reich), was characterized as a latent homosexual whose repressed tendencies explained not only "his ruthless ambition and lack of scruple" but also his compulsion to follow Hitler "with a passionate enthusiasm that beclouded all reason and legal or humane concepts of human rights."[35] Finally, while Eichmann's pathological nature was revealed for many in his "talon-like hands," "reptilian eyes," cold nerves, and utter lack of affect, he was at the same time described as meek, frightened, and nervous, a mere mouse of a man rather than a "big, strong 'German-type.'"[36] Indeed, for those who listened to his testimony in translation, his was often the voice of a woman.[37]

While gender may *not* have been a salient category of analysis at the time of either trial, its presence and play in both cases and usefulness for understanding otherwise occluded dynamics seems clear.[38] That it might also help to explain some of what was in play in the criticism leveled against Arendt seems equally apparent in retrospect. "The overwhelming reality of being a Jew anywhere in the world during Hitler's reign was *impotence*,"[39] and this would have lasting consequences in shaping the political landscape throughout the postwar years of state formation and building. Indeed, during the war, Ben-Gurion and the Mapai in Palestine along with organized American Jewry had each pursued a set of priorities that took precedence over working to rescue the Jews of Europe even while what could be known about the full extent of the Nazi pogroms was known if not fully grasped. As one of the leaders of the Jewish Agency in Palestine put it, "We read, we sigh, . . . [we] go on."[40] While memorials for those who perished were planned as early as 1942—when most were still alive—and while the possibility of reparations was discussed, little was done, officially, to address or impede the slaughter of European Jewry: saving the persecuted in exile, Ben-Gurion insisted, was not the job of those attempting to build the Land of Israel, indeed, their plight was relevant only insofar as it advanced or forestalled the Zionist project in which he and others understood themselves to be engaged. However, once the war ended and the state was founded, the sense of impotence and complacency that engulfed the Jewish leadership in Palestine gave way, Ring argues, to guilt, recrimination, and a decades-long process of cultural reckoning that would "dominate the politics of the Eichmann trial" and, in the end, frame Ben-Gurion's efforts to set (a version of) the historical record straight. The story would be retold, the history reinflected, and the past reclaimed. It would become the basis for a culture of remembrance—or as some have described it, a "cult of memory"—that would celebrate the resistance and martyrdom of a people, transform what had been a pervasive sense of helplessness into a narrative of abandonment and betrayal, and secure the fledgling state's right to advance its claims and stand its ground in a clearly hostile world, politically, morally, and militarily.[41] In this context, as historian Peter Novick suggests, implicating some Jews in the deaths of others or foregrounding the absence of a substantial Jewish resistance, as Arendt had done, was seen as potentially undermining what he describes as Israel's newly acquired "moral capital" and "furnish[ing] a ready out for those ... who ha[d] never faced up to their full responsibilities in permitting the Nazi Holocaust to go unchallenged until it was too late."[42] That it was a woman who contested the official story—Ben-Gurion's setting straight of the record—challenged the political purposes to which it was being put and questioned the authority of its authors was obscene, intolerable, and unforgivable. "Our enemies have for years been engaged in a campaign of whitewashing the culprits and blaming the victims," wrote Jacob Robinson, an assistant to Justice Jackson at Nuremberg and one of several consultants aiding Hausner during the trial. "The latter, brutally murdered not so long ago, are now being killed for a second time by the defilers. Among these enemies Hannah Arendt now places herself."[43]

Killed for a second time? In what sense are the kinds of questions Arendt posed, however sharp, analogous to murder? For the Israeli reporter Haim Gouri, writing daily over the course of the trial for the newspaper *Lanchav*, the moral landscape was not yet so perfectly neat or conclusively settled. Amid the litany of betrayals and indictments—what the British and the Allied forces did or failed so miserably to do—the outlines of another story, otherwise "hidden in the shadows," was emerging. And this "dark confusing story"[44]—as Gouri described it— concerned the leaders and representatives of Jewish communities across eastern Europe "all behaving as if normalcy had not yet broken down," negotiating, "playing their accustomed roles, conducting business with the murderers of their own people in hopes of being allowed to carry on, somehow, with their lives."[45] From this story Gouri appears to have discerned what Arendt had also seen as pivotal: not so much complicity, cooperation, and betrayal by the Judenräte, although such questions overshadowed the state and the trial, as we have seen, and circulated throughout Israeli society in many guises, moral as well as political.[46] More significant still in the aftermath of Auschwitz was what a detailed account of the actions of the Jewish Councils might contribute to a larger understanding of the workings of totalitarian domination. Arendt explains: "I have dwelt on this chapter of the story, which the Jerusalem trial failed to put before the eyes of the world in its true dimensions because *it offers insight into the totality of the moral collapse the Nazis caused in respectable European society—not only in Germany but in almost all countries, not only among persecutors but also among victims."*[47] This total "moral collapse of respectable society" suggested to Arendt just how feeble were the traditional mores, customs, and habits typically considered an indisputable and self-evident infrastructure of civil(ized) life in times of crisis and under conditions of terror.[48] And it throws into relief an altogether more sobering and complex moral terrain than the territory that the prosecution occupied over the course of the trial or that Arendt—accused of having defiled the memory of the dead or "whitewash[ed] the culprits and blam[ed] the victims"—found herself occupying following its conclusion. For us, at least for the moment, the question is this: How did the discursive field become so quickly and dramatically circumscribed such that there came to exist only two positions from which one might speak, the position of victim or victimizer, of innocent or perpetrator? And in what ways, we might ask further, did this constraint of discursive possibilities serve to stabilize a wide spectrum of commitments and practices whose net effect was both to obscure and to escape questions of common responsibility?

What emerged during the Eichmann trial and acquired a certain momentum in its aftermath was a sweeping simplification of the meaning of the Nazi genocide with radical anti-Semitic evil on one side and radical (Jewish) innocence and bravery on the other. This morally reductive discourse would become more or less institutionalized by the 1970s, the basis for what Novick refers to as the "sacralization" of the Holocaust[49] (its transformation from a historical event to a mythic, metaphysically framed one, unique(ly evil) and therefore outside of history, incomprehensible and therefore beyond interpretation, inexplicable and unimaginable and therefore beyond representation).[50] But even in its nascent form, this materially reductive discourse worked against ambiguity or the unsettled and unsettling questions that Arendt claimed were now given features of contemporary life. As she saw it, the Nazi genocide and Eichmann's part in it were not just the most recent chapters of a much larger and longer story detailing the natural and inevitable destruction wreaked by anti-Semitism, the "most horrible pogrom in Jewish history." Arendt's claim, rather, was that the Nazi genocide represented something unprecedented; and it was unprecedented because it entailed an attack first and foremost on human plurality or what, she argued, constitutes not only the precondition for shared human life in the world, but a fundamental source of its meaning. Given the organization and logic of the Nazis' extermination policies, she suggested in a letter to

Figure 1.3. Eichmann listens as he is sentenced to death by the Court. United States Holocaust Memorial Museum, Washington, D.C., courtesy of the Israeli Government Press Office.

Mary McCarthy at the time of the trial, the death factories would not have shut down once the Jews—or the Poles, or the Gypsies—had been annihilated in their entirety. Retreating from a position she had advanced a decade earlier in *The Origins of Totalitarianism*, Arendt had come to believe that "extermination per se was more important than anti-Semitism or racism"—more important, in other words, than the particular ideologies that ostensibly rationalized it and could be (as they were) amended, reformed, and rescripted to accommodate the changing needs and vision of the regime.[51] As Arendt understood it, then, "the crime against the Jewish people was *first of all a crime against the human status,*" although most failed, in her view, to fully see or appreciate the implications of this significant if nuanced difference. As such—as an attack on human diversity, "without which the very words 'mankind' or 'humanity' would be devoid of meaning"—it was a matter that vitally concerned and inescapably involved not just the Jews and not only Israel but the international community as well.[52]

> Had the court in Jerusalem understood that there were distinctions between discrimination, expulsion, and genocide, it would immediately have become clear that the supreme crime it was confronted with, the physical extermination of the Jewish people, was a crime against humanity, perpetrated upon the body of the

Arendt and the Trial of Adolf Eichmann

Jewish people, and that only the choice of victims, not the nature of the crime, could be derived from the long history of Jew-hatred and anti-Semitism. Insofar as the victims were Jews, it was right and proper that a Jewish Court should sit in judgment; but insofar as the crime was a crime against humanity, it needed an international tribunal to do justice to it. . . . If genocide is an actual possibility of the future, then no people on earth—least of all, of course, the Jewish people, in Israel or elsewhere—can feel reasonably sure of its continued existence without the help and the protection of international law.[53]

III.

In the chapter that follows, I want to take a somewhat closer look at Arendt's reassessment of the role played by ideology in the persecution and genocide of the Jews—her sense, in other words, that "extermination per se was more important than anti-Semitism or racism"—while leaving for still later a consideration of her claims about the *banality* of evil. Before proceeding, however, and by way of concluding this general overview of Arendt's report and its critical reception, several issues merit the foreground. For Arendt, clearly, the Eichmann trial represented a missed opportunity on at least two, related fronts. Orchestrated from the beginning by Ben-Gurion to foster an emerging Israeli national identity and emerging national interests, the proceedings constituted, in her view, a state-sponsored spectacle, didactic in design and staged to underscore what she described as a host of "superficial and even misleading lessons" despite the relentless (and not altogether wasted) efforts of the judges to "faithfully serve Justice."[54] As primarily a show trial—a characterization commentators since have categorically rejected or sought to refute[55]— it squandered the opportunity that Eichmann's capture offered to begin to make judicial sense of what she insisted was a "special type of crime," administrative massacre; and "a special type of criminal," one who has no intent to do wrong, who does not act from base motives, and "who commits his crimes under circumstances that make it well-nigh impossible for him to know or to feel that he is doing wrong."[56] On a second, equally significant and related front, the trial also squandered the opportunity to recast genocide as a *"crime against humanity"*—as a matter of international responsibility that exceeded the scope of any one state's jurisdiction, required an internationally binding means of address, and demanded a clear-eyed reassessment of conventions that rendered millions of stateless, hence vulnerable and expendable, people someone else's problem.[57] "State-employed mass murderers," she argued, " must be prosecuted because they violat[e] the order of mankind, not because they kill millions of people. . . . Nothing is more pernicious to an understanding of these new crimes, or stands in the way of the emergence of an international penal code that could take care of them, than the common illusion that the crime of murder and the crime of genocide are essentially the same."[58] For Arendt, therefore, the Eichmann trial squandered the opportunity to mobilize the world around a set of questions Israel was uniquely positioned to raise. For lack of imagination and understanding, the trial "failed as a precedent for a way of thinking and comprehending."[59]

In the end, obviously, we cannot know whether the development of such a precedent in the context of this trial would have made an appreciable difference in shaping global responses to subsequent atrocity.[60] However, what we do know is that "totalitarian instruments," as Arendt referred to them, have long outlived their original regimes. In virtually every decade since the Eichmann trial—with the last decade of the twentieth century being by far the most deadly—genocide or "genocidal acts" in Cambodia, Iraq, Bosnia, Rwanda, Kosovo, and, most recently, Darfur have been perpetrated and, for the most part, dismissed, ignored, accommodated, and even encouraged.[61] These genocides have unfolded and continue to unfold notwithstanding the insistent and incessant assertion, "Never Again," that has accompanied a growing "Holocaust consciousness" at least since the late 1960s and despite an overwhelming enthusiasm for institutionalizing a set of lessons about moral accountability and responsibility in the building of memorials too numerous to count or name. As Power observes, "In 1979 President Jimmy Carter declared that out of the memory of the Holocaust . . . , an unshakable oath with all civilized people . . . [had to be forged]." And every U.S. president since Carter has joined him in promising "that never again w[ould] the world stand silent . . . [or] fail to act in time to prevent the terrible crime of genocide."[62] That the world mostly does stand silent even as leaders flock yearly to commemorations that honor a refurbished past renders the vow "Never Again" a curiously empty gesture. It promises to forestall what has already happened, naturalizes a certain production and distribution of suffering, tolerates the ever increasing number of superfluous people who have no place within established structures or societies, and normalizes the racial and religious conceits, political dislocations, and economic miseries from which atrocity blossoms. Thus it is that if "never again" refers to anything with certainty now, it is, as David Rieff's notes, only this: "'Never Again w[ill] Germans kill Jews in Europe in the 1940s.'"[63]

2   Ideology and Atrocity

Eichmann claimed to have been only a "transportation officer" in the elaborate bureaucracy that was the Third Reich. The details of his story and the nature of his position as he set out both for the Court in Jerusalem appeared only to frustrate the judges, mock the suffering of survivors, insult the memory of the dead, and enrage the prosecution, so inadequate was his account of the phenomenon he was being called on to explain. His job, he said, was to organize and coordinate the movement of bodies and trains across Europe. That the trains were transporting human beings for "labor service" or death was something over which, he insisted, he had no control: his orders were to deport for "resettlement," and this is precisely what he did, neither more nor less. If Eichmann went to his death without grasping what it meant to have been a "transportation officer" of human cargo, the prosecution in Jerusalem similarly failed, at least in Arendt's view, to grasp how occupying such an ostensibly innocuous position was enough to place Eichmann at the epicenter of genocide—a diligent participant in the organization of mass murder, one of the greatest criminals of the period. The crime, she argued, was unprecedented, and so too the criminal, but what explains the conditions that produced them? How is mass murder made routine? How does it become part of the rational functioning of an orderly society?

I.

In an exchange with Karl Jaspers, occasioned by an article Jaspers had written on the question of German guilt in the context of the Nuremberg hearings some years before the *Origins of Totalitarianism* was published, Arendt followed the understandable compulsion to see in the crimes of the Nazis something so monumental as to resist both reason and representation. How was one to account for crimes that appeared to defy tradition, destroy extant moral frameworks, and mock the life-sustaining ethos of juridical practice?[1] What forms of address were now possible in the aftermath of an event that "changed the basis for the continuity of the conditions of life within history?"[2] The genocidal project of the Nazi regime left in its wake ruptures across the shared human world, and it was precisely in these ruptures, Arendt explained to Jaspers, that the regime's true monstrousness was reflected:

For these crimes, no punishment is severe enough. It may well be essential to hang
Göring, but it is totally inadequate. That is, this guilt, in contrast to all criminal
guilt, oversteps and shatters any and all legal systems. That is the reason why the
Nazis at Nuremberg are so smug. They know that, of course. And just as inhuman
as their guilt is the innocence of the victims. Human beings simply can't be as innocent as they all were in the face of the gas chambers (the most repulsive usurer was as
innocent as the newborn child because no crime deserves such punishment). We are
simply not equipped to deal on a human, political level, with a guilt that is beyond
crime and an innocence that is beyond goodness or virtue. This is the abyss . . . into
which we have finally stumbled. I don't know how we will ever get out of it.[3]

While acknowledging the metaphysical pull of Arendt's position, Jaspers
assumed a more critical posture toward what he suggested was her questionable, even specious flirtation with a kind of mythic grandeur. Such grandeur
he refused outright. "I'm not altogether comfortable with your view," he wrote,

> because guilt that goes beyond all criminal guilt inevitably takes on a streak of
> "greatness"—of satanic greatness—which is, for me, inappropriate for the Nazis as
> all the talk about the "demonic" element in Hitler and so forth. It seems to me that
> we have to see these things in their total banality, in their prosaic triviality, because
> that's what truly characterizes them. Bacteria can cause epidemics that wipe out
> nations, but they remain merely bacteria. I regard any hint of myth and legend
> with horror, and everything unspecific is just such a hint. . . . Your view is appeal-
> ing—especially as contrasted with what I see as the false inhuman innocence of the
> victims. But all this would have to be expressed differently (how, I don't know yet).
> The way you do express it, you've almost taken the path of poetry.[4]

Jaspers's reading would obviously shape Arendt's later efforts to account for
Eichmann, explain his deeds, and defend her claims against the many critics of
both. In fact, she would contend in a reply to Gershom Scholem's disparaging
response to her analysis of Eichmann that evil was, as Jaspers had suggested,
very much like a fungus: while it spread across the world, laying waste, it was
without depth or demonic dimension. Indeed, ostensibly echoing Christian
thinkers since Augustine, it was only the "good," she subsequently maintained,
that could have depth and be radical. In the meantime, however, and clearly
given pause by Jaspers's critical appraisal, Arendt responded:

> I found what you say about my thoughts on "beyond crime and innocence" in what
> the Nazis did half convincing; that is, I realize completely that in the way I've
> expressed this up to now I come dangerously close to that "satanic greatness" that
> I, like you, totally reject. But still, there is a difference between a man who sets out
> to murder his own old aunt and people who . . . built factories to produce corpses.
> One thing is certain: We have to combat all impulses to mythologize the horrible,
> and to the extent that I can't avoid such formulations, I haven't understood what

actually went on. Perhaps what is behind it all is only that individual human beings did not kill other individual human beings for human reasons, but that an organized attempt was made to eradicate the concept of the human being.[6]

The tension Arendt articulates in this exchange with Jaspers between the importance of understanding "what actually went on" and the impulse to "mythologize the horrible" remains forcefully at play even today, well over sixty years since the war's end, in the uneasy, dissonant relationship between an ever more detailed academic scholarship of the period and the graphic images of Nazi atrocity that circulate as a constituent part of the popular imaginary, often as a stand-in for historical understanding. And the tension clearly animated the Eichmann proceedings as well: the prosecution built its case against Eichmann around survivor testimony in order to foreground a comprehensive and exhaustive account of suffering and heroism while the judges acknowledged having had to reassemble the case through documents in order to render a judgment firmly anchored in a "legal analysis of the facts."[7] However, in 1946, when Arendt and Jaspers exchanged these thoughts on the International Military Tribunal at Nuremberg, the verdicts against the major war criminals had not yet been handed down, the proceedings had not yet been published, and the documents collected by the prosecutors at Nuremberg had not yet been archived. In other words, what was known about the *full* extent of Nazi criminality was largely dependent on what could be seen—on the not yet organized, not yet fully narrativized visual record that had begun to emerge, indeed explode, with the liberation of the concentration camps.[8] To be sure, accounts of brutality, persecution, and murder had been circulating in the West since at least 1943. But these accounts were incontrovertibly confirmed only when reels of film and lurid photographs together provided a shocking portrait of political terror: "the careful and calculated establishment of a world of the dying in which nothing any longer made sense."[9]

Both photograph and film captured and were subsequently put in the service of a story of chilling perversity for which those who first entered the camps insisted there could be no words, no comprehension, and, like Arendt, no punishment severe enough. But if the magnitude of the horror left journalists, military personnel, war correspondents, and congressional delegations speechless, the images of corpses, open graves, clothing, hair, eyeglasses, and shoes still seemed to speak volumes. "Let the world see," General Eisenhower declared when he required all civilian news media and military combat camera units to visit the camps and record their observations in print, pictures, and film. But see precisely what? What was the broader interpretive scheme Eisenhower assumed was shared and in place that would make these images make sense? Was the carnage they depicted what an *organized attempt at eradicating the concept of the human being* looked like? Were they a portrait of *inhuman guilt [that] over-steps and shatters any and all legal systems?* Was it plausible to see in such images something akin to the ravaging effects of bacteria, a certain prosaic triviality, as Jaspers put it? In the immediate aftermath of the war, atrocity images from the camps confirmed for publics of both continents the shocking form and scope of Nazi criminality in all its depravity. But what these images could not convey with any specificity—and thus what made them a rich medium for stories about the demonic other or dark forces beyond human reach—was how and why millions had come to participate in a continent-wide killing enterprise.

Arendt turned her full attention to this question in the *Origins of Totalitarianism*. First published in 1951 and concerned to explain the political components and historical trends that congealed to create the conditions of possibility for Nazism, the work retained, for all its insight, a certain infatuation with the monumental.[10] Totalitarianism, Arendt argued, was a novel form of political organization whose emergence was facilitated by the convergence of a number of forces. Among these she included (1) late-nineteenth-century European imperialism, with its idea of expansion and its dual pursuit of power and profit;[11] (2) racism, which emerged as imperialism's ideology or principle of social organization and functioned to legitimize the exploitation, displacement, and murderous subjugation of indigenous African populations; (3) the collapse of the nation-state (under the impact of imperialism), with its increasingly incompatible guarantees of ethnic solidarity and equality of rights; and (4) the alliance between excess capital and those Arendt calls "the mob," the socially idle and economically dispossessed (the *déclassés* of all classes) who became the unscrupulous adventurers and settlers of the so-called dark continent. Also at play in the mix of forces that facilitated totalitarianism's emergence were the pan-nationalist movements (Pan-Germanism and Pan-Slavism), which set their sights on continental rather than overseas expansion and an ethnobiological reorganization of national boundaries with colonial holdings of racially inferior populations; and, finally, anti-Semitism, which Arendt argues emerged as a distinctly nineteenth-century political ideology in the context of the pan-movements and, in effect, positioned European Jews as race rivals, a community constituted across centuries and distinct national territories through blood and a sense of unique historical destiny. Arendt explains:

> What drove the Jews into the center of these racial ideologies more than anything else was the . . . obvious fact that the pan-movement's claim to chosenness could clash seriously only with the Jewish claim. It did not matter that the Jewish concept had nothing in common with the tribal theories about the divine origin of one's own people. The mob was not much concerned with such niceties of historical correctness and was hardly aware of the difference between a Jewish mission in history

to achieve the establishment of mankind and its own "mission" to dominate all other peoples on earth.[12]

For Arendt, it was the mix of these forces—imperialism, racism, the collapse of the nation-state, economic dislocation, Pan-Germanism, and anti-Semitism—that *together* created the conditions for totalitarianism's emergence. They did not cause it—in her view, there was nothing inevitable about Nazism—but they were clearly visible constituents of the phenomenon and worked together to render the solutions it ostensibly offered both plausible and possible. Taking her lead from what she characterized as Montesquieu's discovery "that each form of government is set in motion and guided in its action by its own innate principles," Arendt set out to discern amid totalitarianism's dense administrative layers its constitutive components and distinct "essence." And her argument was that totalitarianism's essence was (motion implemented by) terror, while its principle of action was ideology—"the logicality of ideological thinking," or in the case of Nazism, specifically, scientific racism organized around the notion of racial struggle for world domination. Where ideology provided a comprehensive account of the world, terror was its instrument and deployed to ensure that reality and the otherwise unpredictable individuals who inhabit it conform to and consistently reflect the higher laws and imperatives of Nature or History.[13] The object, in other words, of totalitarian domination was in large measure to disable and rehabilitate populations: its aim was to extinguish the possibility of spontaneity or initiative because either could impede or forestall the expression of extra-worldly designs; its aim was to immobilize victim and executioner alike in order to render them suitable mediums for the roles Nature or History has called on them to play. In Arendt's words, terror "eliminates individuals for the sake of the species; it sacrifices men for the sake of mankind—not only those who eventually become victims of terror, but in fact all men insofar as this movement, with its own beginning and its own end, can only be hindered by the new beginning and the individual end which the life of each man actually is."[14] From this Arendt concluded that the tyranny of logicality—the grand movements of History or Nature for which human beings are merely the raw material—promised to eventually consume all equally: "Anti-Semitism only prepared the ground to make it easier to start the extermination of people."[15] And this is what constituted the real horror, the unprecedented and radical evil, of the totalitarian political universe that was most fully expressed in the defining institution of the camps. For the camps were in effect laboratories for the remaking of human nature: under scientifically exacting conditions, they "created ghastly marionettes with human faces" on the one hand and fostered the delusion of omnipotence on the other, in both cases rendering the human in all its variety and unique individuality superfluous.[16] In time, all inhabitants of the totalitarian universe, Arendt argued, would be rendered superfluous and were, in the meantime, schooled in their own potential superfluousness; required to embrace and internalize it with the recognition that the extermination of so-called subhumans or those unworthy of life was merely a prelude to one's own eventual elimination as just so much biomedical waste material according to the changing needs and demands of Nature or History.[17]

As Arendt saw it, therefore, at least in 1951, in order to fully grasp the phenomenon of totalitarianism, one needed to avoid historical commonplaces, especially the impulse, as she put it in a letter to Eric Voglin, "to deduce the unprecedented from precedents."[18] Totalitarianism represented a radical historical break. Its techniques of terror and domination were deployed as a way of life and into every corner of life, even as it also interpellated subjects into a larger whole through what she called "ideological propaganda," enlisting them to perform their providential part in a cacophonous symphony of death. But in explaining totalitarianism's nature or mapping the constitutive principles that set and kept it in motion, Arendt only vaguely acknowledged the infrastructure of mass slaughter that had to have been constructed across discursive domains well in advance of the actual practice if only to stabilize the cultural chains of signification, indeed that had to have been in place to rationalize the practice or enable its emergence as a viable policy for alleviating perceived social ills. She insisted instead that institutionalized mass murder could not be explained even in the fabricated senselessness of the totalitarian universe except as an expression of ideological rigidity: it benefited no one, it was militarily counterproductive, and it was organized and implemented in ways that defied any scale of utility. Mass murder, then, remained for Arendt, at least at this stage in the development of her account, decidedly otherworldly. Thus while *The Origins of Totalitarianism* may have gone some distance in arresting the impulse Jaspers observed to "mythologize the horrible," it hardly escaped the lure.

In what remains of this chapter, I want to turn to a set of studies initiated primarily by the German historian Götz Aly and his numerous coauthors but including other contemporary scholars as well in order to gain a better understanding of the otherwise dissonant picture and claims Eichmann presented in Jerusalem. Working from newly opened archives and proffering reinterpretations of otherwise available documents and historical material, Aly reconstructs what he insists was an elaborate network of economists, demographers, agricultural experts, regional planners, labor deployment specialists, geographers, social scientists, and statisticians—the great majority of whom were university based and, in the beginning, non–party members—who worked more or less in concert to address what was perceived at the time to be Germany's "overpopulation problem" in the east and southeast of Europe (Poland, the Ukraine, and western Russia). From the policy studies and administrative reports of these professionals—most of whom joined the various planning commissions of American and British occupying forces following the war—emerged what Aly refers to as "the economy of the Final Solution." This he reads as a set of partially implemented programs and failed strategies designed to alleviate a population surplus—with "surplus" being understood primarily as a question of productivity rather than density and as including the unemployed (and unemployable) as well as propertyless—that experts estimated was somewhere between 30 million and 50 million people. Aly seeks to discern the "logic" of reasoning—which enabled, for example, one to identify "every second rural Pole as 'nothing more than dead weight'"[9]—and the policies such reasoning generated in order to develop an account that might more precisely reconstruct the vision of the perpetrators. He explains his approach:

> Because the retrospective interpretation of Nazism as a rule follows the perspective of the victim, the obviously negative aspects of racial politics are generally regarded as an absolute. As understandable as this is, such a one-sided view leads historical analysis astray and causes it to almost ignore the 'positive' aspects of Nazi population policies. . . . Nazi ideology gained its effectiveness not from isolated, government controlled hatred of Jews or the mentally ill, Gypsies or Slavs, but from the totalitarian unity of so-called negative and positive population policies.[20]

Aly's assessments are instructive as well as provocative in considering how the pursuit and failure of economic and utilitarian goals in the context of social modernization efforts—efforts conceived and designed to *make the world better*—could have facilitated the mass murder of human beings and allowed it to appear, over time, to be an administratively plausible and practical necessity, *merely* "the price one pays for progress."[21] Moreover, the arguments he crafts draws our attention away from the obvious centers of power (leadership) and the mesmerizing centers of destruction (the camps) to notice the incremental building (and reorganization) of complex, expanding, multilayered, and ill-fitting infrastructures that aimed to translate and standardize the meaning and value of reproductive bodies across economic, legal, educational, medical, and scientific domains. As such, his approach not only moves to the foreground the material effects of otherwise innocuous systems of classification and registration; it brings into excruciating focus the effects of practices of knowledge collection and the mechanisms as well as conditions of knowledge production that were and can be easily ignored or dismissed as irrelevant to the spread and nature of terror during this period.[22]

There are two parts to this story. The first part more or less rehearses Aly's account and foregrounds the centrality of "economic factors" in shaping and, in his view, ultimately fostering the conditions or prerequisites for state-directed mass murder. The second turns to other recent scholarship to highlight an integral constituent of the "economic equation" (as well as of policy formation across the fields of education, demography, health, and social welfare) that Aly's analysis recognizes but understates: this includes notions of natural inequality, social hierarchy grounded in "race science," a politics and ever expanding policy of exclusion, "a world view [of which anti-Semitism is only a part] that divided [humanity] into worthy and unworthy populations."[23] What is crucial is not ideology per se but rather the ways in which systems of classification worked to stabilize and distribute particular configurations and practices of power. And, finally, a critical turning point in each instance is the period between September 1939 (following the defeat and territorial partition of Poland) and September 1941 (following the German invasion of Soviet Russia). During these two years, the area under German control expanded four times and in all directions.[24] What ensued with conquest and annexation under cover of war was a massive effort to (forcibly) repatriate some 500,000 ethnic Germans with the long-term goal of redistributing nationalities across Europe in order to thereby "rationalize" European social and political as well as economic life.[25] This effort, which took for granted the death of tens and, later, hundreds of thousands clearly failed. But according to Aly it was precisely as a result of the *succession* of failures and the *compromises* they necessitated—the repeated modification of numerous, far-reaching "restructuring" projects along with continuously amended interim policies—that an administrative apparatus initially set up to relocate and settle "biologically distinct" ethnic populations became an apparatus of mass murder:

> What to the victims must have seemed the horrible efficiency of the bureaucracy of death appeared very different in the eyes of the perpetrators. In the contemporary view of the deporters, the same story was seen as an unbroken series of defeats, an inability even to approach their goals, once established. . . . The activities of Himmler, Heydrich and Eichmann can . . . be described as a chronology of failure. As early as 24 January 1940, as Himmler sought in vain to resettle [approximately 60,000] Baltic Germans in the time allotted [approximately 8 weeks], Goebbels noted, "Himmler is presently shifting populations. Not always successfully."[26]

With the signing of the nonaggression pact with the Soviet Union in August 1939 and the subsequent conquest and partition of Poland in September 1939, the Reich leadership initiated an ambitious project to repatriate half a million ethnic Germans from the east and south of Europe within a fifteen-month period. Responsibility for implementing this project of ethnic redistribution, known as "home-into-the-Reich," fell to an eventually vast administrative apparatus overseen by Himmler (in his capacity as Reich Commissar for the Strengthening of the German Nation), Heydrich (in his capacity as head of the Main Office for Immigrants and the Main Office for Resettlers), and later Eichmann (whose Department IVD4 was responsible for all matters of emigration and evacuation).[27] Implementation entailed from the beginning deportation to the east of large numbers of Poles and Jews, whose farms, businesses, homes, and household effects were shuttered, demolished, or reallocated as compensation to repatriated Germans whose property and possessions—amounting to more than three billion reichmarks—were appropriated, in turn, by the Reich and exchanged for oil and foodstuff in the interest of its foreign trade balance with Russia, Romania, and Italy.[28] Significantly, the first mass murders were related to these initial population transfers in late fall 1939 and involved ten thousand to fifteen thousand psychiatric patients institutionalized in West Prussia and occupied Poland. As Aly observes, these murders took place *not* in the context of the well-documented "euthanasia" program, which began the following year and is often cited as the first movement in a meticulously scored "symphony of death." Rather, they occurred in response to the need to create transit shelter for Baltic and Volhynian German settlers and, according to Aly, were neither planned in advance nor apparently ordered from above. Horrific though these murders were, they represent precisely the kind of tacitly approved, on-the-ground improvisation or compromise necessitated by circumstance along the way toward realizing what was considered a far grander, more encompassing scheme of ethnic unity, prosperity, and peace.[29] In other words, while implemented on behalf of one vision, such measures set the conditions for quite another. Aly explains:

> These first mass murders stood in close connection with the general resettlement policy. A concrete order to kill the mental patients did not exist. Obviously, the participants acted on a tacit understanding, which only required a vague expedient direction. By autumn of 1941, a total of 30,000 people had already been murdered for the purpose of "making space for ethnic German resettlers." Before the functionaries of resettlement built the camps for the extermination of the European Jews, they had practiced mass murder for two years and gained the certainty that many of the participating German officials and the German public as well condoned these practices.[30]

To get a more concrete picture of the chaos or potential for chaos that attended Germany's ethnic redistribution project and Aly's argument with respect to it, consider the following: to the west in Poland were the territories annexed by Germany, to be demographically cleansed for the sake of economic reorganization and agrarian redevelopment. It was to this annexed territory that ethnic Germans from the Soviet-occupied east and (eventually) South Tyrol as well as so-called ethnic aliens (primarily young Polish children but also individuals of "eligible stock" under the age of forty-five) "deemed suitable for Germanization" were initially (to be) (re)settled.[31] And it was from this territory that Poles and Jews were deported to the General Government in the east, under the administration of Hans Frank. While Jews were sent to ghettos, temporarily established until territory outside or on the periphery of German interest could be identified and permanent, economically self-sufficient "Reservations" were established, the Poles were sent to transit camps where they were "processed and classified according to racial group" and either assimilated (sent back to the old Reich) or forced into service as a "reservoir of unskilled labor" to be tapped as needed for menial and seasonal work.[32] A densely populated, economically truncated area, the General Government would become the site for the murder of every third person who died in the Nazi genocide.[33] Finally, according to the terms of the nonaggression pact, the Soviet Union occupied the easternmost third of Poland, thereby reclaiming a significant share of the territory it lost in 1920.

To render these massive population transfers that began across Poland immediately after German annexation and occupation (historically) comprehensible, Aly contends that they must be seen in context—as an expression of an internationally endorsed notion of national self-determination, as a response to the perceived threat of "Bolshevism," and, most significantly in terms of the analysis he develops, as part of a larger, utopic effort to create an economically viable, agriculturally efficient, ethnically contiguous region. And while anti-Semitism was unquestionably a factor in the execution of these transfers, Aly argues that they were not solely or even primarily driven by it: "The common images of an insane racist state and a central or long since determined plan for extermination [do not] correspond . . . to reality."[34] Rather, as he reads them, the population transfers entailed two, inextricably linked and frequently at odds objectives: resettlement and deportation. And it is the interaction of these two objectives, once the transition was made from planning to implementation, that goes some distance to explain not only the increasingly more radical treatment of Jews as the war progressed but also the prolonged formative process that created the conditions for genocide: "When, beginning in the autumn of 1941, German authorities spoke of 'deportation', 'displacement', 'resettlement', or 'evacuation' of Jews while now in fact meaning murder, this should not be seen merely as an effort to camouflage their actions; it also serves as an indication of the *evolution of events* leading up to the Holocaust."[35]

If racial ideology or "eliminationist" anti-Semitism did not constitute the sole or definitive criteria by which plans for the region were originally organized, in Aly's view economic criteria grounded in demographic science most certainly were definitive. Well in advance of the German invasion of Poland, economists from the United States, Great Britain, and France had scrutinized the country's prospects for economic development and cataloged its problems in terms similar to accounts later proffered by German strategists. Without exception, rural overpopulation was identified as Poland's most severe problem. Coupled with widespread poverty and permanent unemployment that left over "a quarter of the Polish population living on the brink of starvation," a semifeudal class structure, and a complex ethnic mix, riddled with tensions, the country itself appeared vulnerable to civil war and communist revolution. In order to boost agricultural productivity, build urban centers, transition to industrial manufacturing, produce surplus capital, foster commerce, establish a stable tax base, and generate a middle class—in order, in other words, to unify and modernize a region that had achieved nationhood only by treaty at the end of World War I—economists from the West proposed redirecting population groups within the country while Poland's conservative leadership sought ways to "export" what it maintained were the country's extraneous populations—identified, significantly, as "Jewish"—without, however, also exporting this population's wealth. Indeed, as early as 1937, Polish officials had pursued talks with Palestine about Jewish emigration and had also entered into negotiations with France for use of Madagascar as a possible settlement site.[36] The radical character of these and other proposed solutions underscores the extraordinarily dire and clearly reactionary conditions of a country that geographically at least had come to be considered by Western powers as "the key to Europe." And, significantly, they also anticipate the kind of reasoning that shaped the projects subsequently pursued following the invasion of German forces. As Aly and Heim observe, "By 1939, the on-going discussion in Poland and in the international arena about issues of migration, overpopulation, and the transfer of population groups had thrown up all the key socio-political and economic arguments that would later influence the deliberations and decisions of the German occupying power in Poland."[37]

As with discussions in the international arena, the deliberations and decisions of the German occupying forces were organized for the most part around addressing Poland's "overpopulation problem" but referenced, specifically, a mathematical formula first articulated at the turn of the century by Paul Mombert.[38] Mombert's formula purported to calculate the "optimum" population size of a region, not by density, but by linking population numbers to economic resources—what he referred to as feeding capacity—and standard of living. As Aly and Heim explain it, Mombert's idea was a simple one and worked in both a descriptive and a prescriptive (not to mention reductive) fashion: "if the population [grew] in size, then in order to feed the extra mouths either the standard of living ha[d] to fall or the feeding capacity ha[d] to be increased."[39] By the same token, if the population shrank in size or was made to shrink especially in those sectors deemed marginal and/or unproductive, then feeding capacity would increase and along with it the standard of living. Taking this formula and numerous variations on it as their point of departure and in a direction Mombert had at one time cautioned against, the many economic, demographic, and agrarian experts who served the occupying authorities in Poland estimated that "every second rural Pole was nothing more than 'dead weight.' By their figures as much as 75% of the population in some regions of the country could be considered superfluous"[40]—that is, unproductive and/or unproductively employed and therefore of no benefit to Germany's (industrial) economy.[41] And it was the same throughout the conquered territories as Germany expanded its sphere of interest. Thus, for example, economists estimated that between 12 million and 15 million agrarian workers would have to be "transferred" from the land in southeastern Europe (50 million people if one included their families). And later, in anticipation of the invasion of the Soviet Union and as part of Germany's planned attack, a network of economists, demographers, agricultural experts, social scientists, statisticians, and various other state functionaries equally as elaborate as any set up in Poland proffered equally as deadly plans in which "population" also figured as one among many manipulable variables. War would be waged, land would be freed for colonization, and the economy would be "rationalized" with the "natural reduction" of the region's extraneous populations through planned famine, or as one nutritionist characterized it, a "scientifically proven method." According to estimates, "extraneous" included a staggering total of some 30 million inhabitants from the Balkans and western Russia. Aly elaborates:

> The plans, which were unparalleled in their clarity, never mentioned the word
> 'race', but constantly referred to the logic of economic circumstances. 'Negative
> demographic policy' was the imperative of the hour, with hunger acting as a form
> of geo-strategic tourniquet. These plans, which were developed some months
> before the 'Final Solution of the Jewish Question', once again emanated from
> Goering's Four Year Plan agency. The two million Soviet prisoners of war who
> died of starvation in German camps before the end of 1941, did not die because
> of any problems in the food supply, but were victims of deliberate murder. In
> November 1941 Goering remarked that 'this year twenty to thirty million people
> will starve in Russia. Perhaps that's a good thing, since certain people will have to
> be decimated'.[42]

Assumed was the notion that "certain people [would] have to be decimated" in the process of restructuring the European continent under German hegemony, during and after the war. But more significant still was the assumption, prior to the invasion of the Soviet Union in fall 1941, that the decimation of particular populations would in large measure occur *naturally* over the course of resettlement and from any number of causes—exposure, starvation, insufficient medical care, forced labor, forced marches, epidemics, substandard living conditions, and abandonment in uncultivated, infertile regions.[43] This is what Aly describes as "death by conventional means in unconventional circumstances." And given the unquestionably wretched circumstances of these forced population transfers, huge numbers did die. However, what crosses an important threshold in the evolution of state-directed mass murder is the building of extermination camps, the conversion of forced labor camps into death camps, the eventual construction of a crematorium with fifteen chambers at Auschwitz, the systematizing of murder through gassing that began in December 1941 with the shutting down of the Lódz ghetto. With these practices, murder became a technology and matter of policy. As such, they reflect the pursuit of a qualitatively different, altogether more radical course of action, generated, in Aly's view, by the complete impasse reached by administrative efforts to secure *territorial solutions to "demographic problems"*—in every respect, a deadly refiguring of the Reich's various economic and population schemes. In 1940 Heydrich characterized the "biological extermination" of Jews as an "undignified" option for a "civilized nation" even while also asserting that "Jews were of no use . . . to the Reich." And Himmler would echo this view, asserting that the physical extermination of a people was a method employed by Bolsheviks and thus fundamentally "unGerman."[44] By the end of 1941, however, the so-called resettlement policy had been suspended (by Himmler) and a program of organized mass murder had begun, at least experimentally. By May 1942, this program was fully in place and more or less routinized.

The shift from a territorial or total solution to a physical or "Final Solution," according to Aly, emerged only gradually with the invasion of the Soviet Union and the eventual collapse of the resettlement programs. Briefly rehearsed: With the invasion of Poland, massive population shifts were instigated that entailed the "return" of ethnic Germans to land and homes made available by the deportation of Poles and Jews to points east, primarily the General Government. But immediately there were problems: coordinating the transports in virtually all directions simultaneously, for example, and on the scale that had been called for, proved impossible given the limited capacity of the rail system. Delays and bottlenecks hindered implementation of the resettlement plans and required schedules to be revised many times over: psychiatric patients were murdered to make room for German returnees—something that would happen repeatedly over the course of the next year and a half—but even so, there were critical housing shortages that left German returnees languishing in transit camps awaiting placement.[45] In addition, there was what Heydrich referred to as the "unauthorized exodus" of Poles seeking to escape relocation, with at least 40 percent of deportees in some areas simply evading transport and going underground; and Jews, as they were evacuated to the General Government, were held in mass detention, robbed and often destitute but in any case rendered economically unproductive and superfluous—precisely what at least some administrators maintained they were to begin with.[46]

The General Government functioned as a collection point, as Hans Frank put it, a "dumping ground," for masses of humanity from the east and southeast of Europe. With emigration no longer feasible or possible for some four million Jews now under German jurisdiction, ghettos were established in so-called Jewish residential districts as a provisional measure until more permanent settlements or colonies on the periphery of German interests could be found.[47] Indeed, with the defeat of France in May 1940, Madagascar emerged as the territorial antidote, or "foreign policy solution," to Germany's perceived Jewish problem. A French colony off the coast of Africa in the Indian Ocean, the island would enable the establishment of a Jewish homeland under German sovereignty but far from European soil and, according to at least some proposals, " financed by English and American Jews [after the war] as restitution for Versailles." Although subsequently abandoned in favor of an "eastern solution"—in anticipation of the defeat of the Soviet Union, other territories were expected to become available for settlement—excerpts from a report submitted by the demographer Friedrich Burgdörfer suggest that the possibility of establishing a colony in Madagascar was not only taken seriously but also regarded as feasible on condition that the Reich prevailed against Britain:

> At the last census (1.7.1936) Madagascar has a population of 3.8 million, which, in a total land area of 616,000 sq. km, is equivalent to 6.2 persons per sq. km. The total number of Jews being considered for resettlement is only 2.7 million greater than the present population of the island. If the island were to be given over exclusively to the Jews the presence of 6.5 million Jews on the island would increase the population density to just 10 persons per sq. km. If the intention is to resettle the 6.5 million Jews there in addition to the existing indigenous population, the mean population density would rise to around 16 per sq. km, which is the average figure for the earth's surface as a whole—and slightly more than one tenth of the population density of the German Reich. Even this figure should be well within the natural capacity of the island.[48]

Clearly, quite a lot depended on the Madagascar Plan: with the "expulsion" of Jews to a permanent site—however murderous the process would most assuredly be—the ghettos would be cleared, creating room for displaced Poles; and with the relocation of Poles to what had been ghettos, German settlers from southeastern Europe could then be accommodated. But the proposal was dropped for military reasons within months of being put forward, and the only other territory considered to which Jews might be deported—the Pripet Marshes, Siberia, or the icy northwest of the Soviet Union—required victory in a war that was being prepared for but had not yet been declared.[49] Nevertheless, even as plans for a Jewish settlement on the peripheries of empire stalled (and were eventually dropped), according to Aly, such plans had a significant material effect in shaping subsequent thinking and policy: they worked to further legitimize "ever more radical steps towards ethnic segregation" and to increasingly separate settlement questions with respect to Jews from the program of general resettlement. With over a million people deported to the General Government over the course of 1941 and the buildup of the Wehrmacht units in preparation for war with the Soviet Union, an already desperate set of conditions in the region turned catastrophic. Resources were diverted to support the widening scope of military needs; transports were curtailed; food shortages intensified; returnees in transit camps still awaiting farms were diverted into "practical work"; Poles were moved into forced labor; and the ghettos—which had suddenly become the permanent fixture they were never intended to be—were now expected to become economically viable and self-sustaining even while, as Aly and Heim observe, they

> possessed virtually no resources that would have allowed the people confined within [their] walls to produce the means of supporting themselves in the longer term. Within the ghetto itself, formally an impoverished residential area, there were very few factories or workshops. The transfer of production facilities into the ghetto from the outside had been forbidden by the Germans. Raw materials for the production of goods of any kind had already been taken away from those shut up inside—insofar as this was possible. Everything they needed in this regard had to be purchased via the transfer agency, along with their day-to-day food supplies.[50]

Economists and settlement staff, each with very different agendas, had disagreed from the beginning over the function and operation of the ghettos, with debate focused largely on whether, to what degree, and precisely how these sites were to be subsidized (in anticipation of territorial solutions); at least some administrators argued that they should be allowed simply to deteriorate as "a means for liquidating the Jewish people." And even as they became a more permanent mechanism for the detention of larger and larger numbers of Jews, such questions were by no means settled. In the early months of 1941, efforts were made to harness the labor potential of the ghetto to various work programs amid an ongoing debate about "whether Jewish labor represented an asset valuable enough to be preserved."[51] And while these programs ultimately failed for a variety of reasons, of lasting and fatal consequence was a hierarchy they introduced into ghetto life between those fit for work and thus economically useful and those unfit for work and thus "surplus to requirement." A variation of this calculus had already been brought to bear in hospitals and institutions for the mentally and chronically ill: between 1939 and 1941, the notion that a person's economic usefulness was the measure of their worth and thus claim to life or space, literally, was pivotal in legitimizing the murder by gas of some seventy thousand institutionalized German nationals identified by physicians as unlikely ever to be discharged or to "do enough work to offset the cost of keeping and feeding them."[52] And in the context of the ghettos, where cutting expenditures and consumption came to be considered a matter of some urgency in the context of war making and the numerous shortages attending it, an individual's claim to life came to be determined, similarly, by his or her productive capacity: those who could work had access to at least some rations; those who could not either died from starvation or were among the initial transports to the newly operational death camps.[53] As Aly and Heim observe, by the end of the year, following the invasion of the Soviet Union and on into 1942 when the onslaught against the ghettos had begun and systematic selections had become routine, what awaited those identified as "unfit for labor"—primarily women, children, the sick, and the elderly—was hardly open to doubt. Representing a massive hemorrhage of increasingly scarce capital, they became what the authors chillingly describe as the "priority victims of the German policy of annihilation."[54]

By the time the Wannsee Conference was held in January 1942, the initial transports to the first dedicated extermination center, Chelmno, had already perished in gas vans; the *Einsatzgruppe*, or special units of the Security Police (SD), and *Waffen-SS* had moved east into Russia alongside advancing troops, ruthlessly "cleansing" newly conquered Soviet territories of "all communist elements," military and civilian alike, "but especially Jews"; the "selective mass executions of those seen as 'unfit for labor' [had begun] in western Ukraine, in western White Russia, and in the Warthelandl"[55] and, finally, a program to deport German Jews to the eastern territories was in the early stages of implementation. Wannsee appears, then, to have been only an explicit acknowledgment of what was a previously determined, gradually intensifying, and ongoing if nevertheless implicit course of action. Significantly, however, a number of contemporary historians proffer alternative framings that modify or complicate the more easily reached assumption that genocide had been a foregone conclusion from the start. Jürgen Matthäus, for example, offers a cautious word with respect in particular to the mass shooting campaigns of the *Einsatzgruppe:* "What might appear from a post-Holocaust perspective as a centrally planned and uniformly applied pattern of stigmatization, dispossession, concentration and annihilation was in the first months of Operation Barbarossa an incoherent, locally and regionally varied sequence of measures."[56] And this view is echoed by Arno Mayer, who, despite the different inflections he brings to events during this period, notes that certainly before the conference but even after it "the drive against the Jews was not uniformly exterminationist."[57]

With the broader framing, the Wannsee Conference emerges as a constitutive moment in the formulation of policy not because an intensification of the genocide long decided elsewhere required relevant administrations to be informed about the changed conditions or details of extermination.[58] In fact, the killing technologies that would come to distinguish the Nazi genocide as a genocide were still being developed at the time of the conference, as was the ostensibly scientific classification scheme that would enable those overseeing deportation to clearly identify the racially marked body. As Mark Roseman notes, "the problem of defining who was a Jew had vexed the Nazis" from the beginning, and the full confusion of provisionally resolved battles of definition were fully reflected in the proliferation and growing incoherence of social and political as well as legal categories.[59] Heydrich would (attempt to) address this incoherence at Wannsee in the context of acknowledging that a Final Solution of the Jewish Question—which now included some 11 million Jews from across Europe—was imminent.[60] In addition, he advised those in attendance—the backbone of the government administration—that efforts to implement this solution would be closely monitored and, in contrast to previous arrangements, coordinated exclusively by officials under his direction. And, finally, he revealed what the Final Solution of the Jewish Question would entail: primarily the exploitation of Jewish labor in the East.

> In the course of the final solution and under appropriate leadership, the Jews should be put to work in the East. In large, single-sex labor columns, Jews fit to work will work their way eastward constructing roads. Doubtless the large majority will be eliminated by natural causes. Any final remnant that survives will doubtless consist of the most resistant elements. They will have to be dealt with appropriately because otherwise, by natural selection, they would form the germ cell of a new Jewish revival.[61]

As Christopher Browning notes, "Despite the euphemisms—separation of sexes, labor utilization leading to large scale natural diminution, and finally appropriate treatment of the surviving remnant that could not be released to begin a renewal of the Jewish race—the genocidal implications [of Heydrich's directive] were unmistakably clear."[62] Indeed, so clear were the implications of the meeting that Eichmann—who was "by far the lowest in rank and social position of those in attendance"[63] and whose participation, as he reports it, was limited to taking notes and preparing the minutes—later maintained that he experienced "a kind of Pontius Pilate feeling."[64] In his words, "Here now, during this conference the most prominent people had spoken, the Popes of the Third Reich. . . . [The] dream [of creating distinct ethnic land settlements] was over." "I had never thought of such a thing, such a solution through violence," he continued. "I now lost everything, all joy in my work, all initiative, all interest."[65] Forced to execute both orders and people but without animus or even "[his] own thoughts in this matter," he considered himself, on reflection, utterly "free of guilt."[66]

III.

Aly's analysis of the "political economy of the Final Solution" has been criticized by some and dismissed by others for ignoring anti-Semitism and the place occupied by European Jewry as "Germany's first and primary target."[67] While acknowledging the original and provocative character of Aly's analysis, for example, Omer Bartov contends that efforts to "explain the origins of the Holocaust without any attempt to analyze the impact of traditional antisemitism, the regime's anti-Jewish propaganda and indoctrination, and the attitudes of the men who were actually organizing the genocide is to misunderstand much of what the Holocaust was about."[68] Bartov continues: "From where the victims stood, there was no doubt in their minds that they were not being killed merely as a bureaucratic abstraction, but as the worst enemy of the Germans and as the lowliest creatures on earth: as Jews."[69] Saul Friedländer finds that in focusing exclusively on the eastern territories and ignoring the treatment and deportation of Jews in Western Europe, Aly's account leaves too much out to be convincing.[70] Browning, while noting that Aly and Heim's research "provides the impetus for reexamining important issues," nevertheless questions both the picture they present of "a close knit group of 'planning intelligentsia' working cooperatively and successfully toward a common goal of eliminating Jews" and the role they afford economic calculation in moving "the persecution of the Jews beyond pogrom and massacre to the Final Solution."[71] And finally, both echoing and adding to these sentiments, historian Dan Diner contends that Aly and Heim fail at the most basic level of methodology to adopt enough critical distance from the corpus of documents they marshal in support of their utility-centered thesis to accurately discern the documents' historical meaning or significance.[72] In Diner's view, it is utterly predictable that such documents might consistently offer an economic rather than racial rationale for population transfers and so-called ethnic resettlement plans, but they must be read for what they are: rhetorical subterfuge, which, in the end, works both to obscure and to justify the implementation of an already determined and determining eugenic and racist program:

> Among the documents Aly and Heim have discovered, a considerable number do indeed propose, in one manner or another, an economic justification for the mass killing and its antecedent measures; the evidential character of such documentation, its usefulness for reconstructing the Final Solution in its entirety, is nevertheless extremely doubtful. This holds true particularly for material "affirmatively" appropriated by the authors: an adaptation of its vantage accompanied by utter disregard of the historian's constant need for critical distance from his or her sources. Virtually without exception, Aly and Heim take the arguments of Nazi academic subalterns . . . literally.[73]

And Diner takes his objections still further.[74] More egregious than the lack of scholarly distance he sees in Aly and Heim's reading of documents, but related to it, is their failure to appreciate the *specificity* of the Nazis' murderous plans—the Nazis' obvious clarity about who constituted their worst enemy and what they were going to do about it—as well as the authors' suggestion that the murder of European Jewry was only the first stage in what would ultimately have become a more comprehensive program to rationalize Europe's ethnic distribution while also addressing its "overpopulation" problem. In this Aly and Heim echo one of Arendt's observations in *The Origins of Totalitarianism*, and for that matter in *Eichmann* as well, about the nature and real horror of the totalitarian universe and the logic of genocide—that the singling out of some lives as "unworthy" is merely a prelude to the designation of other lives as unworthy according to the changing needs and demands of the state, indeed, the changing needs of a state that, following Foucault, takes life as its object and objective.[75] Bartov concurs with Arendt on this point:

> The urge to cleanse society of all deformity and abnormality was truly a promise of perpetual destruction. In this quest for perfection, everyone was potentially tainted, and no proof of ancestry could protect one from allegations of pollution. Even in a totally *judenrein* universe, the definition of health could always exclude more and more members of society, whose elimination would promise a better future for the rest.[76]

It was an evolving array of disciplinary as well as regulatory mechanisms, techniques, and technologies that secured the regime and enabled its efforts to take charge of individuals and populations in the name of life and health. Agencies tasked with knowledge collection and its organization proliferated within Germany and across the conquered territories, generating ever more elaborate categories of classification and systems of stigmatization. Their aim was not only to manage conventionally dependent or newly marked (and marginalized) individuals and populations—the criminal, indigent, asocial, and insane, as well as those deemed racially undesirable or genetically degenerate. It was in addition to track, measure, appraise, and quantify for future policy initiatives the makeup and behavior of the so-called *Volk* with the long-range goal of rationalization and national revitalization or maximizing the nation's fitness across all facets of individual and collective life.

By way of illustration, consider the observations of Friedrich Zahn, president of the German Statistical Society. Writing in 1941, Zahn had this to say about the place and promise of advanced statistical techniques:

> [The National Socialist Regime] has moved man into the foreground, not man as free individual, but man as biologically, socially, economically, and culturally connected with the community. . . . [I]mportant demographic and medical statistical studies have been undertaken in the areas of family, tribe, race, hereditary sciences, homeland studies, and national characteristics (affiliation, dialect, language, family names). . . . [T]he census of 1933 provided the basis for statistical studies of the family that correspond to the existing family policies. Population analysts and demographic statisticians have been pushing for such a program for decades, but it was not actually implemented until the rise of the Third Reich. The census of 1939 developed this program even further by determining the biological make-up of the family through a series of cross-sectional and longitudinal studies. Additional data for these studies were drawn from physical examinations of soldiers in the German military, the results of studies of boys and girls in the youth brigades, and from special examinations conducted by health departments, university institutes, and company physicians. The statistical evaluation of the Reich's occupation competitions should also be noted. Over time, all of these sources illuminate the society's overall state of health and quality of life. It ranges from hereditary health to hereditary illness, promoting the growth of a healthy hereditary core of the German *Volk* and preventing the proliferation of the weak. . . . Studies conducted by the Department of the People's (*Volk*'s) Health at the *Deutsche Arbeitsfront* [the sole labor organization in Nazi Germany] deserve special recognition, as the questionnaires they developed serve to ensure the health and productivity of the present generation and the productivity of every individual into old age in working at the highest level of efficiency for the well-being of the ethnic German community (*Volksgemeinschaft*).[77]

From Zahn's optimistic and forward-looking depiction of the Reich's efforts to map and monitor bodies, we can see clearly the way in which otherwise unremarkable processes of knowledge collection and production anchored ever more finely honed diagnostic or normalizing systems across social worlds—economic, medical, educational, and legal arenas, to name only the most obvious.

Agencies overseeing such processes—the Ministry of Health, the Reich Commission to Protect the German People, the Reich Office for Research on Ancestry, the Office on Race and Migration, the Office on Race and Resettlement, the Reich Office of Statistics, the Department of Population Management and Welfare, to list only a few—these agencies and the densely structured apparatuses of control produced and sustained as well as naturalized through them were part of the ongoing, working, indeed, permanent infrastructure of the regime through which a "global remodeling" of collective life was to be achieved. And a constitutive component of this global remodeling was the notion that the elimination of life would be a necessary means and condition for definitively improving it.[78]

That Diner assumes a very different view of the matter is no surprise in part because he takes the destruction of European Jews rather than the ostensibly more abstract goal of population management to have been the overriding objective of the regime. As such, the speculative suggestion that Germany would have continued its genocidal march ignores what he regards as a basic historical fact: the death camps in which Polish Jewry met its end were razed right after the slaughter and therefore could not have been employed to serve a more comprehensive program of annihilation.[79] Informed by what he sees as an "implicit anticapitalist polemic" concerned more with contemporary political contests than discerning what he contends are the true historical facts of the matter, the account Aly and Heim advance not only trivializes the past in its gross and ahistorical generalizations. It leads, in addition, to "disturbing misjudgments" with respect to the Final Solution as it was "actually implemented." And with this it seems we reach the heart of the matter for Diner: "To interpret the destruction of Europe's Jews exclusively as a consequence of mere negligence, of unpremeditated action, is unacceptable to Jewish memory."[80]

IV.

The issue of standpoint and the production of historical knowledge— or rather what will count as such (and for whom)—is clearly pivotal in the critical assessments of scholarly efforts to make sense of the complex and often contradictory processes that precipitated what all nevertheless agree was atrocity on a grand and tragic scale. Diner himself acknowledges the now commonplace notion that all historical accounts are situated and richly mediated. "The design of any historical project," he writes, "is always linked to some paradigmatic perspective."[81] And we can assume that this is the case with his work just as he underscores the anchoring function of perspective in the work of others. But he appears curiously unreflexive with respect to the interpretive protocols he brings to the event and which then necessarily inform his rejection of the critical framework Aly and Heim marshal to address it. "Perspective" (shaped by a broader standpoint) will have something to do, obviously, with what gets described as misjudgment, with what "vantage"—to use Diner's language—is authorized and thus can be "affirmatively" or legitimately adopted, with what accounts pass as credible, and with what counts as foreground or background in the reading and rendering of Nazi atrocity. As we saw in the previous chapter, the standpoint of the persecuted, and by this is meant primarily Jews, was precisely what the military tribunal at Nuremberg was said to have ignored and what some maintain was finally authorized (indeed, produced) by the trial of Eichmann.[82] It is what Bartov insists one must occupy to fully understand what the Holocaust was all about. It is what Diner argues "endows the event with something like historical meaning."[83] It is what Arendt maintained prevented the court in Jerusalem from fully grasping the unprecedented character of the crime that confronted it. And, finally, it is what Aly's analysis displaces, or perhaps more accurately, seeks to reposition, in reconstructing events from the perspective of the perpetrator. Aly's argument, as we have seen, is that it is only by incorporating this perspective—by reconstructing the internal logic of the regime's vision and the constellation of practices that shaped and were in turn shaped by it—that the formative conditions of the Nazi genocide can be discerned.

Aside from the formidable, narrative challenges such an approach poses, attempting an archival reconstruction of the perpetrator's perspective clearly leaves Aly and Heim vulnerable to what looks at first blush to be Diner's most devastating objection—that in neglecting to lift the obvious veil of linguistic deception that must necessarily shroud their sources, their analysis is "tainted by National Socialist reasoning."[84] The charge is clearly designed to undermine the status of their inquiry as "history" and discredit any claim it might make to represent the past as it (might have) happened. On the other hand, Aly and Heim understand their account to be at odds with received historical thinking given their point of departure, foregrounding the links between negative and positive population policies on the one hand and the utterly disastrous efforts to implement these policies on the other; between "Auschwitz and visionary German projects of the time for a modernized and pacified Europe."[85] And while this understanding does not render their inquiry immune to critique, it does call attention to the ways in which the radical outcome that has come to be called "the Holocaust" trains our attention and ostensibly provides the conditions from which it emerged with a certain coherence, organization, and necessity these conditions could never have had as they took shape. It calls attention, speaking now more generally, to a tension that riddles historical scholarship between what historian David Carr refers to as the real and "the real." Carr explains:

> Seeking to "locate" an action in the real world, with respect to time, the historian inevitably situates it in relation to the events that really followed. For the agent, however, the act was not so situated, and the genuine understanding of the action seems to require taking seriously the agent's point of view. But this means that the very attempt to represent the reality of an action requires that it be located in a time whose future reality was very different from what really happened. . . . The temporal setting of an action is not limited to its future. The agent's view of where his action comes from, of what led up to it and caused or motivated it, may differ as radically from the historian's conception of what really happened as the action's real future may differ from its intended consequences.[86]

While not discounting anti-Semitism or the persecution of Jews—Aly and Heim are quite clear that European Jewry bore the burden of each failed policy and change of plans, expelled and robbed without exception—they nevertheless argue that answering the question of "who" will not tell us "how." Anti-Semitism, in their view, cannot account for and was not the central factor leading to the Nazi genocide: there was no evidence of an overall coherent plan orchestrated from Berlin to murder European Jewry (quite the contrary), no central decision, no state-sponsored, well-coordinated, or single-minded effort, at least initially. During a 1998 interview at Yad Vashem, Heim elaborated:

> Sociologists, space planners, economists, agricultural planners, and historians . . . didn't just act because they were anti-Semites, although many of them were. They were mainly driven by a utopian idea of a modern efficient economy to make Poland an efficient part of greater Europe, ruled by the Germans. The main aim of these planners and experts was not to solve the "Jewish Question[.]" . . . [E]xcluding the Jews from the economy was just a tool for realizing their economic projects. In their perspective, they had to exclude part of the population from the economy, and even out of society, because in their calculations there were too many people, and Nazi racial antisemitism provided the criteria of who to select to be pushed out.[87]

In this and their joint rendering, as we have seen, anti-Semitism is not *the* story even while it becomes an essential constituent of the story and critically shapes its outcome. What Aly and Heim offer instead is a reading that situates anti-Semitism in a larger context of and as part of a deadly dynamic between economic and population schemes designed to rationalize production across the continent while also creating a new, utterly segregated ethnographic order. And what bears special emphasis here is that rationalizing production was not only or simply about the effective utilization of raw materials or the efficient organization of agriculture and industry. It also entailed organizing and rationalizing the allocation and use of human material—something that is often seen as part of and thus lost amid the gruesome details of atrocity, or, as Foucault has put it, "the murderous splendor" of the regime. This process—of "distributing the living in the domain of value and utility"—required registering, evaluating, classifying, and tracking individuals as well as population groups, in order to better assess and integrate comparative costs, risks, and productive capacity, in both a social and a biological sense, and brought demographers, economists, and regional planners, if not in harmony with, then certainly within working proximity of their professional counterparts in medicine, anthropology, and race science. Laboring bodies, reproductive bodies, racially marked bodies, bodies deemed genetically productive and/or pernicious—all were among the readily available and consumable raw materials that could be mobilized, disciplined, resettled, exploited, and discarded by offices and functionaries as needed.[88] Such was (and is) the prerogative of the state. In this respect, racial science—begun long before the Nazi rise to power and practiced throughout the West during this period—as well as the policy initiatives and regulatory norms and strategies generated by it were essential components of the Reich's ethnic and economic modernization programs.[89] And it is in the evolution and eventual collapse of these partially pursued and imperfectly implemented programs and the ever more radical networks of terror they fostered both within Germany and throughout the conquered territories that one can begin to piece together the confused, twisted, and protracted process that produced mass murder as an administratively plausible and apparently practical "necessity."

V.

When the Allied powers were drawing up the roster of defendants to prosecute at Nuremberg, they sought to include a cross section of the Nazi leadership. The prosecution of prominent Nazis was of course given; but the tribunal also sought to bring to trial representatives of the regime's many organizations and groups—candidates who contributed to the twelve or more years of Nazi oppression across Europe but whose crimes were without precise geographic localization.[90] Significantly, but perhaps not surprisingly, statisticians, sociologists, engineers, architects, space planners, economists, agricultural planners, and historians were not among those selected for trial even while the elaborate biodemographic reconfigurations of land and populations primarily in the east envisioned by experts in each of these fields were an integral component of the constitutive rationale for what became administrative mass murder. Indeed, individuals who played a central role in drafting and guiding the initial implementation of plans for the global remodeling of Europe—and whose practices, as Aly argues, were essential to establishing the formative conditions of genocide—drifted back into private life once the war ended and turned their quite considerable skills in human geography and regional planning, registration and categorization toward rebuilding the country—in the service of yet another vision that would "make the world better."[91]

Aly and Karl Heinz Roth note that a similar elision exists in the scholarly literature on the period. As they observe in their study of Nazi census taking, while "the murder of millions of Jews has been researched more intensively than any other historically relevant topic . . . many of the bureaucratic and scientific techniques used by the Nazis have not been taken into account. This is probably because they are, in many respects, considered normal techniques of the modern state—used to be sure, in extreme cases, but by no means considered shady."[92] The issue Aly and Roth foreground in this passage is not about a failure to appreciate the practices of the technocrat or banal bureaucrat who went about his work writing ordinary but lethal memos, nor are they advancing some version of the popular, thoroughly clichéd view that those who served the Nazi state were merely cogs in a machinery of death. Rather their emphasis is on the immanent logic of forms of rationality, modes of relations, mechanisms of management, and techniques of power that regularly produce and distribute order and suffering as a matter of course; forms of rationality, modes of relations, mechanisms of management, and techniques of power that were and remain, at bottom, essential and naturalized—which is to say virtually invisible—features of all modern states.[93]

Consider for the moment in this regard a conversation that transpired between Eichmann and his Israeli captors shortly before he was executed. Eichmann was asked in his capacity as a former "expert" in Jewish Affairs what he thought the Jews might have done to resist or subvert the Nazis' program in all its various phases. His response is telling. The Jews, he answered, could have resisted by disappearing:

> We would have been at a loss if they had disappeared before being registered and concentrated. The number of our commandos was very small, and even if the local police had helped us with all they had, their chances would have been at least fifty-fifty. A mass flight would have been disastrous for us.[94]

Certainly on the face of it and regarded retrospectively through the lens of extraordinary atrocity, this response seems, as the Court found a great many of Eichmann's responses in Jerusalem, cynical and dissembling: from the sealed world that was Europe under Nazi siege, to where precisely could a stateless and otherwise marked population have escaped? But Eichmann's response assumes a somewhat different cast and resonance when read through the lens Aly provides and considered in terms of the kaleidoscope of institutions and agencies generating, implementing, and revising on an ongoing basis the regime's population policies, regulatory strategies, and resettlement schemes. What it foregrounds is not primarily a helpless passivity in the face of imminent slaughter. What it foregrounds is how utterly dependent the government-driven program of genocide was on processing individuals through perfectly conventional and familiar registration practices—practices that under normal or even extreme (perhaps especially extreme) circumstances, most individuals would have no reason to distrust (and few resources to resist if they did).

And, in some sense, that is the point: as Aly and Roth note, "every act of extermination was preceded by an act of registration."[95] These practices refined and were in turn refined by ever more elaborate, identity-based classificatory schemes, utilized throughout the West and regarded, at the time, as scientifically based and sound. And in the normal course of things, such schemes are accepted as the unremarkable tools of asset management and a routine component of modern statecraft. They help render the social field legible and thus permit states to take inventory, mobilize resources, rationalize production, and achieve greater efficiency in the distribution of services and the redistribution of wealth. That rendering the social field legible also facilitates the disciplining of populations through bodily mapping and self-disclosure and may more easily enable the targeting and application of lethal force against groups deemed "biopolitically" suspect is precisely what leads Aly and Roth to closely scrutinize and track how and through what mechanisms systems of counting and sorting work and expand. These systems organize, administer, and sustain the lifeworld, to be sure; but what the Allies missed at Nuremberg and what continues to be ignored or discounted is the absolute centrality of such systems to Auschwitz. They are its precondition. And they are in the end, to conclude this chapter following Adi Ophir, what makes Auschwitz an integral part of the industrial revolution, an industrialized process in a world of manufacture. Ophir elaborates:

> Auschwitz was the site of a plant deploying familiar technologies of space management, of the classification and management of human beings, of the processing of organic and inorganic materials. It was seemingly, but only seemingly, an impossible combination of slaughterhouse and distillery, prison camp and industrial plant, slave camp and mechanized meat-packing plant. Auschwitz must be thought through on all these continuities combined, even if it turns out that on each separate continuum Auschwitz is located at the extreme point, that it manifests an apex of what the continuum measures.[96]

3   Thoughtlessness and Evil

What makes judgment possible, Arendt argued, are the purging effects of critical thought, the disassembling of received customs, rules, opinions, codes of conduct, and established values that may otherwise come to function as banisters of a sort to which we grow habituated and on which we may depend, not as the cultural conventions they represent, but as part of the given architecture of the world. Critical thought is the undoing of the ostensibly given, the perpetual scrutiny of "fixed habits of thought" and of "entrenched moral beliefs and cultural standards ossified into inflexible general precepts." This scrutiny creates, in turn, an "open space for discernment." As Arendt put it, "You remain in a way empty after thinking. . . . And once you are empty, then in a way which is difficult to say, you are prepared to judge. That is, without having any book of rules, under which you can subsume a particular case, you have got to say 'this is good,' 'this is bad,' 'this is right,' 'this is wrong.'" As a practice that "loosens the hold of universals," thinking prepares us for judging, for saying what is and for meeting "whatever we must meet . . . head-on, without any preconceived system."[1]

I.

In 1972, a three-day conference on the work of Hannah Arendt was held at York University.[2] Arendt was invited to attend the conference as its guest of honor but declined, preferring instead to attend as a participant along with a select group of other thinkers—which, of course, she was permitted to do. In the context of an exchange on the tensions in her work that suffuse the relationship between *thinking* and *acting*) the discussion momentarily settled to query the calling of the political theorist, turning specifically to consider whether teaching, writing, or theorizing could be regarded as forms of political action. Arendt argued that they could not be; indeed, to conflate thinking and acting or theory and practice was, if not delusional, then certainly dishonest.[3] Each activity not only constituted a fundamentally and necessarily distinct "existential position"; thinking and acting each also entailed fundamentally and necessarily distinct postures of engagement with and disengagement from the shared world of human affairs. In her view this difference was plainly underscored by the fact that "you can only act in concert and . . . only think by yourself."[4]

64

Political economist Christian Bay took umbrage at Arendt's formulation and called the group's attention to her account of Eichmann and what he regarded as the clear implications of this account for political education. *Eichmann in Jerusalem* stood out as Arendt's most serious work, he suggested, at least in part because of the great force with which she was able to demonstrate "how Eichmann is in each one of us."[5] If such was the case—and for him and others, certainly, the pervasive complacency of an American electorate in the face of political abuses, corruption, scandal, and social injustice seemed to suggest that it could be—it was clearly the job of the political theorist, indeed his or her highest calling, to join thinking and acting in a struggle for justice and human survival. As Bay saw it, this entailed, among other things, working specifically to instruct and compel one's students *and* fellow citizens to "find ways of coping with, combating, and surpassing Eichmann in ourselves."[6]

Arendt rejected Bay's rendering of her analysis of Eichmann along with the conclusions he drew from it. She described both as a fundamental and, in almost every important respect, ludicrous misunderstanding of her encounter in Jerusalem.

> You like my book *Eichmann in Jerusalem* and you say that I said there is an Eichmann in each one of us. Oh no! There is none in you and none in me! This doesn't mean that there are not quite a number of Eichmanns. But they look really quite different. I always hated this notion of "Eichmann in each one of us." This is simply not true. This would be as untrue as the opposite, that Eichmann is in nobody. In the way I look at things, this is much more abstract than the most abstract things I indulge in so frequently—if we mean by abstract: really not thinking through experience.[7]

Despite Arendt's efforts to set the record straight in this exchange with Bay,[8] her account of Eichmann as a disturbingly average, petty, deferential, careerist bureaucrat of middling intelligence—driven *not* by ideological convictions or sadistic impulses but in large measure by the desire to better himself—seemed to many a fitting description of what individuals living disaffected, narrowly circumscribed lives had and could again become in the context of modern technocratic, bureaucratic societies. And marshaled to support this popularized view were the experiments of Stanley Milgram. Conducted in the early 1960s at Yale University, Milgram's experiments appeared to capture subjects willing to deliver harmful, ostensibly painful, and, in some cases, deadly electric shocks to protesting victims (actors) simply on the say-so of white-coated authorities. The favored interpretation at the time—marshaled in the context of the divisive popular debate over the Vietnam War but frequently invoked since—was that under the *right* circumstances otherwise law-abiding individuals were entirely capable of "becoming agents of destructive processes" in ways similar to many

Germans during the war.[9] As Milgram explained in the opening chapter of his 1974 book, *Obedience to Authority*, "Arendt's conception of the *banality of evil* comes closer to the truth than one might dare imagine. The ordinary person who shocked the victim did so out of a sense of obligation—a conception of his duties as a subject—and not from any peculiarly aggressive tendencies."[10]

The notion that Eichmann could have been anyone—given the "right" circumstances—and that the Holocaust, therefore, could (have) happen(ed) anywhere was perhaps one of the most widely assumed and even embraced misconceptions of Arendt's work. And, curiously enough, it persists in contemporary scholarship. Consider in this regard Daniel Goldhagen's book, *Hitler's Willing Executioners: Ordinary Germans and the Holocaust*.[11] In this work, Goldhagen argues that while the genocide of European Jewry became Germany's national project only in 1933 with the popular election of Hitler, this project was nevertheless fueled by a centuries-long obsession with driving or removing the Jews from Europe. Goldhagen claims that anti-Semitic ideology—what he calls "eliminationist antisemitism"—was the essential, decisive, indeed, sole, factor in precipitating and sustaining a continent-wide killing enterprise for which the war itself was merely a pretense. And he understands himself to be arguing against a vision that he maintains now dominates intellectual discourse of the perpetrators as "numb, inane one-dimensional men," a vision for which he sees Hannah Arendt principally responsible.[12] Similarly, historian Michael Allen begins his study of the complex organization and workings of the German war economy by taking critical aim at what he describes as Arendt's historically uninformed and politically misguided portrait of Eichmann, in part because this portrait "fixed for the next forty years and likely more, popular conceptions of the Nazi bureaucrat."[13] Indeed, far from being the "classic, atomized 'organizational man,'" Allen argues, Eichmann along with other functionaries who staffed the SS administration were anything but atomized or disaffected automatons: they were, on the contrary, ideologically dedicated and fanatical in their commitment to the genocidal project of National Socialism.[14] Finally, historian Yaacov Lozowick's study, *Hitler's Bureaucrats*, pursues a line of argument similar to Allen's. He likewise rues the lasting influence of what he believes are Arendt's erroneous distortions of the historical record and aims to set that record straight by showing, once and for all, that "there was nothing banal about the evil of Eichmann and his comrades."[15] Resuscitating the dramatically different renderings of the former Nazi official that emerged from the proceedings in Jerusalem, Lozowick observes (or laments) that whereas Hausner's view of Eichmann as the "personification of satanic principles" resides somewhere in the general vicinity of historical truth, "in the duel of explanations" since the trial it is rather Arendt's account of the official as a "normal" nondescript bureaucrat that has "won hands down." In his reading, history gives us "a group of people completely aware of what they were doing, people with high ideological motivation, people of initiative and dexterity who contributed far beyond what was necessary."[16] And yet:

> Generations of educators, journalists, preachers, politicians and scholars have adopted as fact that the main difference between most of mankind and Adolf Eichmann is the specific historical situation: Most of us, exposed to the historical winds which pushed Eichmann, would probably have been carried away, as he was. . . . Arendt and her followers . . . wish us to accept that in spirit we are all potential accomplices: there but for the grace of circumstance, go we.[17]

Although Arendt's account of Eichmann may be vulnerable to the kinds of misreadings Allen, Lozowick, and Goldhagen among others develop, it nevertheless remains curious that a position she clearly disavowed and described as belonging to a book she never wrote and no one ever read, continues to be invoked as if she herself held and promoted it.[18] Rather than simply dismiss or ignore such misreadings, we might pause for the moment and ask instead how they actually contribute to contemporary inquiries: for what version(s) of the world are they needed, and what versions do they generate?

Clearly, we might answer this question in a number of ways. But we would find each such answer inescapably anchored in some combination of the conventionally accepted (if also variously contested) morality tales that the Holocaust has been called upon to tell over the course of the past fifty years and that we have already encountered in some form or another in earlier chapters. For example, described as a problem of blind obedience and individual conformity, Eichmann situates us at the extreme end of dangers identified by Alexis de Tocqueville or the classical liberal theorist John Stuart Mill in the mid-nineteenth century: social tyranny, social conformity, apathy, and intolerance on the one hand, coupled with the illegitimate use of state power or political tyranny on the other, together jeopardize a shared world in ways Tocqueville or Mill could not have begun to imagine. Not surprisingly, this is at least one of the ways in which this past shows up in the United States, a country that understands itself to be among the world's liberators rather than perpetrators and in all ways the antithesis of Nazi Germany in its defense of pluralism, individual rights, civil liberties, and the conditions for democratic self-governance. And note that what is perfectly consistent with the logic of this story are conclusions similar to those that Milgram and legions of researchers since have drawn from his experiment regarding the perils of individual complacency, indifference, and obedience to authority. In other words, there is a reason that Milgram's findings, which see "evil" as a situational attribute, seem "closer to the truth" and, more to the point, that the book Arendt never wrote has enjoyed such lasting resonance.[19] The notion that Eichmann could have been anyone given the "right" circumstances produces a known and conventional moral universe whose coherence, while perhaps violently shaken by the scope of Nazi atrocity, reemerges curiously intact. It is a universe in which the perpetrators are, in the end, what we apparently need and expect them to be: individuals who have grown complacent, alienated, narrowly careerist and/or deferential to authority but who are still capable of choice and, by every significant measure, responsible. In this world, Anne Frank's much-quoted insistence that "people are really good at heart" prevails.[20]

That is on the one hand. On the other and by way of further example, consider again the extent to which Eichmann and the atrocities for which he stands symbolically have been an important (though obviously not exclusive) vehicle for Israeli nationalism and the assertion of righteous state power under the auspices of security. On this discursive field, monstrosity rather than conformity is a narrative necessity: Eichmann and his comrades must be, are required to be, as Hausner depicted them, the "personification of satanic principles." For the more monstrous the threat (once was), the more innocent the victims, the more righteous the claims of the militarily achieved and maintained state acting on behalf of all wronged Jews everywhere, both living and dead, against past and future terror.[21] Indeed, the more monstrous the threat, the less questionable either the claims of the state or what can be done to secure and defend them. On this field, establishing ideology in the form of "eliminationist" anti-Semitism as the primary force and focus of Nazi policy is critical: so long as anti-Semitism persists, mass murder such as once occurred—that is, mass murder in its unprecedented singularity—could again take place. And insofar as anti-Semitism is genocide's ever present (and only) condition of possibility, preemptive measures—however harsh—are justified against those who are perceived to be potential slaughterers or persecutors. On this point Zygmunt Bauman elaborates:

> Those who need to be disempowered may not be kith and kin of the perpetrators of the Holocaust, neither bodily or spiritually, and may in no juridical or ethically sensible way be charged with responsibility for the ancestor's perdition; it is after all, the heredity of the 'hereditary victims', and *not* the continuity of their assumed victimizers, which makes the 'connection.' Yet, in a world haunted by the ghost of the Holocaust such assumed would-be persecutors are guilty in advance, guilty of *being seen* as inclined or able to engage in another genocide. They need commit no crime; standing accused or just *being suspect*, true to the message of Kafka's *The Trial*, is already their crime, the only crime needed to cast them as criminals and to justify harsh preventative/punitive measures.[22]

According to Bauman, a world "haunted by the ghost of the Holocaust" is one in which the Holocaust will never stop being prophesied, is one in which, we might add, evil is not merely criminal but diabolical as well as fanatical, and not only ever present, but discursively (and politically) required.[23]

To get a concrete sense of what Bauman is describing when he speaks of a world "haunted by the ghost of the Holocaust," recall the controversy that erupted in 1985 when the otherwise media savvy former President Ronald Reagan announced that he would commemorate the fortieth anniversary of VE day by visiting a German cemetery at Bitburg—at which were buried fallen members of the *Waffen-SS*. Reagan (or his handlers) explained the visit as a gesture of reconciliation between a victorious power and its former adversary—a gesture that was intended, more specifically, to acknowledge Germany's hopeful future (in alliance with the United States against Soviet incursion) while also remembering its young draftees who fell at Leningrad ("soldiers to whom Nazism meant no more than a brutal end to a short life"); memorialize those mostly good Germans who had suffered under the yoke of "one man's totalitarian dictatorship"; and recognize the many millions who were "terrorized by the acts of a hated regime." When asked why he had not chosen a concentration camp to commemorate the end of the war or at least a site associated with the Holocaust, the president explained that he did not want to reawaken the passion of past quarrels, that is, open old wounds or feelings of guilt. And while persuaded eventually to "balance the symbolism" of his visit to Bitburg by adding Bergen-Belsen to his itinerary, Reagan was nevertheless accused of having reenacted "the complacency of governments and national leaders during the World War II years [by once again] reject[ing] the desperate cries of Jews for rescue."[24] His visit was said to have intolerably distorted history—now reconstructed and marshaled to serve the administration's reinvigorated cold war battle against communism—and ignored or simply erased what many commentators insisted was its principal lesson. As Martin Marty reflected in a *Los Angeles Times* article that appeared shortly after the commemorative event:

> Bitburg is likely to reinforce Jewish fears and resolve. Bitburg was a nonviolent, calculatedly gentle and solemn event, yet one might say that 1985 raised sharply the possibility of Jewish "storycide." The dictionary does not include or need that term, but the world needs such a concept. If a story sustains Judaism, then to distort, neglect, mute or forget that story would be to help end the people and all it holds dear. . . . Have we made the point of the Holocaust story so weakly, so forgettably? After only 40 years, can a President and his advisors, people adept at manipulating symbols, have so misunderstood ours? Can they not have learned other ways to "reconcile" than to walk past the SS graves and "balance" the death of drafted German youth with the weight of 6 million innocents led to death? If our story is thus downgraded and devalued, and if that story matters for our existence, are we secure? Will we survive when greater tests come?[25]

69   Thoughtlessness and Evil

The administration may have sought—as the *Wall Street Journal* put it—to "lay some of the ghosts of the past to rest." And there are many things that we might say about the utterly inept and arrogant way in which it failed to appreciate (or worse yet, comprehend) the complex histories and density of stories that constitute the Holocaust and anchor competing claims over how and by whom it will be remembered.[26] But as Bauman and Marty both make clear on behalf of very different arguments (and agendas), the very ghosts the administration sought to appease—much like the Eichmann Arendt claimed never to have seen or described—are now discursively indispensable to postwar political and national identitites. And indispensable as well to a particular version of the world that hears in their continued haunting sacral mystery, meaning, and an ominous if ineffable prophesy of horrors yet to come. But where Marty sees this haunting as a matter of survival, Bauman sees in it instead a dangerous diversion that works to mythologize genocide and obscure "the ground in which it might be genuinely rooted." In this, he echoes the insight that informs Aly's work, as we saw in the previous chapter, and like Aly seeks to redirect our attention away from the mesmerizing horrors of Auschwitz to the conditions that make such horrors possible. Bauman continues: "While we know quite well that prejudice threatens humanity and we even know how to fight and constrain the ill intentions of people poisoned with prejudice, we know little about how to stave off the threat of murder which masquerades as the routine and unemotional functioning of orderly society."[27]

And here is where we return to Arendt, reframing the question of how mass murder becomes part of the routine functioning of an orderly society by considering the responsibility of functionaries who administer such order: if Eichmann is not "everyman" given similar circumstances or a "beast in the jungle" as Hausner described him during the trial, how are we to think about him, and why might it matter? It was in observing and listening to the actions and explanations of Eichmann in Jerusalem—this transportation officer whose job it was to move human freight from one place to another—that Arendt encountered what she came to describe as the "banality of evil." This "banality," she claimed, was "borne out by the facts of the case," even while it "contradicted prevailing theories and understandings concerning evil" and thus seemed hardly plausible.[28] However, rather than dismiss the notion because of its utter implausibility, Arendt turned a critical eye instead to conventional understandings that rendered it so, to accounts of good and evil that relied on what was, in effect, a Manichaean framework and as such were fundamentally and irreducibly theological. As Dana Villa explains, a diabolical or "absysslike evil requires an author (human or transhuman) of similar depth and proportion"[29] who is embodied in some form and tirelessly pursues the destruction and corruption of what is good and innocent. In Arendt's view, such a figure was not the accused—was not the Eichmann that she, or the prosecution, or the foreign press, for that matter, actually encountered on the stand in Jerusalem even while the prosecution and press alike read Eichmann's unexceptionally flat and disappointing demeanor as merely the most cunning of ruses, further evidence in the end of the very evil he seemed in appearance to lack.[30]

Arendt acknowledged that "it would have been very comforting indeed to believe that Eichmann was a monster."[31] This would certainly let the rest of us off the hook and, as the journalist Harry Mulisch observed, "allow us to believe in the Devil even if it was no longer possible to believe in God."[32] But Arendt saw in him something she maintained was far more terrifying and consequential. What "stared one in the face at the trial," she argued, was not monstrosity but "sheer thoughtlessness," and it was precisely this thoughtlessness or shallowness, Eichmann's lack of "diabolical or demonic profundity," that forced one, in her view, to reconsider accounts that required him and others (in the Nazi leadership like him) to be both diabolically and demonically profuse, somehow larger than life, "the most abnormal monster[s] the world has ever seen."[33] To be sure, among those who served the Third Reich, there were thugs, fanatics, racists, sadists, and perverts—about this Arendt did not argue. But the vast majority, she contended and others since have confirmed, were probably more like Eichmann—quite commonplace or ordinary people who routinely engaged in quite extraordinary criminal acts. They constituted, as did Eichmann, a "new kind of criminal." And in order to ascertain precisely how and in what ways, in order to determine both the nature and the implications of this new criminal and his crime, one was required, as she later formulated it, to dispense with metaphysical dualisms and "approach the problem of evil in an entirely secular setting."[34]

II.

Early in her report on the Eichmann trial, Arendt notes that half a dozen psychiatrists had been called upon to examine and assess the mental state of the former Nazi official and found him a more or less well-rounded man of "positive ideas"— "more normal than I am after having examined him . . . one of them was said to have exclaimed while another found that his whole psychological outlook, his attitude toward his wife and children, mother and father, brothers, sisters, and friends was 'not only normal but most desirable.'"[35] The consensus among these specialists was significant: Eichmann could not be regarded as either legally insane or morally deranged; he was neither feebleminded, cynical, hopelessly indoctrinated, fanatically anti-Semitic, nor in possession of an obviously criminal "nature."[36] Pathology of the sort they were apparently prepared to find or uncover was nowhere in evidence. But still, there was something Arendt maintained these experts missed or failed to recognize, something decisively more troubling than his otherwise "normal," unremarkable demeanor. And this she described as a twofold incapacity. Throughout the proceedings, she argued, Eichmann displayed an inability not only to think—by which she meant an inability to take in or consider the world from another's point of view—but also to speak, to "utter a single sentence that was not a cliché."[37] This inability to talk without cliché or the use of "stock phrases" was something for which Eichmann himself repeatedly apologized in court. "Officialese," he offered, "is my only language."[38] And it was also something for which the judges repeatedly reprimanded him: "they . . . told the accused that all he had said was 'empty talk'—except that they thought the emptiness was feigned, and that the accused wished to cover up other thoughts which, though hideous, were not empty."[39] In Arendt's reading, this was not the case: there was no hidden or hideous evil lurking beneath or behind the defendant's nondescript exterior, no mask to be removed or depths to be unearthed and examined. As she explains:

> The longer one listened to him, the more obvious it became that [Eichmann's] inability to speak was closely connected with an inability to *think*, namely, to think from the standpoint of somebody else. No communication was possible with him, not because he lied [as the judges and prosecution maintained] but because he was surrounded by the most reliable of all safeguards against the words and the presence of others, and hence against reality as such.[40]

What precisely were the "safeguards" that so insulated Eichmann? Because Arendt did not specify them in the context of her report on the trial, it is to subsequent writing that we turn to reconstruct her meaning. But we begin, first, by briefly underscoring what she did *not* mean in part because of the nearly irresistible impulse as readers to simply shift registers and reformulate the notion of "thinking from the standpoint of somebody else" as a problem of empathetic identification. This reflexive reinterpretation follows from the constitutive (though not uncontested) place empathy occupies in conventional accounts of moral development as well as conventional understandings of what anchors moral sensibility.[41] A reading of Eichmann through the optics of such accounts would go something like this: had Eichmann been able to empathize with those he sent en mass to their death; had he been able to see them or feel-with or feel-for them as individuals with whom he shared a common humanity; had he dealt with names and faces rather than lists of nationalities, then—and here we find ourselves inadvertently reentering the fictionalized world of Anne Frank's good-hearted people—things might have taken a different turn. In other words, within the frame of such reasoning, there is a chain of assumption that moves from proximity to compassion or pity and from compassion to moral response. And the philosopher Arte Vetlesen suggests why: proximity, he explains, typically "possesses the power to call the bluff of dehumanization."[42]

In the case of Eichmann, this power of proximity clearly failed: Eichmann met regularly with the leadership of the Jewish Councils and described his encounters with Council members as both "normal and human" and, at times, even "friendly."[43] They were not a mere abstraction even while the changing lists and figures that leaders were required to submit to him of people to be transported might have been: and still he persisted, apparently unfazed and disinterested, although guided in his work, as the Court later learned, by what he more or less accurately identified as a version of Kant's categorical imperative, a version "for the household use of the little man."[44] That he could meet with members of the Jewish Council and enlist its leaders in expanding Nazi terror against those whose trust they bore—without apparent feeling for the suffering he inflicted, many times multiplied—appears only to underscore, as it did certainly for the Court and has for generations since, the extent of his depravity or, as Vetlesen puts it more on point, his *insensitivity*. Taking issue with Arendt's rendering of the figure of Eichmann, Vetlesen elaborates: "The capacity [Eichmann] failed to exercise is emotional rather than intellectual or cognitive; it is the capacity to develop *empathy* with other human beings, to take an emotional interest in the "human" import of the situation in which the persons affected by his actions found themselves."[45]

Arendt proffers an altogether less confident assessment than Vetlesen and other contemporary moral theorists of the political potential of moral sentiments. Indeed, in *On Revolution*, a comparative study of the French and American Revolutions, she takes critical aim at the idea that human emotions could be either a site or a source of guidance in public affairs, and highlights by way of example the terror (of virtue) let loose during the French Revolution when the revolutionary enterprise of founding freedom gave way to the project of alleviating human suffering.[46] Overwhelmed by the "spectacle of people's suffering,"[47] and overcome with "the passion of compassion" in the presence of such suffering, those who championed the revolution jettisoned the tedious struggle over institutions and constitutions and, in Arendt's rendering of the story, turned their efforts instead to lifting the yoke of need and necessity.[48] From this shift in focus followed rage and sheer terror. Arendt explains: compassion does not typically "set out to change worldly conditions in order to ease human suffering"; it emerges, rather, in response to particulars, to the specific anguish of specific persons in the form of mutual suffering, and, for this reason, it typically compels by abolishing distance between people. However, when generalized and mobilized in the service of worldly change, using Arendt's language now, it becomes both impatient and boundless: "it will shun the drawn-out wearisome processes of persuasion, negotiation, and compromise, which are the processes of law and politics, and lend its voice to the suffering itself, which must claim for swift and direct action, that is, for action with the means of violence."[49] And there is more. For where compassion may initially have "summoned the resources of the heart against indifference and injustice," in the context of the French Revolution, it was pity—what Arendt calls the perversion of compassion—rather than solidarity that "reached out to the multitude" and bound the few to the many. In contrast to solidarity, which Arendt sees as an alternative to pity and which can be "aroused by suffering but is not guided by it," pity cannot exist without the presence of misfortune and both glorifies and sentimentalizes those in its grip (they are the virtuous, the wise, and/or the more truly authentic). Where solidarity can "deliberately and dispassionately establish a community of interest with the oppressed and exploited," in part, she explains, because reason guides and constrains it, pity shuns institutional order and convention and demands redress on behalf of the dispossessed. But its claims and imperatives, emotion-laden and thus always volatile, know no limit. In this respect, Arendt maintains, pity "possess[es] a greater capacity for cruelty than cruelty itself": it razes whatever obstructs its path and silences whoever might frustrate its claims. In Arendt's words: "Measured against the immense sufferings of the immense majority of the people, the impartiality of justice and law, the application of the same rules to those who sleep in palaces and those who sleep under bridges . . . [is] like a mockery."[50]

In Arendt's reading, therefore, emotions can prove and have proven fickle, boundless, and easily co-opted in political life. And for this reason it is unlikely that she would then have seen in the presence or absence of particular emotional responses or faculties a possible antidote to (rather than vehicle for) totalitarian terror. In other words, for Arendt, it was not Eichmann's lack of affect—his lack of compassion or his impaired capacity for empathy—that struck her during the trial and led her to describe him in her trial report as someone unable to "think from where he was not." As she would later recall, what was in evidence at the trial, indeed, what was most telling was Eichmann's persistent self-abandonment, his inability to take in the reality that was right in front of him, his refusal to engage in what she calls a "thinking dialogue." For as Arendt construes it in her later work, *thinking from where one is not* is primarily a practice of self-examination and accountability. Such thinking, she maintains, requires a certain retreat from the world so that the mind can turn toward itself—and this, in order that we might then critically scrutinize our actions and interactions over the course of daily life. At the center of this critical engagement whose condition of possibility is solitude are the assumptions and convictions that shape activity; the fixed habits of thought and entrenched belief, the many varied and often inconsistent stories each of us might tell ourselves about who we are and what we are doing.[51] And part of the process of such reflection entails imagining, representing, making present to ourselves what is absent—the views of others as a countervailing set of claims and perspectives not, primarily, for the purpose of establishing affective ties with other individuals or knowing where they stand or what they might feel but as a way of determining and evaluating (by contrast) where one stands oneself. This process Arendt describes as "training one's mind to going visiting." She explains:

> I form an opinion by considering a given issue from different viewpoints, by making present to my mind the standpoints of those who are absent; that is, I represent them. This process of representation does not blindly adopt the actual views of those who stand somewhere else, and hence look upon the world from a different perspective; this is a question neither of empathy nor of counting noses and joining the majority but of being and thinking in my own identity where actually I am not. . . . Imagination [or representational thinking] alone enables us to see things in their proper perspective[,] . . . to put that which is too close at a certain distance so that we can see and understand it without bias and prejudice, to be generous enough to bridge certain abysses of remoteness until we can see and understand everything that is too far away from us as though it were our own affair. This distancing of some things and bridging of others is part of the dialogue of understanding, for whose purposes direct experience establishes too close a contact and mere knowledge erects artificial barriers.[52]

The "dialogue of understanding" Arendt refers to in this passage is one in which individuals engage with the ever present witness or "observant other of [their] own conscience."[53] And the conscience she references is not the voice of god or some intuitive moral sense or even reason; nor is it simply the psychically registered norms and values of society. In each of these instances, right conduct ultimately comes down to a matter of obedience whether it is reason or some higher power, by whatever name we call it, telling us "what to do and what to repent." Arendt instead takes her model (or metaphor) for conscience from Socrates. On returning home each night, she tells us, Socrates claimed to encounter "a very obnoxious fellow," someone he described nonetheless as a friend or close relative with whom he shared a house and an ongoing if sometimes fraught conversation. Waiting only with questions (rather than advice or direction) and refusing to be put off, Socrates' friend is the one to whom he insists he must give an account of himself each day and with whom he cannot risk living in discord. As he explains matters to one of his interlocutors in the *Gorgias*: "It would be better for me that my lyre or a chorus I directed should be out of tune and loud with discord, and that multitudes of men should disagree with me rather than that I, *being one*, should be out of harmony with myself and contradict me."[54]

Arendt refers to the practice of self-examination depicted in this passage from the *Gorgias* as the Socratic "two-in-one." By this she means to underscore a particular kind of encounter of the self with itself, the self engaged in a "thinking dialogue" whose aim, she argues, is not truth—which would altogether retire the need for thinking—but consistency or what Socrates calls "harmony." Such consistency, while a condition of living peacefully with myself—keeping company with that obnoxious person who waits for me at home—is also only provisional, an ongoing if tenuous achievement given the basic deconstructive character of the thinking dialogue "which relentlessly dissolves and examines anew all accepted doctrines and rules," opinions and beliefs.[55] "The business of thinking," writes Arendt,

> is like Penelope's web; it undoes every morning what it has finished the night
> before. For the need to think can never be stilled by allegedly definite insights
> of "wise men"; it can be satisfied only through thinking, and the thoughts I had
> yesterday will satisfy this need today only to the extent that I want and am able to
> think them anew.[56]

How much easier it may seem, Arendt notes following Socrates, to avoid one's own company as we will certainly seek to if we are at war with ourselves; indeed, "blissfully fortunate" is the person, says Socrates, who never goes home and examines things and is thus able to elude her observant other. Although such a person may then fail to develop a distinctive humanity and only sleepwalk through life—for in Arendt's view, thinking is "the dematerialized quintessence of being alive"—hers will also be an untroubled (if meaningless) existence, lived entirely on the surface of things according to conventional rules of conduct, prevailing trends, or prescribed fashions. It is in the encounter of the self with itself—where I am both actor and onlooker, subject and object—that I engage and negotiate difference; and it is in the thinking dialogue between me and myself that I am then compelled to critically consider and come to terms with it, dismantling and renarrativizing my life and history and the assumptions and convictions that structure both.

If "thinking as such" is for Arendt essential in the constitution of a meaningful life or the development of our distinctive humanity, it tends also (under most historical circumstances) to be a politically irrelevant, socially inconsequential activity. Generally speaking, she observes, "it does society little good. . . . It does not create values; it will not find out, once and for all, what 'the good' is; it does not conform but, rather, dissolves accepted rules of conduct."[57] Moreover, thinking can be and frequently is considered dangerous and, by some, even "nihilistic" in effect because it entails a relentless, critical questioning of received norms, accepted doctrines, conventional practices, and cultural sentiments—"undo[ing] every morning what it has finished the night before." And Arendt acknowledges the risks "inherent in the thinking activity itself," although she rejects the notion that nihilism is its product.[58] But times in which thinking comes to be considered especially dangerous or is denounced as nihilistic tend also to be precisely those times when it ceases to be a politically marginal activity—times, in other words, of political emergency when, as she puts it following Yeats, "Things fall apart; the center cannot hold." At such moments, the purging effects of critical (self-)examination comes up against and sometimes collides, brutally, with entrenched ideas, national pieties, or moral certainties and the often dogmatic insistence that further thinking is not only unnecessary, but crippling, subversive, and even treasonous: "When everybody is swept away unthinkingly by what everybody else does and believes in, those who think are drawn out of hiding because their refusal to join in is conspicuous and thereby becomes a kind of action."[59]

In such a context when, as Arendt puts it, the "stakes are on the table," the critical engagement that distinguishes the activity of thinking creates an open space for discernment and works to orient individuals. Although thinking itself is not productive—it neither creates nor promotes particular values, particular rules, or particular notions of the good—Arendt tells us that in politically turbulent times it provides a critical vantage and equips individuals with what may well be the only compass available for navigating conditions of moral collapse and terror.

III.

So where does this leave us with Eichmann and Arendt's claim on the one hand that it was "sheer thoughtlessness . . . that predisposed him to become one of the greatest criminals of the period" and her insistence on the other that in this *thoughtlessness* lay a story about the banality of evil. The issue, clearly, is not—as it seems to have routinely become in studies of the Nazi leadership or the regime's midlevel administrators—what precisely Eichmann (or Albert Speer, or Joseph Strangl, or countless other prominent officials) knew and when he (they) knew it; or what he felt and didn't feel.[60] Nor is it a question of Eichmann's intelligence as some critics have understood Arendt and gone to great lengths to counter: as she explains it, "Thinking in its non-cognitive, non-specialized sense . . . is not a prerogative of the few but an ever-present faculty in everybody; the inability to think is not a failing of the many who lack brain power but an ever-present possibility for everybody—scientists, scholars, and other specialists in mental enterprises not excluded—to shun that intercourse

Figure 3.1. Eichmann giving testimony at his trial, 1961. Courtesy of
the Yad Vashem Photo Archive, Jerusalem, Israel.

with oneself whose possibility and importance Socrates first discovered."[61]
Sheer thoughtlessness in the case of Eichmann has rather to do with his refusal
at any number of significant junctures over the course of his career—and some
eighteen years afterward—to engage the world as it was, to say *this is wrong* even
as he described for the Court any number of instances that threw into painfully
sharp relief the broader meaning and unmistakably dreadful consequences of
his job as a "transportation officer" for dispossessed populations across Europe
and for European Jewry in particular, his special area of expertise.

The Wannsee Conference—however we might understand what transpired
there—is one such instance. As Eichmann and numerous biographers since
have told it, he preferred a territorial solution as the cornerstone of German policy but when the "Popes of the Third Reich" determined that a physical solution
was now to be coordinated and implemented, Eichmann expressed misgivings

Thoughtlessness and Evil

to his superior but ultimately complied. *"Who was he to judge?* Who was he 'to have [his] own thoughts in this matter'?"[62] But there is more—as when he insisted to his interrogators in Jerusalem that he harbored no malice toward Jews and offered as evidence his refusal to watch them being asphyxiated in a gas van at Chelmno. As he described his reaction, "I couldn't look . . . my knees were buckling under me . . . I was badly shaken." Reporting back to Müller, his immediate superior, about the killing process at Chelmno, Eichmann claims to have expressed alarm, *"This can't go on, one can't do this."*[63] And later, again to Müller, after witnessing a mass shooting at Minsk, Eichmann maintained that he was horrified and experienced if only momentarily something akin to doubt:

> The solution . . . was supposed to have been a political one. But now that the Führer
> has ordered a physical solution, obviously a physical solution it must be. But we
> cannot go on conducting executions as they were done in Minsk and, I believe, in
> other places. Our men will be educated to become sadists. We can't solve the Jew-
> ish problem by putting a bullet through the brain of a defenseless woman who is
> holding her child up to us. . . . My unconditional, my absolute allegiance underwent
> a change. . . . [W]hen the so-called solution of the Jewish question became more
> violent[,] . . . when the gassing and shooting started[,] . . . I said to my superior: . . .
> This isn't what I imagined, it probably isn't what any of us imagined because it's not
> a political solution.[64]

Finally, in terms of instances in which the broader meaning and clear consequences of Eichmann's job were before him in stark relief, there is a story he recounted for his interrogators prior to the trial that commentators since, including Arendt, have found especially revealing, although for somewhat different reasons. As Eichmann describes it, he was called to Auschwitz by the camp's commandant, Rudolf Höss, on behalf of Bernard Storfer. Storfer was an international banker and prominent member of the Jewish leadership in Vienna who had collaborated with Eichmann to organize the illegal emigration to Palestine of some 2,200 Jews from Prague (in December 1939). Arrested late in the war (1944), deported to Auschwitz, and assigned to a labor gang, Storfer sent an appeal for help to Eichmann through Höss. And Eichmann agreed to meet with him:

> I said to myself, O.K., this man has always behaved well, that is worth my
> while. . . . I'll go there myself and see what is the matter with him. . . . With Storfer
> afterward, well, it was normal and human, we had a normal, human encounter. He
> told me all his grief and sorrow: I said: "Well, my dear old friend [*Ja, mein lieber
> guter Storfer*], we certainly got it! What rotten luck!" And I also said: "Look, I really
> cannot help you, because according to orders from the Reichsführer nobody can
> get out. I can't get you out. Dr. Ebner [chief of the Gestapo in Vienna] can't get
> you out. I hear you made a mistake, that you went into hiding or wanted to bolt,

which, after all, *you* did not need to do." [Eichmann meant that Storfer, as a Jewish functionary, had immunity from deportation.] I forget what his reply to this was. And then I asked him how he was. And he said, yes, he wondered if he couldn't be let off work, it was heavy work. And then I said to Höss: "Work—Storfer won't have to work!" But Höss said: "Everyone works here." So I said: "O.K.," I said, "I'll make a chit to the effect that Storfer has to keep the gravel paths in order with a broom," there were little gravel paths there, "and that he had the right to sit down with his broom on one of the benches." [To Storfer] I said: "Will that be all right, Mr Storfer? Will that suit you?" Whereupon he was very pleased and we shook hands, and then he was given the broom and sat down on his bench. It was a great inner joy to me that I could at least see the man with whom I had worked for so many long years, and that we could speak with each other.[65]

Characterizing this episode as one "filled with macabre humor surpassing that of any Surrealist invention"—for within six weeks of Eichmann's joyful reunion, Storfer had been shot and killed—Arendt was compelled to wonder whether Eichmann's narrative wasn't simply "a textbook case of bad faith, of lying self-deception combined with outrageous stupidity[.]"[66] That he could so fail to grasp the circumstances of this meeting, the larger or even more immediate context that brought *his dear old friend* Storfer to be pleading for help on a gravel path in Auschwitz; the desperate and degrading situation that was hardly a matter of happenstance or simple misfortune, as Eichmann intimated (*what rotten luck! . . . I hear you made a mistake!*); that Eichmann failed to grasp even some eighteen years after the encounter the ways in which his actions and Storfer's fate were linked or the ways in which Storfer's situation at the time of the meeting implicated the operation he, Eichmann, had overseen throughout the war suggested, in Arendt's view, an utter dearth of imagination. And by characterizing it as such, she meant to underscore, as we have seen, Eichmann's inability to "bridge certain abysses of remoteness," to understand what was happening as though it were his own affair or to think from where he was not—even after having years during which he might have figured it out. In the absence of imagination, Arendt argues, we cannot "take our bearings in the world"; it is what provides, in the end, "the only inner compass we have."[67]

The story with Eichmann, therefore, as Arendt tells it, is that he refused to engage in the kind of thinking activity that she insists would have allowed him not only to tolerate the doubt he claimed to have experienced at Chelmno or the ditches in Minsk but also to use this doubt as the disruptive opening it presented for (re)considering the meaning of the trite bureaucratic formulas, rules, codes, and directives that together organized and continued to organize his sense of who he was and what he was doing. That Eichmann's identity was so constituted was clearly evidenced for Arendt in his insistence throughout the trial that "he would have had a bad conscience only if he had not done what he had been told to do," that is, only if he had broken with the formulas, rules, codes of expression, and directives that had come to constitute his sense of self.[68] Along these same lines and equally as telling was the fact that some two decades after the regime's collapse, Eichmann still insisted that *officialese* was his only language and still could not give a coherent account of himself—of what he said and did—that was not riddled with clichés or stock phrases or rendered in terms of the ever-present pile of documents that accompanied him in prison and court as if these papers provided definitive points of reference to some unfamiliar story, except the story if there was one was supposedly his own. Indeed, when considered through the lens that Arendt provides, there was, in the end, no personal story to be told, in part, because there was no thinking subject to tell it.

> What causes a man to fear [conscience] is the anticipation of the presence of a witness who awaits him only *if* and when he goes home. Shakespeare's murderer says: "Every man that means to live well endeavors . . . to live without it," and success in that comes easy because all he has to do is never start the soundless solitary dialogue we call "thinking," never go home and examine things. This is not a matter of wickedness or goodness, as it is not a matter of intelligence or stupidity. A person who does not know that silent intercourse (in which we examine what we say and what we do) will not mind contradicting himself, and this means he will never be either able or willing to account for what he says or does; nor will he mind committing any crime, since he can count on its being forgotten the next moment.[69]

Eichmann held tenaciously to an empty oath and rules of conduct that together worked to insulate him from encountering his own witness, the ever-present, observant other. Indeed, as Arendt puts it, "he and the world he [had] lived in [were] in perfect harmony."[70] Thus he could arrange for the displacement, deportation, and eventual death of hundreds of thousands across Europe and still maintain in all sincerity, without duplicity, that he was innocent of the charges brought against him: "Officially I had nothing to do with [the gassing] and, unofficially, I wasn't interested. . . . I am responsible for the things my orders obliged me to do. . . . I have no desire to evade that responsibility. But, I refuse to take responsibility for things I had no orders for and which were not in my department."[71] In contrast to Eichmann, there emerges in Arendt's report another figure, Anton Schmidt, whose story was first told during the trial in the context of survivor testimony and who she takes as an example of someone clearly guided by his own judgment against what were the nearly unanimous opinions and inclinations of the world around him: "how utterly different everything would be today in the courtroom," Arendt reflects, "if only more such stories could have been told."[72] Schmidt was an army sergeant overseeing a patrol in Poland whose task it was to recover German soldiers who had been separated from their units. In the course of sweeping for soldiers, Schmidt was said to have encountered members of the Jewish underground; and rather than turn these partisans in, he opted to help them by supplying forged papers and trucks. This he did successfully without extracting or accepting payment for some five months until he was arrested and executed.[73]

Where Eichmann could not have imagined acting in any other way than he did—"I obeyed my orders without thinking, I just did what I was told. That's where I found my—how shall I say?—my fulfillment. It made no difference what the orders were"[74]—Schmidt obviously could and did take his bearings from elsewhere. Indeed, in a context that aimed to level difference, silence speech, and extinguish spontaneity and in contrast to Eichmann and all the many others who argued that opposition to the Nazi regime was virtually impossible and when possible "practically useless," Schmidt became, to use Arendt's language, his own witness. In times of political emergency this in itself can become an opening and act of resistance. But it was only the first of such acts for Schmidt. For while the character of his action suggests that he began what Arendt infers was a silent, solitary dialogue with himself, he seems also to have extended the conversation in ways and directions others at the time may have considered morally meaningful but also dismissed as politically pointless: he joined and died in solidarity with marked others to counter a regime that sought "to abolish the most basic material conditions for thought, identity, and agency."[75] For Arendt, the political lesson to be drawn from his example was clear: "Under conditions of terror most people will comply but *some people will not.* . . . Humanly speaking, no more is required, and no more can be reasonably asked, for this planet to remain a place fit for human habitation."[76]

IV.

In the final section of this chapter, I want to return to the question of empathy. I noted earlier that with respect to Arendt's claims the question of empathy shows up in basically two ways: it constitutes a common transliteration of what Arendt described as Eichmann's lack of imagination and inability to think where he was not; and it shows up as part of a critique of what Arendt missed or simply dismissed in marshaling what Vetlesen refers to as a "cognitively based" model to explain the dramatic asymmetry between the ordinary, even commonplace character of the defendant and the monstrous deeds for which he was being tried. In either rendering, the problem is not that Eichmann was thoughtless—and within this frame, thoughtlessness is typically equated with general intelligence or analytic competence, a significant departure from Arendt's explanation of the notion. The problem, rather, is that Eichmann could not *feel* for those who suffered at his hand or respond to the claim their suffering placed on him. In this view, then, his was an emotional rather than cognitive failure. Vetlesen, who champions such a reading, elaborates: "Eichmann failed to *perceive* the Jews as human beings and he did so because he failed to develop empathy toward them, to take an emotional interest in the human import of the situation in which they found themselves."[77] Indeed, for Vetlesen—and here he speaks both to and from conventional assumptions (versions of which have circulated since at least the eighteenth century) about the critical place of empathetic feeling in the constitution of a relationally situated but autonomous "enlightened self": empathy is an essential human faculty, in his view, "humanity's basic emotional faculty, at work in an unimpaired exercise of moral judgment."[78]

Leaving aside the question of whether and in what sense empathy can be said to be a faculty or (universal) moral property—the point is only that it has long been regarded as instrumental in the constitution of moral sensibility and as an essential constituent of "civilized" coexistence—I want to call attention to the way in which this ostensibly clarifying shift, or in Vetlesen's case, alternative formulation, fundamentally transforms the constitutive terms of the problem that Arendt insisted was Eichmann. For reading Eichmann's failure as a failure of empathetic identification restores to him precisely the dark depths that Arendt insisted were absent and whose absence then incited her efforts to articulate an entirely secular, demythologized account of the criminal and his crime. "I was struck by a manifest shallowness in the doer," she explains, and this shallowness "made it impossible to trace the uncontestable evil of his deeds to any deeper level of roots or motives. The deeds were monstrous, but the doer . . . was quite ordinary, commonplace, and neither demonic nor monstrous."[79] Pathology, however, changes everything (or at least reinstalls a more familiar conceptual landscape): it produces the well-adjusted, appropriately empathic, compassionate norm even as it casts Eichmann (reassuringly) as a departure from this norm so that an evil or perverse nature can be said (once again) to ground obviously evil deeds. Eichmann's especially flat demeanor, his nondescript self-representation, his nervous tics, crooked grimace, or formal and deferential continence when speaking may well reveal a shallow personality, as Arendt maintained. But within a conventional frame that sees in empathy a civilizing sentiment that distinguishes the pathological from the well adjusted, they are symptoms as well and evidence—the most cunning of ruses. They tell us something about the man who secured rolling stock to transport "human cargo" while being utterly indifferent to the meaning and implications of what

Figure 3.2: Court scene during the Eichmann trial, 1961. Courtesy of the Yad Vashem Photo Archive, Jerusalem, Israel.

he was doing: "*Officially I had nothing to do with [the gassing] and, unofficially, I wasn't interested.*" The scope of atrocity demands that he have an interest or at least some remorse, and his lack of empathy begins to explain why he might not experience or express either.

Even accounts that are guided by or aim to adopt Arendt's reading of Eichmann, it seems, cannot easily escape producing "thoughtlessness" as an absence of empathy or rendering what she argued was a political failure (a question of solidarity) as primarily a moral one (a question of sentiment). Consider in this regard *The Specialist*, the 1999 documentary by Eyal Sivan and Rony Brauman that elaborates Arendt's argument while also inadvertently reproducing precisely this confusion. The film draws from 350 or so hours of videotape that was shot during the trial by filmmaker and television news director, Leo Hurwitz, and broadcast daily across the globe but most extensively in the United States.[80] Considered part of the Steven Spielberg Jewish Film Archive but stored for some thirty years in an unused basement bathroom at the Hebrew University law faculty, the videotape had been spliced, sold, lent piecemeal, and left to deteriorate until the early 1990s, when Sivan and Brauman along with a team of technicians commenced to restoring and reassembling it. Once transferred to a digital format, they turned their attention to "making a movie,"

Figure 3.3: The court looks on as a film is being screened as evidence during the trial of Eichmann, June 8, 1961. United States Holocaust Memorial Museum, courtesy of the Israeli Government Press Office

based on what Sivan characterized as a "courtroom drama."[81] Although the film used only Hurwitz's raw footage, the intent of the filmmakers was not to reconstruct the original narrative structure of the trial according to the temporal or chronological scheme of day-to-day sessions. Rather, through selective editing and image enhancement they sought, in their words, to "lay down a grammar" that would allow the drama of Arendt's narrative to emerge along with its main protagonist, Eichmann. As Sivan and Brauman explained in a postproduction interview, much of the trial as it unfolded in 1961 had very little to do with Eichmann, and yet he was his own "best accuser."[82] By bringing Eichmann into focus (literally) and allowing him to give an account of himself, one could, in their view, turn his defense against him. The result of their editing, remixing, and enhancement efforts, then, is both a two-hour compilation of Hurwitz's footage and what Sivan and Brauman characterize as a two-hour *composition* organized by and around questions of responsibility and obedience. Indeed, as Sivan put it in response to charges that what he had produced was nothing more than a "perverse fraud," "all images are from the archives"—which is to say the documentary relies exclusively on Hurwitz's footage—"but no image [in *The Specialist*] exists in the archives"—in other words, all the original footage that was used was enhanced in one way or another and thus altered.[83]

The sequence to which I want to call attention comes some twenty-five minutes into *The Specialist* when the prosecution elected to show footage from numerous documentaries originally produced by U.S., British, and Russian troops as they moved across Germany, Austria, and Poland liberating what were primarily at that point in the war labor/death camps. Originally shown at Nuremberg—to bear witness in ways that words and testimony simply could not—they were introduced into the record in Jerusalem for similar reasons. As Hausner explained, survivor testimony about the death camps was threatening to overwhelm the legal proceedings: "Words no longer conveyed their full meanings, and it looked as if in two or three more days of this we might lose control of our nerves and give way to hysteria. Instead of more evidence I showed a film that lasted about an hour."[84]

The sequence from *The Specialist* that depicts the screening of the liberation footage begins with Hausner introducing the film and noting that he will explain for the Court what it is they are seeing; his narration will replace the film's original and otherwise sparse sound track. The lights dim, and the camera finds Eichmann earnestly taking notes. He will be visible only intermittently and always in shadow while images from the screen on which the film is being projected reflect off the glass booth in which he sits, a ghostly presence. As Hausner describes what have become, for contemporary viewers at least, easily conjured scenes of atrocity—mounds of bodies, shoes, eyeglasses, and suitcases—we watch Eichmann as he watches the screen, his head nodding to one side and then the other as if he might be falling asleep. The film stops, and, in the shadows before the lights are turned on, Eichmann's mouth subtly twitches. We hear Hausner apologize to the Court for subjecting spectators to such a distressing experience even as he also insists that viewing the film was necessary.[85] The judges look down, in the classical repose of shame, clasping their heads, averting their gaze from the scene of the courtroom. Hausner grasps the armrests of his chair as if to stand; he pauses, looks to the floor at his feet, and then collapses back into himself as if exhausted by the emotions wrought in him by the spectacle. The camera cuts to Eichmann. Looking vacantly out across the courtroom, he performs an utterly banal gesture, one he would hardly perform had he been aware that the camera was trained on him at this moment (if indeed we are being shown a shot of the moment following the screening): he absently reaches up to his face and unceremoniously scratches his nose. He blinks and shifts his eyes from right to left, composed and perhaps apprehensive but hardly overcome.

Eichmann's expressions throughout this sequence stand in their ambiguity and in marked contrast to those of the judges and the prosecution whose

Figure 3.4. Eichmann at trial, 1961. Courtesy of Yad
Vashem Photo Archive, Jerusalem, Israel

gestures and countenance leave no doubt as to their state of *feeling*. Eichmann's
apparent lack of affect, his ostensibly apathetic demeanor during the viewing
of these films in Jerusalem—especially when juxtaposed to the judges' loss of
composure—seems to reveal a perverse humanity. He looks at the images but
neither sees nor seems to grasp the story that is readily if painfully apprehended
by others in the courtroom. And this, in some sense, discloses his guilt *and* a
monstrosity his appearance and ordinary demeanor do not otherwise betray, at
least for those watching him watch the debased and debasing outcome of orders
he denies having given. As a French journalist wrote of the screening of these
films at Nuremberg, so too with the Eichmann trial: "It was not a matter of
showing the judges a document about which they already had in depth knowledge. It was about bringing the criminals suddenly face to face with their colossal deeds. Thus, as it were, throwing the assassins right into the mass graves
organized by these butchers of Europe and observing the reactions that these
shocking images would provoke."[86] That they produce no apparent reaction in
Eichmann speaks volumes.

What Sivan and Brauman aim to present is the portrait of a bored, detached administrator, a transportation specialist, a bureaucrat. And by their own account, they aim to do this, following Arendt, without offering any exploration of Eichmann's inner character or psychological disposition. Yet in the sequence I have just set out, atrocity images are presented to the Court—depictions of apocalyptic horror, as they were described by the press—as graphic evidence of the consequences of Eichmann's work. And yet Eichmann himself remains apparently unmoved and indifferent throughout; indeed, it appears he can barely stay awake. In the words of a reporter for the *New York Times*: "Eichmann sat through eighty minutes of filmed horror today without flinching or batting an eye. A ghostly figure in the dimmed courtroom, the former Gestapo (secret police) officer, on trial for his role in the murder of millions of Jews, looked steadily from his glass cage. . . . The man who said he could not bear the sight of blood, who said he hated visiting death camps, was the very model of composure. . . . At the end of the films, after the three Israeli judges hurried to the chambers, Eichmann—the man who headed the Gestapo section assigned to the annihilation of Jews—picked up his pile of green folios and walked steadily from his cage."[87]

Because he does not see, or, perhaps more accurately, is not made to perform his "seeing" (as he might have been through editing), in a manner that is legible—a manner that conveys if not shame or remorse then at least discomfort in the company of suffering and the obvious anguish of those in whose presence he watches the film—a question of inner character or moral character necessarily overtakes the scene. The judges return to their chambers in tears, Hausner tells us, "for the first time since the trial began" while Eichmann displays only a cool reserve.[88] In this densely constructed sequence, how can we not read the twitch of his mouth as a sneer? or the shift of his eyes as the sign of psychopathology? (particularly since contemporary spectators for whom Sivan and Brauman are restaging this trial do not need to see the images to know what their moral claim is and how to respond; contemporary viewers have been schooled in the meaning of such images or schooled to see and experience in the spectacle of catastrophe a morally transformative, morally transcendent lesson). Still, the most fundamental crime of Arendt's shallow bureaucrat in this rendering, if we follow the logic of the sequence, is not Eichmann's affect so much as his apathy. And this, in turn—Eichmann's failure to demonstrate feeling or empathy, which even the *New York Times* could not fail to note—seems to betray precisely what the filmmakers sought to challenge by reconstructing the visual record some thirty years after the event, Eichmann's inhumanity or Hausner's insistence that while Eichmann may have been "born human," he could no longer be regarded as such:

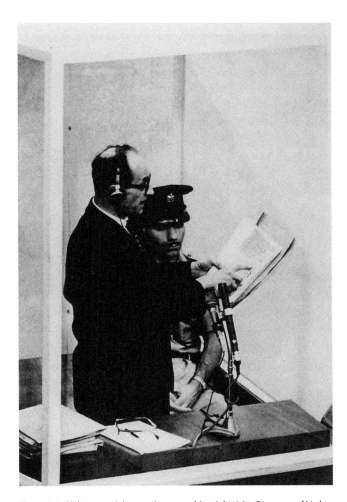

Figure 3.5. Eichmann giving testimony at his trial, 1961. Courtesy of Yad Vashem Photo Archive, Jerusalem Israel

Here stands before you the destroyer of a people, an enemy of mankind. He was born human, but he lived like a beast in the jungle. He committed atrocities so unspeakable that he who is guilty of such crimes no longer deserves to be called human. His crimes go beyond what we consider human. They go beyond what separates man from beast. I ask the Court to consider that he acted with enthusiasm, out of his own free will, and with passion. Right to the end. I ask you to sentence this man to death.[89]

Hausner's is a portrait of monstrosity and, in the end, curiously, so too is Sivan and Brauman's (despite their controversial effort), although obviously Eichmann through the optics of Sivan and Brauman's film is not Eichmann

Figure 3.6. Eichmann taking notes during his trial, 1961. United States Holocaust Museum, courtesy of the Israeli Government Press Office.

through the optics of Israeli nationalism. Nevertheless, the figures that each conjures are related. *The Specialist* attempts to recover one of the missed opportunities Arendt identified in her trial report and offers contemporary viewers a certain critical distance to consider anew the nature of Eichmann's "criminality" or what was otherwise treated during the trial as self-evident and foregone. With this critical distance and the film's refusal to provoke through emotional immersion and trauma, there is, then, room for the pedantic and at moments seemingly abject administrator that is Eichmann to emerge clearly (albeit through skillful editing) or at least in ways the filmmakers' contend were obscured or contained by Hausner's performance. In addition, the film refuses to extract for viewers—and works against viewers easily extracting for themselves, notwithstanding the rhetoric and truth-generating technique of the documentary medium—the now-conventional moral lessons for which Eichmann and the trial have come to stand in as a kind of rhetorical shorthand.[90] But even with these decidedly striking interventions, the apathetic indifference of Sivan and Brauman's Eichmann—alongside and in contrast to Hausner's "flint-hearted plotter"—fails still to capture Arendt's reading of the criminal and his crime. Thoughtlessness is not indifference or the absence of (normal human) feeling; more feeling (however demonstrated) is not a substitute for critical thinking (although it may be a constitutive component of it). It will not bridge what Arendt described as "certain abysses of remoteness"; it will not provide a compass from which we might take our bearings in the world; and finally, it will not render the evil of which she spoke explicable even if resuscitates a metaphysics that renders a figure like Eichmann both more and less horrifically legible.

4 "Crimes against the Human Status"
Nuremberg and the Image of Evil

We saw in chapter 1 that the Eichmann trial was made to bear a host of burdens well beyond the otherwise highly choreographed spectacle of criminal prosecution. Whether by chance, opportunity, or design, the proceedings were put in the service of a number of consequentially distinct agendas for regionally distinct audiences, with the focal point throughout being the "story of the great destruction."[1] In the presence of the world and the one man said to have been responsible for overseeing the whole monstrous affair, this brutal story was rehearsed to shame, educate, and inspire. Its telling was also finally to correct the legal record, to set right what some insisted were the glaring inadequacies, misconceptions, and misrepresentations of the Allied case against prominent members of the Nazi leadership in the initial postwar trial before the International Military Tribunal at Nuremberg. For while the accomplishments of the tribunal may initially have appeared considerable in terms of establishing a detailed, more or less coherent and (therefore) plausible account of National Socialist criminality, the "authoritative and impartial" record that emerged was later said to have ignored or simply marginalized the systematic mass murder of European Jewry. And it was not simply a matter of the record being incomplete. If one takes, as the Jerusalem court and countless commentators since have taken, the annihilation of European Jewry to have been the principal aim, indeed the definitive crime, of the Nazi regime—for which the waging of war was merely a pretense—the stark omissions of the narrative produced at Nuremberg meant that the full magnitude and significance of Nazi criminality remained entirely outside the legal frame. As legal scholar Mark Osiel observes, "Historians and political analysts have been dismayed . . . that the Nuremberg Court would subsume the most unparalleled features of the defendants' wrongs under longstanding doctrines in the law of war, reducing the Holocaust merely to one among several methods employed for the 'waging of aggressive war.'"[2] And in basic agreement with Osiel, political scientist Gary Jonathan Bass writes that while the establishment of an International Tribunal reflected the Allies' shared desire for justice,

> it is often forgotten that [their] efforts to punish Germany were undertaken mostly out of anger at the Nazi instigation of World War II. One of the great ironies of

Nuremberg's legacy is that the tribunal is remembered as a product of Allied horror at the Holocaust, when in fact America and Britain, the two liberal countries that played major roles in deciding what Nuremberg would be, actually focused far more on the criminality of Nazi aggression than on the Holocaust. Nuremberg was self-serving in ways that are usually forgotten today.[3]

With the bringing to justice of Adolf Eichmann, therefore, the marginalized and silenced were said to have been allowed, at long last, to emerge centrally, not only to rewrite a legal history, but also to become "the speaking [and acting] subjects of [their own] history."[4] In words echoed repeatedly by lead prosecutor and general attorney, Gideon Hausner, throughout the Jerusalem proceedings, Prime Minister Ben-Gurion elaborates:

> This is not an ordinary trial nor only a trial. Here for the first time in Jewish history, historical justice is being done by the sovereign Jewish people. For many generations it was we who suffered, who were tortured, were killed—and we who were judged. Our adversaries and our murderers were also our judges. For the first time Israel is judging the murderers of the Jewish people. It is not an individual that is in the dock at this historic trial and not the Nazi regime alone but anti-Semitism throughout history. The judges whose business is the law and who may be trusted to adhere to it will judge Eichmann the man for his horrible crimes, but responsible public opinion in the world will be judging anti-Semitism which paved the way for this most atrocious crime in the history of mankind. And let us bear in mind that only the independence of Israel could create the necessary conditions for this historic act of justice.[5]

I.

In this chapter, I want to take a closer look at the Nuremberg proceedings. Like the Eichmann trial, these proceedings entailed a certain performance of law; they staged a judicial purging broadcast twice daily on German radio that made possible, as Tony Judt puts it, the distilling of "*German* guilt . . . into a set of indictments reserved exclusively for German Nazis, and then only a select few."[6] The military trials spanned nearly half a decade and were designed to distribute responsibility across the regime's leadership in order to mete out punishment, denazify as well as educate morally an otherwise recalcitrant population, and, finally, produce in the process the foundations for democratic order. No modest goals, these—but modest could hardly describe the grim mess of the now-occupied postwar landscape. The sheer scale of destruction and dislocation defies imagination: some 45 million dead across the continent alone, the built environment all but decimated, massive homelessness, food shortages, famine, and disease. Indeed, consider just some of the numbers: 750,000 orphaned children in need of care, 11 million POWs in need of processing, and approximately 20 million displaced persons in need of refuge, a figure that does not include the 15 million Germans forcibly expelled from east central Europe, East Prussia, and Poland in the war's aftermath.[7]

It is against this backdrop that the first, and the only *international*, of twelve trials convened at Nuremberg, resulting in the indictment of seven criminal organizations and twenty-four prominent or prominently placed members of the Nazi regime—the "Grand" criminals as Churchill described them—on one or more of four counts.[8] The counts emerged from lengthy negotiations between the four prosecuting parties—Great Britain, the United States, France, and the Soviet Union—in the weeks after the war and are part of what became known as the London Charter. Refiguring loss and reorganizing suffering into a coherent legal idiom marginally resonant across disparate juridical traditions, the four counts were (1) Conspiracy to Wage Aggressive War (participation "in the formulation or execution of a common plan" involving the commission of Crimes against the Peace, War Crimes, or Crimes Against Humanity within Germany and the occupied territories);[9] (2) Crimes Against the Peace ("the planning, initiation, or waging of a war of aggression" in breach of the Kellogg-Briand Pact of 1928);[10] (3) War Crimes (violations of the laws and customs of war including murder or ill treatment of civilian populations and/or prisoners of war); and (4) Crimes Against Humanity ("murder, extermination, enslavement, deportation, and other inhumane acts committed against any civilian population, before or during the war"). In addition, the London Charter (Articles 9 and 10 specifically) identified half a dozen key groups or organizations—the SS, for example, and the Gestapo, as well as the Security Police—that would be charged and tried (and represented by counsel) alongside the major defendants.[11] A conviction against any of these groups or organizations would subsequently enable prosecutors in successor trials across the four occupied zones to more easily indict additional individuals, for complicity at least, by virtue of their membership in an organization whose criminal nature and thus illegality had been established by the court. As legal scholar Stephen Landsman explains, "While defendants were to be tried for their own crimes, they were also viewed as representatives of or stand-ins for the organizations with which they were associated. . . . [In this respect, their] guilt was not theirs alone but to be ascribed to a host of others."[12]

Like the Eichmann trial, therefore, Nuremberg constituted a particular kind of political spectacle in the service of particular ends having something to do with justice or at least its appearance however imperfectly enacted. What these ends were or are conceived as having been (by no means necessarily the same thing) are still matters of considerable scholarly debate. For this reason

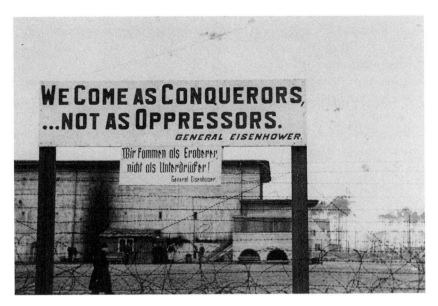

Figure 4.1. A sign in front of a U.S. military installation, Berlin, 1945. United States Holocaust Memorial Museum, Washington, D.C., courtesy of Aviva Kemprer.

and from the outset, I want to emphasize that my aim in this chapter is not to enter directly or stake a claim in these debates whether on questions having to do with Nuremberg's legitimacy (did the tribunal in effect create crimes in order to punish them?); its shortcomings (did injunctions against introducing any material that might demonstrate that Allied forces had committed war crimes analogous in scale and destruction to those for which the defendants were being tried compromise the proceedings?);[13] or, finally, its ultimate success (or failure) in establishing a legal apparatus that provided at least the basis for a new international moral and political order. The literatures on these and other related issues are vast, stretch across careers and disciplinary domains, and seem to be ever expanding in the context of continuing efforts to discern (or establish) a credible, internationally binding basis for judging and condemning real-time atrocities across the globe. Rather, in this chapter I want to look more closely at what some might regard as a relatively minor or incidental component of the overall legal effort in terms of its bearing on the case, to wit: the use made during the Nuremberg proceedings of documentary film footage and images that were assembled by U.S., Soviet, and British forces as they encountered and liberated concentration camps in their movement from the east and west toward Berlin. The footage has everything to do with how (and for what) "the Nazi regime was given official 'criminal status'" and, thus, with Nuremberg's legacy at least as this legacy lives on in popular memory and understanding;[14] indeed, the footage has been instrumental in shaping what Telford Taylor, chief prosecutor throughout the course of the secondary series of twelve trials at Nuremberg, described as "the ethos of Nuremberg"— in other words, what people believed happened in the context of the trial as opposed to what actually transpired.[15]

Most of us are familiar with this very footage: it is regularly recycled on cable channels, incorporated in most World War II docudramas, featured in history units designed for middle and high school students, and is on an endless replay loop at the many museums now commemorating the period.[16] Its monochromatic starkness continues to facilitate a seamless collapse of the moral and visual fields and to enlist spectators in the telling of an uncomplicated black-and-white story.[17] At the same time, it is also the still much championed look of American benevolence, authority, and national identity. At Nuremberg and notwithstanding the observations of Osiel and Bass, among other commentators, the footage was similarly read as evidence of evil and atrocity even if it was also *seen* quite differently—and seen quite differently for mostly obvious reasons. On the one hand, as Douglas Lawrence points out, the footage had yet to be contextualized and narrativized: it would be the task of the prosecution to lay down a grammar and translate what were horrific images of a crime scene into a vernacular that was legally and culturally coherent.[18] On the other hand, if the prosecution saw in these films a story whose main through line had to do with atrocities committed in pursuit of world domination rather than the Holocaust, this is because the Holocaust as such did not yet exist as the self-enclosed event and self-evident narrative it has taken well over fifty years to produce. In 1945 at Nuremberg, the screened footage was yoked to a case and context that linked crimes against humanity to the brutality of an aggressive, imperialist war, driven by fierce nationalism and sinister militarism and fed by "pathological pride, cruelty, and a lust for power" in the pursuit of empire that left millions dead or enslaved.[19] In subsequent years, particularly following the Eichmann trial, the representational resources or economies of meaning would expand: crimes against humanity would be uncoupled from aggressive war and the footage reserviced not only to tell a very specific story about Hitler's war against the Jews, but to depict, sentimentalize, and mythologize a mid-twentieth-century rupture that was nevertheless bridged with the war's end through a reaffirmation of humanity's bonds and collective destiny. Obvious but certainly worth mentioning is that the conditions of possibility for either or both readings had not yet fully congealed when assistant trial counsel, James Donovan, introduced the first of three films into the record at Nuremberg a mere eight days into the proceedings.[20]

From all accounts, the turn to visual texts in the opening days of the trial marked an abrupt shift in the prosecution's strategy. Although the Allied team had intended to screen the films once the proceedings were under way, their presentation in the initial phase of an effort to reconstruct the anatomy of Nazi aggression—or well in advance of a narrative that might have anchored or contextualized the mass atrocity they depicted—was something of an improvision. Indeed, as Taylor recalls, the introduction of visual texts so early in the proceedings was "dictated not by logic but by felt necessity";[21] it came in response to an impatient press and the need to expose by other means the true horror and depravity of Nazism that the prosecution's tedious recitation of events predating Europe's devolution into war had muted. Thus, as he introduced the films, Thomas Dodd aimed to reorient the Court by inviting it to see the visual landscape as merely a more graphically rendered legal one:

> This is by no means the entire proof which the prosecution will offer with respect to the subject of concentration camps, but this film which we offer represents in a brief and unforgettable form an explanation of what the words "concentration camp" imply. The subject arises appropriately in the narrative of events leading up to the actual outbreak of aggressive war, which . . . was planned and prepared by Nazi conspirators. We propose to show that concentration camps were not an end in themselves but . . . an integral part of the Nazi system of government. . . . We intend to prove that each and every one of these defendants knew of the existence of these concentration camps; that fear and terror and nameless horror of the concentration camps were instruments by which the defendants retained power and suppressed opposition to any of their policies, including of course their plans for aggressive war.[22]

Under the direction of Supreme Court justice and chief of counsel at Nuremberg, Robert Jackson, the prosecution's strategy for the trial entailed developing its case against the accused through the meticulously kept records of the Nazi regime that Allied forces had amassed at the war's end and that the American staff for the prosecution had culled in the months prior to trial.[23] Informing this approach was Jackson's concern that allegations of Nazi atrocity could easily be discredited: even those tasked with coordinating evidence "had [initially] discounted the most serious claims of Nazi brutality on the theory that such claims had been exaggerated for wartime propaganda purposes."[24] For this reason, the chief justice had insisted that the documents be allowed to speak for themselves and that the prosecution construct its case *without* the emotionally compelling but evidentially compromised, because biased, testimony of those who had suffered under the boot of Nazi rule.[25] Better for justice and posterity that the defendants hang by their own words and record whatever they now claimed regarding either.[26]

Theoretically at least, an exclusive reliance on documents may have been a sound strategy. But from the opening sessions, the approach involved the prosecution in a presentation of evidence that proved tedious and disorganized—a presentation that was mired in detail, difficult to follow, appeared to lack clarity, and, from the point of view of the press at least, entirely without impact. This was not the great spectacle of reckoning that "the largest group of journalists ever gathered in one place to cover one event" had expected to witness; and it was not long before those assigned to constant coverage of the court "grimly joked that they were the last victims of Nazi persecution."[27] Indeed, writing for the *New Yorker*, Rebecca West described the trial as a "citadel of boredom," nothing less in fact than "boredom on a huge historic scale. . . . [H]owever much a man loved the law he could not love so much of it as wound its sluggish way through the Palace of Justice at Nuremberg."[28]

Moving pictures were thus introduced to revive proceedings that while hardly under way were nevertheless already asphyxiated with fact; and although the early screening of documentary footage upset the schedule of the trial, it also, as one commentator observed, "put [the trial] back on the front page."[29] What the footage ostensibly offered was an unimpeachable account of atrocity from an impeccably disinterested witness, the camera. As such, it served both legal and extralegal agendas and worked simultaneously on several related fronts. Most obviously, perhaps, the footage of the camps provided an illustration of Nazi criminality or at least its aftermath and rendered self-evident the need for and overarching significance of the trial—in effect, a response to detractors, skeptics, and an otherwise apathetic, disgruntled, or insulted German public as to why, as the *New York Times* put it, "the world's conscience crie[d] out for justice and for punishment."[30] That such a "conscience" was something of a chimera produced through such news reporting practices as well as in the prosecution's claim to represent it and act on its behalf is something to which I briefly return later. The film also underscored the ultimate moral rupture and social pathology of Nazi rule in a way not easily captured by document or legal discourse because the "rational mind," as it was explained in court, could not be expected to fully fathom or conjure for itself the horror implicit in or explicitly detailed by either. Finally, the use of film at Nuremberg worked to distinguish the victors in their restrained righteousness from those they would judge: as Jackson put it in his opening address before the tribunal, the Allied powers had opted not to answer atrocity with a "cry for vengeance" or pass those in the docket a "poisoned chalice." Guided by Reason, in the name of Civilization, and with an eye toward History, they would instead "summon such detachment and intellectual integrity [as was required to] fulfill humanity's aspirations to do justice,"[31] however horrific the transgressions of the now-vanquished enemy:

The wrongs which we seek to condemn and punish have been so calculated, so malignant, and so devastating, that civilization cannot tolerate their being ignored because it cannot survive their being repeated. That four great nations, flushed with victory and stung with injury, stay the hands of vengeance and voluntarily submit their captive enemies to the judgment of law is one of the most significant tributes that Power ever has paid to Reason.[32]

II.

Three films were prepared for viewing at Nuremberg, although until relatively recently, with the release of footage shot by Soviet as well as British film crews, only the first of the three was widely known or circulated in the West. These films are *Nazi Concentration Camps* (USA, 1945, 58 min.), *The Nazi Plan* (USA, 1945, 3.4 hr.), and *The Atrocities Committed by the German-Fascists in the USSR* (USSR, 1946, 60 min.).[33] *Nazi Concentration Camps* was shot by the U.S. Army Signal Corps and produced by a prominent Hollywood director, George Stevens, on the order of General Eisenhower, as Allied troops moved through France, Denmark, Belgium, Germany, and Austria encountering what were primarily labor camps, the now better known of which include Dachau, Buchenwald, and Bergen-Belsen. Moving images that we today associate with the end of the war and the liberation of "death" camps, indeed, images that represent what we have come to think genocide looks like. Skeletal men in striped clothing standing behind barbed wire or lying abreast on a sleeping platform, bodies being piled onto carts or lined up in neat rows in an open courtyard, bodies being placed or bulldozed into a mass grave, lampshades made from the skin of murdered camp inmates, piles of hair, piles of shoes and eyeglasses; in short, death and brutality so massive as to seem beyond human comprehension—these images are for the most part taken from the "untainted" visual record that *Nazi Concentration Camps* was, then as now, thought to provide.

The second film shown at Nuremberg, *The Nazi Plan*, was assembled especially for the trial by Bud Schulberg, along with members of the OSS Field Photographic Branch led by yet another Hollywood director, John Ford. It consisted of footage from the Nazi's own archives of propaganda films and aimed to reconstruct for the tribunal the regime's "quest for power and subsequent use of it."[34] These Nazi propaganda films were spliced and edited together to create a continuous narrative that featured in turn each of the accused as conspirators—"re-enacting from the screen some of the events in the course of the conspiracy," as Jackson explained it to the court—secretly preparing (in plain sight) for and then executing a war of aggression with the aim of world domination. And because it was archival footage that formed the basis of this narrative (or renarrativization), *The Nazi Plan* could be seen secondarily to detail the regime's exploits as that story was construed for and marshaled to dupe and incite the German people, Hitler's first victims, as the prosecution repeatedly insisted.[35]

Finally, the third film shown at Nuremberg was *The Atrocities Committed by the German-Fascists in the USSR.* A Soviet production, as the title suggests, this film was also compiled specifically for the trial and was submitted as evidentiary material in anticipation of the testimony of a handful of witnesses, most of whom were Jewish survivors, which Soviet counsel intended to call to the stand.[36] As with the other two documentaries—although "even more terrible," according to Gustave Gilbert, a prison psychologist[37]—it too proffered a visual representation of Nazi criminality that aimed to expand the meaning of "crimes against the peace" as well as "crimes against humanity." Incorporating rare footage of the Soviet liberation of Auschwitz (January 1945) and Majdanek (July 1944)—albeit, in the case of Auschwitz, restaged for the camera—it was designed to "put images to the words of witnesses" and thereby enable the judges and the world at large to more accurately grasp the full scope of violence and suffering as well as destruction and plunder wreaked by German troops as they moved east across Ukraine into the Soviet Union.[38]

About these films chief prosecutor of the secondary series of twelve trials at Nuremberg, Telford Taylor, reports that they were wrenching to watch—even for those like himself who had seen them previously. But beyond "hardening sentiment against the defendants,"[39] they otherwise contributed little in his view to the prosecution's overall effort to definitively establish the individual guilt (or innocence) of any one of the accused: none of the defendants after all were shown on scene at the camps or committing the atrocities whose effects the cameras captured in all their stark horror. In this respect the visual texts were, as Landsman observes, "classically prejudicial." Once spectators were hailed by the spectacle of carnage and were positioned as witnesses to the larger story this spectacle appeared to tell, the connection between the depicted atrocities and the accused was foregone, even if (or precisely because) the connection was established though emotional rather than legal incitements.[40] As the American representative on the bench, Judge Francis Biddle, later wrote about the screening, revealing precisely this process of capture despite a desire to look away: "There was no end to the horrors of testimony. The mind shrank from them, grew tired, rejected the imaginative and systematic cruelties. Or one tried to feel, to share the heroism of the victims."[41]

In addition, and clearly related to the prejudicial impact of film in the courtroom, are specific questions regarding the evidentiary character of visual texts, an issue by no means peculiar to Nuremberg but certainly highlighted by their

Figure 4.2. General Dwight D. Eisenhower and other high-ranking army officers view the bodies of prisoners while on a tour of the newly liberated concentration camp [Ohrdruf], 1945. United States Holocaust Memorial Museum, Washington, DC.

use during the war crimes trial. For although such texts may well provide relevant evidence of some *thing* or event, what that thing or event is precisely and in what sense it might be relevant are often not entirely self-evident from within an analytic rather than evocative frame. That they appear to be self-evidently relevant—or appeared self-evident at Nuremberg—is in large measure a function and effect of the context and documentary medium: this is a medium that is dramatic and didactic, a medium whose operation is about recruiting spectators, emotionally, and interpolating them into the very meaning making practices they otherwise experience as independently established, coherent, and transparently given. As a knowledge-producing strategy—a rhetoric of appeal—documentary is about *showing* rather than *analyzing*; about positioning the viewer and the real in a particular relationship that fosters recognition and identification on the one hand and a sense of moral culpability on the other. To put this another way, as a particular regime of truth, documentary representation places viewers *under conviction*, to borrow a term often used to describe a state or stage of religious conversion, and with this placement or positioning works to direct allegiances while also fostering certain felt obligations.

Consider for the moment and just slightly to the side of this discussion the conditions that helped solidify the development of documentary rhetoric and technique in the first place. As a strategy organizing the social field across discursive arenas, it emerged in the United States of the 1930s, in a context of economic collapse and cultural disenfranchisement and as a constitutive component of Roosevelt's New Deal reorganization of collective social institutions and spending policies. Documentary rhetorics in photography, film, literature, painting, and music, as John Tagg explains, were "tied in a fundamental way to the crisis-driven strategy of the liberal democratic state in its attempt to rebuild a cohesive national audience, to retrieve a sense of shared national experience, and to reestablish the common ground of national interest."[42] Recall briefly by way of example here Dorothea Lange's iconic image *Migrant Mother* (1936), which Lange captured while working for the Farm Security Administration, or William C. Pryor's images (1938) of the mining town of Carbon Hill, Alabama, produced for the Works Progress Administration. Recruiting spectators and placing them under conviction in the way just described, by enlisting loyalties and inciting identifications across disparate social fields, documentary constituted a critical mechanism of crisis management; it was a vehicle for stabilizing confidence, reestablishing authority, fostering civic recognition and relationships, restoring shared values, and, ultimately, procuring consent.[43] Again Tagg: "To be captured by this machinery was to be captured in the imaginary of the benevolent, impartial, paternal State, but to be captured in the act of compassionate looking: an act of decency and the act of a citizen, a civic subject called to duty."[44]

The period following Germany's defeat was not the United States of the 1930s obviously.[45] But the turn to documentary rhetoric and technique shared a similar logic: it was deployed as a mechanism of capture to manage crisis, foster compliance, and shape sentiments in ways that might help establish the conditions for eventual democratization. More specifically and immediately, its function was to facilitate the population's denazification and reeducation; and this task was intimately bound up with the disciplinary management and retraining of the gaze. Thus, for example, in the days and weeks following the liberation of the camps by American forces, Generals Eisenhower, Patton, and Bradley ordered U.S. military units not on the front line to visit the camps and urged journalists and officials from Washington to inspect them as well. The generals also, in effect, transformed these "sites of slave labor and murder into didactic museums" in requiring all German citizens, including children ten years of age or older living in close proximity to the camps, to behold the devastation and human carnage.[46]

Referred to as "confrontation visits," these tours were but one component of a much larger, densely choreographed strategy of rehabilitation whose centerpiece entailed the ostensibly straightforward injunction to "look." It was a strategy, in other words, that entailed repositioning the German public as witnesses to as well as compliant participants in the Nazi criminal project in order to foster shame and incite a sense of guilt and responsibility. The goal was to instill a certain moral literacy, which in turn and time would enable a shift in loyalties to new structures of power (beginning first with the occupation).

Although the confrontation visits ended a short month after they began— unburied corpses posed health risks at the camps, and the sites were needed in any event to accommodate the growing numbers of displaced persons and prisoners of war—they were nevertheless captured on film. And this footage along with footage and photographs from the liberation of the camps became an integral component of the postwar visual landscape; it was reformatted for theaters, posters, and booklets and narratively reframed for pedagogic effect not only in the American zone and sectors in Germany but for civilian and military populations in the United States as well.[47] And notwithstanding the dramatically different positions occupied by these viewing publics, all regarded the images with horror and revulsion. But German audiences for the most part failed to inhabit the morally circumscribed field set out for them as witnesses. Less than three months after the liberation of Ohrdruf, the Psychological Warfare Division found that rather than induce feelings of guilt and remorse among German civilians, the spectacle of the camps and the larger visual catalog of which it became a critical part fostered primarily resentment: "You Americans can hardly understand the conditions under which we were living. It was as if

Figure 4.3. Under the supervision of American soldiers, a German woman shields the eyes of her son as she walks with other civilians past the bodies of 57 Russians, including women and one baby, exhumed from a mass grave outside the town of Suttrop [North Rhine, Westphalia, Germany], May 3, 1945. United States Holocaust Memorial Museum, Washington, DC.

all of Germany were a concentration camp and we were occupied by a foreign power. We were unable to do anything to oppose them."⁴⁸ The civilian population in Germany in large measure refused to look or resisted the capture of the images—resisted seeing and by seeing being morally exposed and culpable. Significantly, and not unlike Eichmann's responses to the many questions put to him by the prosecution in Jerusalem, the standard response of Germans "of all types and social classes" on being shown images of the camps was disavowal: "We do not recognize ourselves in those pictures."⁴⁹ As a result, Judt notes, the reeducation program of the Allied forces "had a decidedly limited impact":

> It was one thing to oblige Germans to attend documentary films, quite another to make them watch, much less think about what they were seeing. Many years later the writer Stephen Hermlin described the scene in a Frankfurt cinema, where

Figure 4.4. German civilians are forced to see the bodies of prisoners exhumed from a mass grave near Namering, Germany, May 5, 1945. United States Holocaust Memorial Museum, Washington, DC.

Germans were required to watch documentary films on Dachau and Buchenwald before receiving their ration cards: "In the half-light of the projector, I could see that most people turned their faces away after the beginning of the film and stayed that way until the film was over. Today I think that that turned away face was indeed the attitude of many millions. . . . The unfortunate people to which I belonged was both sentimental and callous. It was not interested in being shaken by events, in any 'know thyself.'"[50]

III.

Where visual texts had been of limited utility in terms of disciplining the moral gaze of a subject population, they had a decidedly more profound and pronounced impact in the context of the courtroom at Nuremberg. Not only did they lend credibility to the proceedings, the visual texts essentially hijacked them, fixing a certain regime of truth and establishing a certain set of imperatives (and injunctions) about looking that even today remain more or less in place and undisturbable without admonition. That Nuremberg lent itself to, indeed invited, such hijacking can be clearly discerned in the structure of both the legal case and the organization of the courtroom's physical space. On the one hand, as I noted in passing earlier, the traditional rules of procedure and evidence were relaxed in the interest of efficiency and, somewhat ironically, historical truth: the aim as it was imagined by those crafting the London Charter was to create a stage on which the complex story of Nazi criminality could be fully told and this, in their view, required lifting "traditional constraints regarding relevance, heresy, and authentication."[51] As a consequence with respect to the films, in particular, the interpretive and associative possibilities that would otherwise have been more narrowly circumscribed circulated in an utterly unrestrained, uninterrogated manner: the images once viewed reconfigured the indictment only eight days into a nearly yearlong trial, overwhelmed the proceedings they also served however poorly, and rendered a verdict that reverberates, indeed puts viewers under conviction, even today.

On the other hand, the very organization of the courtroom at Nuremberg was configured in its reconstruction for the trial to accommodate (and we could even say feature) a movie screen in precisely the space at the front of the room normally reserved for the judge's bench (and precisely the space where a crucifix is today affixed). This tells us something about the significance of the visual evidence and the power given over to it to shape the meaning of the proceedings whether by chance or design and quite aside from what the transcripts report "actually" transpired. The images stood in judgment and delivered the judgment. For with these images there could be no plausible argument, credible explanation, or convincing response that was not vulnerable, once uttered, to providing ground for the indictment or to being read as evidence of guilt and depravity. Indeed, at Nuremberg, as at each of the subsequent war-related trials through the 1970s, these films and related images were called upon to speak where words failed and *because* words failed.[52] And what the "truth" they espoused demanded in turn was that one look in silence—to better hear what one was seeing—and, having looked, retreat in shame and under conviction.

We saw this demand played out at the Eichmann trial: as expedient as these films may have been for speaking the unspeakable—this is how Attorney General Hausner put it—more important still was Eichmann's encounter with and response to the stark images, the story they told, and the hellish desolation they represented (a desolation he worked to create but, as he tirelessly repeated to his interrogators without apparently grasping its implications, for which he was never adequately compensated with a promotion in rank). Eichmann's apparent lack of affect, his disengaged apathetic demeanor during the viewing of these films in Jerusalem—especially when juxtaposed to the judges' loss of composure—revealed for spectators a perverse humanity. He seemed to look but

Figure 4.5. The Nuremberg courtroom. Note the prominent place occupied by the film screen (1945). United States Holocaust Memorial Museum, Washington, DC.

appeared to those who looked on to be immune to capture. Unable or ostensibly unwilling to see or feel the hail of the images and their indictment, Eichmann's guilt *and* monstrosity, not otherwise betrayed by his ordinary demeanor, were clearly exposed, at least for those watching him watch the debased and debasing outcome of orders he denies having given.

And so it was as well at Nuremberg. The defendants were subjected to close scrutiny by prison psychiatrists Gustave Gilbert and Douglas Kelly as they sat watching the first of the three films in court, their reactions noted at minute intervals.[53] Not unlike the highly choreographed confrontation visits to the camps that German citizens were forced to undertake shortly after their liberation, the screening of the films at Nuremberg staged a similar confrontation, although in the context of the courtroom this confrontation wrote into the trial's record truth's indictment of power and the triumph of the ostensibly self-evident Real over the criminally contrived. Indeed, the cameras in the Nuremberg courtroom featured this indictment and triumph—for while occasionally acknowledging the presence of the defendants, made mere shadow figures in the darkened courtroom by the overwhelming light of the images, the cameras remained trained on the screen, captured by the real even as they (re) produced it.[54] Unlike the session in Jerusalem that sought to place Eichmann under conviction through film, the "machinery of the image that sets the viewer and the real in place"—and thus reveals the interpretive frame as a constructed feat— this machinery was nowhere in evidence at Nuremberg.[55] Before a wordless body, destroyed humanity appeared to speak for itself and lay blame.

It was left to Gilbert and Kelly to record the reactions of the accused. And their notes regarding how and when the defendants broke the gaze—for the issue was not whether they were depraved but rather how or in what form precisely their depravity would manifest—are now part of the International Tribunal's official record. We therefore follow Gilbert's somewhat impressionistic portraits at length—in part to watch him watch the defendants who were, in turn, watching the Allied production, *Nazi Concentration Camps*:

> Schacht objects to being made to look at film as I ask him to move over; turns away, folds arms, gazes into gallery. Frank nods at authentication at introduction of film . . . Fritzsche (who had not seen any part of the film before) already looks pale and sits aghast as he stares with scenes of prisoners burned alive in a barn . . . Keitel wipes brow, takes off headphones . . . Hess glares at screen looking like a ghoul with sunken eyes over the footlamp . . . Keitel puts on headphones, glares at screen out of the corner of his eye . . . von Neurath has head bowed, doesn't look. . . . Funk covers his eyes[. . . .] Ribbentrop closes his eyes, looks away . . . Frank swallows hard, blinks eyes, trying to stifle tears[. . . .]Goering keeps leaning on balustrade, not watching most of the time, looking droopy [. . . .] Funk mumbles something under his breath . . . Streicher keeps watching, immobile except for an occasional squint . . . Funk now in tears, blows nose, wipes eyes, looks down . . . Frick shakes head at illustration of 'violent death'—Frank mutters 'Horrible!' . . . Rosenberg fidgets, peeks at screen, bows head, looks to see how others are reacting . . . Seyss-Inquart stoic throughout . . . Speer looks very sad, swallows hard . . . Defense attorneys are now muttering, 'for God's sake—terrible.' Raeder watches without budging . . . von Papen sits with hand over brow, looking down, has not looked at the screen yet . . . Hess keeps looking bewildered . . . piles of dead are shown in a slave labor camp . . . von Shirach watching intently, gasps, whispers to Sauckel . . . Funk crying now . . . Goering looks sad, leaning on an elbow . . . Doenitz has head bowed, no longer watching . . . Sauckel shudders at picture of Buchenwald crematorium oven . . . as human skin lampshade is shown, Streicher says, 'I don't believe that' . . . Goering coughing . . . Attorneys gasping . . . Now Dachau . . . Schacht still not looking . . . Frank nods his head bitterly and says 'Horrible!' . . . Rosenberg still fidgeting, leans forward, looks around, leans back, hangs head . . . Fritzsche, pale, biting lips, really seems in agony . . . Doenitz has head buried in his hands . . . Keitel now hanging head[. . . .] Ribbentrop sitting with pursed lips and blinking eyes, not looking at screen . . . Funk crying bitterly, claps hand over mouth as women's

Figure 4.6. A sign posted by the British army at the entrance to the Bergen-Belsen concentration camp, May 1, 1945. United States Holocaust Memorial Museum, Washington, DC., courtesy of Madalae Fraser.

naked corpses are thrown into pit . . . Keitel and Ribbentrop look up at the mention of tractor clearing corpses, see it, then hang their heads . . . Streicher shows signs of disturbance for the first time . . . Film ends [. . .] Hess remarks, "I don't believe it." Goering whispers to him to keep quiet, his own cockiness quite gone. Streicher says something about "perhaps in the last days[.]" [. . .] Otherwise there is gloomy silence as the prisoners file out of the courtroom.[56]

Some of the accused acknowledged, some gasped, some glared, fidgeted, shuddered, and hung their heads. But what can this spectacle of aversion in the end really tell us? Moreover, for all the drama Gilbert seemed both to expect and to record, does it matter that the screening of *Nazi Concentration Camps* at Nuremberg was not the first time most of the defendants had encountered this footage; indeed, not the first time they had stood, as the French journalist Joseph Kessel imagined, *at the gates of hell, face to face with their colossal deeds?*[57] The *New York Times* reported that on their initial confinement at the Palace Hotel in the summer preceding their formal arrest and trial, the military officer in charge had arranged for the defendants to watch the film just as the German public had been required at the time to watch it.[58] And at that viewing, according to the *Times,* their responses had been muted: to be sure, Frank is said to have "crammed a handkerchief in his mouth and [not unexpectedly] gagged," but von Ribbentrop walked out of the screening; Streicher wrung his hands, nervously; Doenitz considered the images an affront; and Göring looked bored, later commenting, "That's the type of film that we used to show our Russian prisoners." For the most part, in other words, the accused, like the German public, had been somewhat unsettled and even repulsed by the images— and these reactions they would perform again in a somewhat more practiced manner for the world at Nuremberg. But the so-called Grand criminals of the regime similarly and predictably would not inhabit their proper place in the visual narrative in part because they could not recognize themselves in its interpretive scheme.[59] Where the prosecutors, judges, and world at large saw clearly their hand now graphically displayed in the making of a death world, the defendants saw instead their own bad luck and general misfortune. As former minister of economics, Walther Funk (1937–45), remarked some days after the screening of *Nazi Concentration Camps,* "Believe me, I had no idea of those eyeglasses, watches, and gold teeth. . . . Those deposits must have been sent to the Reichsbank by mistake."[60] Chilling, perhaps. But, in the end, it was Göring who captured best the collective temper: "It was such a good afternoon until they showed that film. It just spoiled everything."[61]

The embodiment of evil or prosaic triviality as Jasper had suggested to Arendt?

IV.

Contemporary scholars from a number of disciplines similarly contend that in the aftermath of the war considerable effort was devoted to institutionalizing an understanding of the Nazi regime that placed it outside the course of a history it was also said to have ruptured, an aberration in its instrumental use and systematic decimation of populations across Europe.[62] It was a criminal state and an egregiously lawless one, radically discontinuous with the moral and political compact that was said to have ushered in modernity in the West and formed the cornerstone of defense against the pernicious, self-aggrandizing, denigrating, and arbitrary claim of power on and against life. In this vein, Arendt wrote to Jaspers: with the death camps the world had stumbled into an abyss from which it might recover but never fully return, so fundamentally altered and precarious did the conditions of human coexistence now appear in the wake of their discovery. And Justice Jackson struggled as well to capture the mood and significance of the immediate postwar moment in his opening address before the tribunal: "The real complaining party at your bar is Civilization. . . . Civilization asks whether law is so laggard as to be utterly helpless to deal with crimes of this magnitude by criminals of this order."[63]

If an important part of the function and performance of the International Military Tribunal at Nuremberg was precisely to ventriloquize civilization's complaints, an equally critical function was to allow the aggrieved but victorious nations to clearly distinguish themselves in character and kind from Germany with its deadly nationalism, brutish militarism, and savage program of imperialist plunder. And this they did, on the one hand, by placing beyond the legal and visual frame "the fact that many of the ideals and policies of Nazism and the German 'criminal state' were not particularly distinguishable in many details from those still operating in the governmental structures and discourses of the Allies."[64] One obvious example in this regard was the turn of Western nations to eugenics throughout the first half of the twentieth century. Underappreciated even today and ignored in its more contemporary iterations, eugenics was considered a scientifically legitimate approach and practice of considerable social and legal utility; it provided a means of rationalizing the social field and a way of explaining the seemingly intractable social problems that plagued liberal capitalist formations but, importantly, was marshaled to serve a *progressive* social vision. Another example, speaking now specifically of the United States, was Jim Crow laws, which married scientific racism and state policy under the aegis of public health:[65] it was not lost on some members of the defense for the accused that Jim Crow had been an early model for lawyers crafting the Nuremberg laws of 1935, laws that initiated the segregation and formal disenfranchisement of Jewish citizens in Germany.

On the other hand, the aggrieved nations at Nuremberg sought to reestablish the "rule of law" in Germany while also making bright and unmistakable the distinction between the rational and the ruthless or the just and the unjust by inscribing as criminal the years from 1933 to 1945. The mostly successful case of the prosecution sought, in effect, to quarantine these years "as a pathological deformation of the great and continuing traditions of western legality and the rule of law."[66] There was a "before Auschwitz" and an "after Auschwitz"; and within this conceptual and even temporal schema, a traumatic rupture whose possibility of repair, speaking more broadly now, was shown to be staged and initiated at Nuremberg. Once restored and administered by reason rather than power, *real* law was neither laggard nor helpless and could contain evil and render justice while also putting the world on notice that no crime of the kind or magnitude exposed at Nuremberg would again escape notice or swift punishment.[67]

David Fraser suggests that this framing of the Nazi state as criminal and the Nazi system as a radical, lawless break for the most part dominates popular historical understanding.[68] And yet significantly, he argues, it is in large measure an invention of the tribunal at Nuremberg; it is a fiction that ignores and even obscures the ways in which the Nazi state and policing system represent a continuation and deepening of already extant state structures and practices that, far from being lawless, were suffused with law.[69] And Auschwitz, he continues, the quintessential pillar of terror that counsel for the prosecution described as one of the fundamental institutions of the regime, was indeed a state institution but one that operated as part of a larger juridical enterprise and apparatus devoted in turn to developing ever more refined systems of classification from which new legal subjects emerged if only then to be destroyed: "Aryan" and Jew" were both first identified in and through law, and an entire jurisprudence subsequently emerged to determine how precisely these interlocking, mutually constitutive categories were embodied and would signify. As Raul Hilberg similarly reflects, it all began with a definition.[70] And the ever expansive specificity of this definition and its consequence were, in the end, fully encapsulated in the legal text that was the tattooed number, etched in the flesh of camp inmates for easy identification in death. What this suggests is that the Nazi project, however horrific, was not outside of but contiguous with Western legal practices. And this in turn raises a question Fraser insists Nuremberg was simply unprepared to address and, for the most part, remains unanswered, to wit: what precisely distinguishes law from Nazi law? In Fraser's words:

> If we cannot mark 1933–1945 as a period of radical disjuncture, if we must admit
> its place in our history and within our legal systems, if the Holocaust was to some

extent at least lawful, then law after Auschwitz takes on a completely new complexion. It is not because the Holocaust was unique that it poses challenges to our legal system or to our conceptions of law and justice. It is the very normality of the Holocaust and of the legal basis of the Holocaust which challenges us. Law must face itself. Law Before and After Auschwitz.[71]

In the course of answering civilization's complaints, "crucial foundation myths" were set in place at Nuremberg; and these myths joined with others, according to Judt, to underwrite the reinvention of democratic Europe and the United States in the postwar years.[72] Law facing itself as an essential constituent in the making of death worlds, as Fraser suggests it must, is about dismantling a set of these myths even as they constitute the brick and mortar of postwar national identities. Part of the argument of this chapter has been that what rendered and continues to render these myths plausible and viscerally unquestionable; indeed, what fixes and situates the period from 1933 to 1945 out-of-time, requiring us to speak of a radical historical break—the before and after of Auschwitz—are the atrocity images, introduced at Nuremberg as both judge and witness. They continue to configure the narrative field, insisting on and guaranteeing a set of stories and allegiances that resist reframing, indeed that indict reframing as revisionist and an affront to the memory of the dead. And of course it is not the images per se but the now largely invisible legal, political, and visual apparatuses that animate and circumscribe their semiotic context. These apparatuses continue to underwrite their privileged status, naturalize their meaning, and authorize them to speak in ways that appear unmediated, indeed in ways that continue to precipitate in spectators a sense of traumatic rupture, of terror and fear as well as silence and shame, alternately read and rendered by some as the necessary core of a historical consciousness that recognizes the inadequacy of historical knowledge. If these images continue to carry with them the imperative to look, with its attendant renunciations, they also significantly entail a prohibition against seeing or seeing specifically beyond the frame. For within this economy of meaning, to move beyond the frame of the image is to fail in the end to grasp fully the sublime evil captured within it.[73] Within this economy there can be no "why," and with this perhaps we might agree—but not because the practices and processes whose outcome the images capture are incomprehensible. It is instead because "why" is not a question that will travel: its pursuit takes us nowhere. So much greater, as Fraser notes, is the challenge of the demythologizing "how" and the familiar, even unremarkable, apparatuses that it then brings within our purview, operating to organize and preserve life even as they also destroy it.

At the beginning of chapter 3, I began the discussion of Arendt's understanding of thoughtlessness by recounting an exchange she had with Christian Bay at a conference devoted to considering the import of her work. This exchange was precipitated by a general discussion of what "thinking is and is good for" but also, more specifically, by Bay's insistence that with the exception of Eichmann in Jerusalem, Arendt's writings on politics lacked "a certain seriousness about modern problems."[1] In his reading, her trial report was a noted exception in an otherwise disengaged corpus of work—an exception because Arendt had provocatively illustrated "how Eichmann was in each of us" or how "Eichmann-like" tendencies constituted a formative component and condition of late-twentieth-century liberal-capitalist subjectivity. From this widely shared but, as Arendt insisted, mistaken reading, Bay drew the further conclusion that such "Eichmann-like" tendencies in oneself, one's students, one's fellow citizens needed to be aggressively combated: individuals had to be educated out of their indifference or "indoctrinated in a pluralist universe," to use his language; compelled to think and passionately care; aroused from apathy and driven to act in the name of justice and on behalf of the dispossessed and disenfranchised. Bay's apparent confidence about what the content or end of critical thinking should be and his plain certainty as to where thinking critically or caring passionately would necessarily lead individuals are striking: were the true and the good so easily settled or so clearly self-evident, what need for further thinking would there then be? Still, Bay's claims are a telling measure of his impatience with Arendt's rendering of a practice that is not obviously "productive" and whose effect we encounter most dramatically in its absence: extreme things, she tells us, are the actual consequences of nonthinking.[2] But of the actual political consequences of thinking? To this query Arendt offered no real answer except to note that a society that has lost respect for thinking is one vulnerable to losing its way:

> I cannot tell you black on white—and would hate to do it—what the consequences of this kind of thought which I try, not to indoctrinate, but to rouse or awaken in my students, are, in actual politics. I can very well imagine that one becomes a republican and the third becomes a liberal or God knows what. But one thing I would hope: that certain extreme things which are the actual consequences of nonthinking . . . will not be capable [of arising]. That is, when the chips are down, the

question is how will they act. And then this notion that I examine my assumptions
... that I think "critically," and that I don't let myself get away with repeating the
clichés of the public mood [comes into play]. And I would say any society that has
lost respect for this, is not in very good shape.[3]

It was Eichmann's thoughtlessness—his refusal to test or examine
received opinions or take his bearings from the awareness he clearly had of what
was happening and how and to whom even while he was not among those who
pulled a trigger, or released the gas, or directly ordered others to do so—that
predisposed him, in Arendt's view, "to become one of the greatest criminals of
the period." However, his failure, his thoughtlessness, Arendt also links to a
failure of judgment for which thinking clears the way.[4] In most instances, judgment "depends on the presence of others 'in whose place' it must think [and]
whose perspectives it must take into account." But where this is not possible—
as in times of political crisis or emergency when the values and standards that
otherwise make a shared common world possible have all but collapsed—one is
simply on one's own. And the question then is whether I will be able to live with
myself doing whatever it is I may be called upon to do regardless of the beliefs
and activities of those around me:

> If you examine the few, the very few who in the moral collapse of Nazi Germany
> remained completely intact ... you will discover that they never went through
> anything like a great moral conflict or crisis of conscience. They did not ponder the
> various issues—the issue of the lesser evil or of loyalty to their country or their oath,
> or whatever else there might have been at stake. Nothing of the sort. . . . [T]hey
> never doubted that crimes remained crimes even if legalized by the government,
> and that it was better not to participate in these crimes under any circumstances.
> In other words, they did not feel an obligation but acted according to something
> which was self-evident to them even though it was no longer self-evident to those
> around them. Hence their conscience, if that is what it was, had no obligatory
> character, it said, 'This I *can't* do,' rather than, 'This I *ought* not to do'. . . . You can
> always counter the 'thou shalt' or the 'you ought' by talking back: I will not or I can-
> not for whatever reasons. Morally the only reliable people when the chips are down
> are those who say 'I can't.'[5]

I.

In the figure of Eichmann—an ordinary man but no ordinary criminal—
Arendt claimed to have observed something about the *banality of evil*.[6] And
commentators since have written volumes on what precisely she meant by the
phrase. She used it, after all, as the subtitle of her report on the Eichmann
trial but insisted at the time that she offered it only as a limited statement of

fact—a "simple" observation about the man in the glass booth—rather than as part of a broader theory or doctrine. Thus, for example, while acknowledging the provocative argument Arendt develops in her report, Peter Baehr simply dismisses the phrase as the kind of "silly cleverness" to which intellectuals are sometimes prone: had Arendt talked about banality *and* evil, he suggests, rather than collapsing the two concepts and thereby "diluting one of the richest normative terms of condemnation in our vocabulary," she would have found herself on much firmer and richer intellectual ground.[7] Other critics prefer the account of evil she offered in *The Origins of Totalitarianism*—that Nazi efforts to render human beings superfluous represented the full gruesome embodiment of *radical evil* for which there could be no humanely recognizable motives and therefore no suitable punishment or earthly forgiveness. These critics denounce her apparent shift in understanding and read her as trivializing the "evil" of the catastrophe while also absolving the accused. Longtime friend and philosopher Gershom Scholem:

> After reading your book I remain unconvinced by your thesis concerning the "banality of evil"—a thesis which, if your sub-title is to be believed, underlies your entire argument. This new thesis strikes me as a catchword: it does not impress me, certainly as the product of profound analysis—an analysis such as you gave us so convincingly, in the service of a quite different, indeed, contradictory thesis in your book on totalitarianism. At that time you had not yet made your discovery, apparently, that evil is banal. Of that "radical evil," to which your then analysis bore such eloquent and erudite witness, nothing remains but this slogan—to be more than that it would have to be investigated, at a serious level, as a relevant concept in moral philosophy and political ethics. I am sorry—and I say this, I think, in candor and in no spirit of enmity—that I am unable to take the thesis of your book more seriously.[8]

More sympathetic readers have made it part of their life's work to explain and more firmly draw precisely the clarifying links that otherwise remain so faint in Arendt's writing and render it vulnerable to misunderstanding. Thus Dana Villa cautions against reading Arendt's claim about the banality of evil in global terms, suggesting instead that it was an observation she offered only with respect to the man before her in Jerusalem: "The 'banality of evil' named *Eichmann's* evil, not the evil of the perpetrators or the Holocaust in general."[9] Richard Bernstein and Margaret Canovan both insist that while it appears Arendt had abandoned the account of evil she offered in her study of totalitarianism, there is in their reading of her work a continuity and compatibility between "radical evil" and her later "formulation," especially if one considers the arc of her arguments over the years regarding the implications of totalitarian terror. Responding to Arendt biographer Elisabeth Young-Bruehl's suggestion that

Arendt's encounter with Eichmann had released her from the nightmare of living with the idea "that monsters and demons had engineered the murder of millions,"[10] both Bernstein and Canovan argue that Arendt "never *had* thought in terms of monsters and demons."[11] And in Canovan's view at least, "banality was really a more accurate way of describing the self abandonment to inhuman forces and the diminution of human beings to an animal species that she had all along placed at the center of totalitarianism."[12]

As we saw in chapter 2, the proceedings at Nuremberg were under way when Arendt wrote to Jaspers insisting that there could be no adequate punishment and thus no real justice for criminals whose deeds defied human comprehension and scales of measurement: "what meaning has the concept of murder when we are confronted with the mass production of corpses?"[13] And it was Jaspers who sensed in her account a certain tendency toward mythologizing Nazi criminality. Indeed, it was Jaspers who offered Arendt a way of thinking about evil that did not flirt with notions of "satanic greatness": "We have to see these things in their total banality because that's what truly characterizes them. Bacteria can cause epidemics that wipe out nations but they remain merely bacteria."[14] And Arendt would herself adopt this language in her response to Gershom Scholem's critical appraisal of her trial report, analogizing evil to a kind of "fungus":

> I changed my mind and no longer speak of "radical evil." It is a long time since we last met, or we would perhaps have spoken about the subject before. (Incidentally, I don't know why you call my term "banality of evil" a catchword or slogan. As far as I know no one has used the term before me; but that is unimportant). It is indeed my opinion *now* that evil is never "radical," that it is only extreme, and that it possesses neither depth nor any demonic dimension. It can overgrow and lay waste the whole world precisely because it spreads like a fungus on the surface. It is "thought-defying," as I said, because thought tries to reach some depth, to go to the roots, and the moment it concerns itself with evil, it is frustrated because there is nothing. That is its "banality."[15]

In this passage from a letter to a friend and colleague, Arendt offers an account that might explain a shift in understanding of high stakes. Without asking her brief explanation to bear too much of the weight of an argument, it seems nevertheless instructive in terms of the issue at hand; for Arendt herself seems to imply in this passage that there had indeed been a time when she regarded the "radical evil" of Nazi criminality to be demonic or demonic-like in depth and dimension. And further, that she had since abandoned that view. Bernstein and Canovan may be quite right to point out that she turned a critical eye toward accounts that attributed an otherworldly character to Nazi atrocity. But readers of *The Origins of Totalitarianism* cannot fail to notice the dominant place occupied by ideology in the work. Ideology is given center stage in the story Arendt tells about totalitarianism, and its power to shape the historical drama of domination as it unfolded is formidable and decidedly extraworldly. As she describes its world-altering and world-destroying capacities, Ideology moves from the outside in, taking hold and somehow capturing a national population and even parts of populations that come under occupation; it—or rather the stringent logicality of an idea whose tenets outside the closed world it creates appear, in Arendt's words, both "stupid and vulgar"—moves individuals who no longer have a sense of themselves as such to subordinate their lives to its laws in ways even they have difficulty explaining once it is all over. There is a kind of possession at work. Moreover, ideology is the explanatory framework and the force that drives the regime, inciting, uniting, and compressing through terror; diabolically fostering and building an earthly hell in concentration camps and torture cellars across Europe, a hell "whose chief difference from mediaeval hell-images lies in technical improvements and bureaucratic administration but also in its lack of eternity."[6] Its *only* purpose is to remake humanity, and terror facilitates the process. Within this narrative, the German mind is captured and conditioned by ideology through propaganda. But what of the leadership? What was its relationship to the forces it unleashed?

> It is an open and sometimes hotly debated question whether the totalitarian ruler himself or his immediate subordinates believe, along with his mass of adherents and subjects, in the superstitions of the respective ideologies. Since the tenets in question are so obviously stupid and vulgar, those who tend to answer this question affirmatively are also inclined to deny the almost unquestionable qualities and gifts of men like Hitler and Stalin. On the other hand, those who tend to answer this question negatively, believing that the phenomenal deceptiveness of both men is sufficient proof of their cold and detached cynicism, are also inclined to deny the curious incalculability of totalitarian politics, which so obviously violates all rules of self-interest and common sense. In a world used to calculating actions and reactions by these yardsticks, such incalculability becomes a public danger.[17]

After the Eichmann trial, Arendt wrote to Mary McCarthy and noted that she thought she had perhaps overestimated the centrality and work of ideology, especially its impact on the individual: Eichmann himself did not seem to her to be either captured or conditioned in quite the exceptionally grand ways she had assumed individuals, especially "the elite" of the regime, as she referred to them, would have to have been to function within what she called an "authentically totalitarian structure."[18] By "authentically totalitarian structure," she meant a structure that had evolved beyond or "transcended" methods of domination that emerged and were refined in the late nineteenth century with colonial expansion. Imperialism of the nineteenth century, she argued, provided the prototype for totalitarianism of the twentieth century—and before that, there was the "extermination of native peoples of the Americas and Australia . . . and the building of empires on the labor of state-owned slaves." As Arendt points out, not even the concentration camps were a novel "invention" of totalitarian rule, at least not in the initial years: "[Concentration camps] emerge for the first time with the Boer War at the beginning of the century, and continued to be used in South Africa as well as India for 'undesirable elements'; here, too, we first find the term 'protective custody' which was later adopted by the Third Reich."[19] But in Arendt's view from the historical vantage point of the late 1940s, all these techniques of domination and the organization of social worlds they fostered and enforced could still be explained in terms of a utilitarian logic or economic as well as political imperatives. In its most developed or authentic form, she insisted, totalitarianism could not be so explained: it had shed utilitarian motive and strategic reason entirely and functioned to destroy humanity even as it sought to remake it according to the laws of Nature and the logic of race struggle.

Without ideology operating in the ways Arendt describes, marshaling terror to hold hostage and clear the way for ever more sinister and refined forms of domination in order to refigure the lifeworld, the tight coherence of her totalitarian universe begins to unravel. Perhaps having a sense of this, Arendt continued in her letter to McCarthy to suggest that rather than ideology, it was instead the extermination policy itself that came to function as the centerpiece of the system: "the content of anti-semitism . . . gets lost in the extermination policy, for extermination would not have come to an end when no Jew was left to be killed. In other words, extermination per se is more important than anti-semitism or racism."[20] But what then explains the extermination policy? Mass murder doesn't just happen for its own sake, however twisted the rationale. Within the framework of her account of totalitarianism, once ideology is decentered and radical evil jettisoned—for radical evil is an effect of ideology's operation—the explanatory resources available to explain how genocide might emerge and become a "plausible solution" narrow, especially since Arendt had also argued at the outset of the work that more conventional rationalities, structures, and techniques of control were inadequate to explain the conjunction of forces that fostered genocide's conditions. She had insisted that totalitarianism marked a radical, historical rupture that defied reason and commonplace explanations; and she had dismissed the possibility of historical continuities, of deducing the unprecedented from precedent or of seeing in "authentic totalitarianism" an adapted, refurbished, but recognizable instantiation of colonial terror, domination, racism, and economic exploitation.

Canovan suggests that "banality" more accurately describes the "self-abandonment to inhuman forces" that Arendt sets out in *The Origins of Totalitarianism* and thus that her insight with respect to Eichmann did not mark a significant shift in understanding. But this reading is not sustained by Arendt's text and is anyway undermined by the language Canovan herself uses: to be sure, "self-abandonment" or an abdication of personal responsibility goes generally to the heart of Arendt's description of evil's banality, but to speak at all about "inhuman forces" implies the distinct presence of something larger than life whose diabolical dimensions make human resistence unlikely. It participates in a kind of mythologizing, and it invokes precisely the "monsters and demons" Canovan also insists Arendt could not possibly have entertained. Clearly, however, one can easily detect in the very description Arendt developed of "authentic totalitarianism" that she was indeed in the company of "monsters and demons," and she appeared prepared to concede, at least in the late 1940s, that the havoc they wreaked in the end "surpass[ed] our powers of understanding."[21]

With the Eichmann trial all this changed. In Jerusalem, Arendt watched the spectacle of the proceedings, and she watched Eichmann as well. She was one of a large audience called upon to witness and, in writing her report, to participate in the creation of a narrative that would organize and definitively lay claim to a past no one had yet mastered. But as we saw in chapter 1, what she produced was in effect a counternarrative—a story that worked against the grain of survivor need, public expectation, political expediency, and traditions of moral and legal thought in advancing the suggestion that "no deep-rooted or radical evil was necessary to make the trains to Auschwitz run on time."[22] Through the optics of thoughtlessness, the broader meaning of the death camps and the unmistakably devastating implications of the practices that brought them into existence could be and, in Arendt's view, would now need to be both reframed and refigured. She arrived in Jerusalem prepared, like others, to stare down a monster and was forced instead to reckon with a man.

Eichmann's highest moral obligation, as he told the Court, was to upheld the oath of allegiance he had taken to the Führer and, within the Nazi SS, to the Reichsführer, Himmler—and this oath, he told the court, he honored faithfully to the end, unlike many of his colleagues who lacked, he said, "the courage of their convictions."[23] When pressed by Judge Reveh about whether maintaining such loyalty in the face of orders that unambiguously entailed mass murder, especially after the Wannsee Conference in 1942, did not provoke an "an inner conflict between [his] duty and [his] conscience," Eichmann conceded that he had at moments experienced a conflict. But "it would be better to call it a split state," he said, "a form of splitting, where one fled from one side to the other and vice versa."[24] The judge asked further: Did this splitting foster mental reservation or perhaps a more sustained introspective process?; did Eichmann at any point understand the practical consequences of his actions as an "emigration

expert" and "transportation officer"?; and was he now finally able to acknowledge to the Court and the world his pivotal role in and responsibility for orches-
trating the mass murder of a people? It was a matter of the facts, Judge Reveh
told Eichmann; could he at least admit to the facts "in order not to be suspected
of wishing to evade things"? Eichmann had repeatedly conveyed to the Court
his desire to impress upon his sons his courage and candor in facing the truth
and telling it in full regardless of the impact such truth-telling might have on
the outcome of his case; if nothing else this would provide them with an honest
and thus accurate record they could use to counter the lies others would inevi-
tably speak against him.[25] Judge Halevi interjected: Did Eichmann understand
that creating such a record required at least acknowledging the facts before the
Court? And better still would be assuming responsibility for them.

With each question from the judges, Eichmann deflected, deferred, quali-
fied, or denied, until finally toward the end of one of the concluding sessions
of the trial, he spoke specifically to their queries. In a fashion that anticipated
Arendt's discussion to a point some fifteen years later when she reflected on
whether and in what sense the activity of thinking "was among the conditions
that make men abstain from evil doing," he offered this account of himself:

> In retrospect, obviously the fact that one was a recipient of orders can no longer
> make any difference. . . . When it came to my innermost self—I in fact now had to
> search my soul, and of course one always searches one's soul—and this is where a
> man judges himself. And I admit that this soul-searching and judging oneself may
> be a hard thing, depending on the mood and the prevailing influences on one—
> sometimes one is inclined to personal cowardice, and one would prefer to shirk this
> business of taking a clear-cut decision about oneself. I am aware of all this [now].
> But if I say to myself, if I remind myself how often I tried to get away and to obtain
> another posting, and how I tried my level best not to go to Berlin, if only because I
> would be separated from my family by this posting, then I tell myself, when I carry
> out this soul-searching, as one does time and again to oneself in hours of quiet.
> I tell myself: Yes, I did everything I could have done. I was a tool in the hands of
> forces stronger than myself. I—let me put it in a somewhat vulgar way—I must
> wash my hands of it in innocence, so far as my innermost self is concerned. That is
> how I understand this. . . . There was nothing to be done.[26]

This is Eichmann at the conclusion of his trial offering the Court and the
world an account of how he lived with himself as the bearer of orders. Over
the course of a decade, the execution of such directives entailed organizing and
plundering Jewish communities across Europe, setting up timetables for trains
to ensure the orderly transport of these communities en masse to the camps
whereupon further larceny was committed against marked bodies with the
extraction from each of hair, gold, and labor. Those who were seen as having

nothing left of use were simply herded into chambers and gassed. But about all this, Eichmann in the end had little to say: he had tried to get away, he told the Court, even as he also insisted that he was bound by his oath to serve; being so bound, he reasoned, he was only an instrument; and being merely an instrument, he was innocent. This he repeated to the judges in Jerusalem over and over; and this they regarded as empty talk and great subterfuge. As we have seen, however, for Arendt Eichmann's "empty talk" signaled something altogether more perplexing and clarifying. It was a portrait of what Jaspers had referred to many years earlier as evil in all its prosaic triviality and what she was now prepared to see as the banality of evil. With every train to Auschwitz, Treblinka, or Tieresenstadt, among the hundreds of camps across occupied Europe, the given condition of human plurality was at one and the same time both acknowledged and refused. And yet for Eichmann, the departure of each train represented only a job well done under increasingly more challenging circumstances. The story of evil's banality was the story of a functionary who facilitated the death of millions without apparent animus or motive and yet never apprehended—not during the war or in the years that followed or standing beside the gallows—what this meant or made him.

II.

Arendt turned to Kant and continental philosophy more generally to work out the phenomenon she believed she had encountered in the figure of Eichmann, to trace the link if there was one between our ability to judge and our faculty of thought. Concerned principally with the banality of the evildoer, she proceeded in the years before her death by drawing an ever tighter inquisitive focus around the constitutive components of subject formation (although this was not her language), in order to begin conceptualizing at the level of the individual what the necessary preconditions of genocide's prevention might entail. What is required to interrupt the practices that enable individuals to ignore and misrecognize (and thus participate in) the processes that produce superfluity rather than plurality as the norm and given of human life together? What is required to interrupt practices of life that destroy its very condition of possibility?

These questions generally inform each dimension of the current study. But the Eichmann trial and Arendt's treatment of it have also taken us in another direction, substantively and thematically, toward considering the ways in which contemporary preoccupations with the Holocaust may contribute to masking and normalizing the totalitarian solutions Arendt was certain would survive totalitarian regimes. The discourse of radical rupture that we have encountered repeatedly across discursive domains and that is central to how the Holocaust has been configured in popular culture and consciousness is pivotal in this respect. This discourse operates, as we have seen, in a number of ways—to quarantine the disciplinary arenas regarded as colonized by the ideologies and agendas of Nazism, to criminalize the state apparatus, or to sacralize the mass murder of European Jewry. As such, it has worked to circumscribe fields of signification; freeze visual, interpretive, and affective landscapes; and dismiss continuities of practices and processes by invoking discontinuities of effect. Terror, traumatic loss, eliminationist anti-Semitism, administrative murder, the fact of the camps, structures of dictatorship, the criminal state—all these things are held to be definitive and unique features of the totalitarian moment; and against all or any of these features, it is said often quite vehemently, "We are not *that*." There can be no argument on this front because it is true or true enough. But at the same time such assertions also miss the point. In suggesting that totalitarian solutions would survive totalitarian regimes, Arendt was not also suggesting that "totalitarian solutions" would manifest in familiar ways, that we would find ourselves under the boot of a Hitler, that some of us would be working hard to ignore the disappearance of our neighbors, or that others of us would be working equally hard to explain away the construction of a labor camp on the outskirts of town. Nazism did not provide such a blueprint, and totalitarian solutions that survive totalitarian regimes will not be an obvious reiteration of earlier forms. New regimes of control, forms of terror, and techniques of domination, Arendt suggested, were likely to evolve in a world called upon to manage and regulate expanding populations, an unstable market, and ever shrinking resources. Under such conditions, how much harder it will be to recognize or affirm a solidarity that assures each their rightful place according to a promise that shapes a necessarily shared world, to wit: alongside, with, and even against each other, we are all here.[27]

As each of the chapters in this study underscore in one form or another, the discontinuities that were so starkly drawn in the immediate postwar period were largely superficial if also rhetorically and politically essential. They served a variety interests, they solved a variety of problems, and they were part of an effort, as Judt notes, to establish serviceable myths that would in turn facilitate the recovery of a war-torn world, across the continent certainly but also in the United States.[28] Many of these myths have since been written into the historical record, their preservation a matter of "sacred obligation" and/or national identity—a matter, in either case, of very high stakes.[29] This has postponed a difficult accounting and understanding of the radical, indeed lethal, potential of mostly obscure practices and processes that we, inhabiting late modernity, do indeed share with *that* earlier and otherwise quarantined period—instrumental and utilitarian rationalities, for example, along with the rational calculation of accumulation and waste; knowledge producing and collecting apparatuses, along with systems of classification so essential to organizing and administering populations; institutionalized mechanisms that both rationalize the production of superfluous people and naturalize the distribution of what Ophir calls "superfluous suffering."[30] We can also add to this list the many techniques of control and regulation that constantly refigure what is called freedom and security, expanding economies of fear so critical to maintaining a compliant population and, not unrelated, a deeply militarized conception of statecraft.[31] There are continuities, in other words, and only from them can sharper and more refined distinctions then be drawn.

But drawing out these continuities and refocusing the interpretive frame is hardly enough. As noted briefly in the context of this book's opening discussion, this interpretive frame must also be broadened to interrupt the contemporary myth that genocide (if a foreign policy establishment is willing to concede that a genocide has happened) always happens "elsewhere"—outside international pacts, systems, and rules of law rather than as an effect of them—a regrettable spectacle precipitated by ethnic or tribal rivalries, civil wars or religious conflicts, situated at some remove geographically, to be sure, but also at a moral, cultural, and political distance. However, as Mark Levine notes, "elsewheres" in the context of contemporary genocides are at best a strategic fiction, a convenient political fantasy and moral alibi. Understanding genocide's contemporary conditions of possibility, he argues, requires foregrounding centrally geopolitical economic interdependencies—those networks of relations, for example, that bring into stark relief the ways that maintaining factories, jobs, and life as usual in one country, paraphrasing Zygmunt Bauman now, most often entails supplying the guns, bullets, and poison gas of genocide in another;[32] or make visible the ways the ten-dollar sweatshirt on offer at Wal-Mart presupposes ever-growing numbers of displaced and ultimately disposable workers as capital roams the globe (with security forces typically not far behind) in search of cheap, docile labor and unregulated, which is to say, "business-friendly" environments. We occasionally catch glimpses of these global relays or networks of relation on the front page of the New York Times, on CNN's continuously updated website, or on any of many other alternative news sites and sources. But there is very little in the ways we collectively think the world that might sustain the linkages, and, indeed, forceful rhetorics and technologies of seeing and not seeing function as well to break, discredit, or simply obscure them. Clearly we are, as Ophir and others note, most surely after Auschwitz. But insofar as the logic that created its condition of possibility is an ongoing, materially and discursively constituent feature of organized life today, securing and enhancing even as it erodes and detroys, that logic ensures that we remain also always before it.[33]

Notes

NOTES TO INTRODUCTION

1. Hannah Arendt, *Eichmann in Jerusalem: A Report on the Banality of Evil* (New York: Penguin, 1963).

2. Hannah Arendt, cited in Jerome Kohn, Introduction to *Responsibility and Judgment* (New York: Schocken Books, 2003), vii.

3. See, for example, Bernard Williams, *Truth and Truthfulness: An Essay in Genealogy* (Berkeley: University of California Press, 2002).

4. D. D. Guttenplan takes to task the testimony of the historian Richard Evans at the trial of the Holocaust revisionist David Irvingon on precisely this issue: "In his book, *In Defense of History* Evans draws an uncharacteristically crude connection between 'the increase in scope and intensity of the Holocaust deniers' activities since the mid-1970s' and 'the postmodern intellectual climate, above all in the USA, in which scholars have increasingly denied that texts had any fixed meaning . . . and in which attacks on the Western rationalist tradition have become fashionable. . . . [A]n atmosphere of permissiveness toward questioning the meaning of historical events . . . fosters deconstructionist history at its worst . . . Holocaust denial is part of this phenomenon.'" *The Holocaust on Trial* (New York: Norton, 2001), 290. See also Richard Evans, *Lying about Hitler: History, Holocaust, and the David Irving Trial* (New York: Basic Books, 2001), esp. chaps. 1 and 4.

5. For an elaboration of this view, see William Bennett, *Why We Fight: Moral Clarity and the War on Terrorism* (Washington, DC: Regnery, 2003). The phrase "pseudosophisticated relativism" is Bennett's, pp. 161–63.

6. Edward Rothstein, "Attacks on U.S. Challenge the Perspectives of Postmodern True Believers," *New York Times*, September 22, 2001, A17.

7. Roger Rosenblatt, "The Age of Irony Comes to an End," *Time*, Special Issue: One Nation, Indivisible, September 24, 2001, 79.

8. Hannah Arendt, *On Revolution* (New York: Viking, 1963), 79.

9. Joan Didion, *Fixed Ideas: America Since 9.11* (New York: New York Review Books, 2003).

10. Stanley Fish, "Condemnation without Absolutes," *New York Times*, October 15, 2001. Available at www.nytimes.com/2001/10/15/opinion/condemnation-without-absolutes.html.

11. Bennett, *Why We Fight*, 10; see esp. chap. 1, "The Morality of Anger."

12. See, for example, Scott McClellan, *What Happened: Inside the Bush White House and Washington's Culture of Deception* (New York: Public Affairs, 2008), esp. chap. 8, "Selling the War."

13. Ron Suskind, "Without a Doubt," *New York Times Magazine*, October 12, 2004. Available at http://query.nytimes.com/gst/fullpage.html?res=9C05EFD8113BF934A25753C1A962 9C8B63.

14. Thucydides, *The History of the Peloponnesian War*, ed. M. I. Finley (New York: Penguin, 1972), 402.

15. "Reckless audacity came to be considered the courage of a loyal ally; prudent hesitation, specious cowardice; moderation, a cloak for unmanliness; ability to see all sides of a question inaptness to act on any. Frantic violence became an attribute of manliness," and so on. Thucydides, *The History of the Peloponnesian War*, 403.

16. James Boyd White, *When Words Lose Their Meaning: Constitutions and Reconstitutions of Language, Character, and Community* (Chicago: University of Chicago Press, 1984), 90.

17. Sheldon Wolin, *Democracy Inc.: Managed Democracy and the Specter of Inverted Totalitarianism* (Princeton: Princeton University Press, 2008), 3.

18. There is, of course, more to this story than I am able to detail here. See Patricia Owens, *Between Wars and Politics: International Relations and the Thought of Hannah Arendt* (Oxford: Oxford University Press, 2007).

19. "The result of a consistent and total substitution of lies for factual truth is not that the lies will now be accepted as truth, and the truth be defamed as lies, but that the sense by which we take our bearings in the real world—and the category of truth vs. falsehood is among the mental means to this end—is being destroyed.... And for this trouble there is no remedy." Hannah Arendt, "Truth and Politics," in *Between Past and Present* (New York: Penguin, 1977), 257.

20. Hannah Arendt, "On the Nature of Totalitarianism," in *Essays in Understanding, 1930–1954*, ed. Jerome Kohn (New York: Harcourt Brace, 1994), 354. For an especially compelling engagement with Arendt's argument on the process and practices by which a "lying world order" gets put in place and its implications, see Peg Birmingham, "A Lying World Order: Political Deception and the Threat of Totalitarianism," in *Thinking in Dark Times: Hannah Arendt on Ethics and Politics*, ed. Roger Berkowitz, Jeffrey Katz, and Thomas Keenan (New York: Fordham University Press, 2010), 73–77; and Cathy Caruth, "Lying and History," in Berkowitz, Katz, and Keenan, *Thinking in Dark Times*, 79–92.

21. To get a feel for how these and related matters have been addressed specifically with respect to the Holocaust, see Alan Milchman and Alan Rosenberg, eds., *Postmodernism and the Holocaust* (Atlanta: Rodopi, 1998); Robert Eaglestone, *Postmodernism and Holocaust Denial* (London: Icon Books, 2001); Hans Kellner, "'Never Again' Is Now," *History and Theory* 33:2 (May 1994): 127–44; James E. Young, *Writing and Rewriting the Holocaust: Narrative and the Consequences of Interpretation* (Bloomington: Indiana University Press, 1990); Marouf Hasian Jr., *Legal Memories and Amnesias in America's Rhetorical Culture* (Boulder, CO: Westview Press, 2000); Saul Friedländer, ed., *Probing the Limits of Representation: Nazism and the Final Solution* (Cambridge, MA: Harvard University Press, 1992).

22. Samantha Power, *A Problem from Hell: America and the Age of Genocide* (New York: Basic Books, 2002), xvi.

23. Darfur is an interesting example in this respect. While recognized as "genocide"—by the president of the United States, no less—intervention has primarily taken the form of economic sanctions. Consider in this regard the bill Bush signed at the end of his presidency (December 31, 1907). As the *New York Times* reports, this bill "makes it easier for mutual funds and other investment managers to sell stakes in companies that do business in Sudan. The bill is aimed at Sudan's oil and defense industries, in particular, and is part of a broader campaign to put pressure on the Sudanese government to end the bloodshed in Darfur." The obvious question is for whose benefit this bill was signed. The interest it represents and the bodies on whose behalf it is ostensibly marshaled seem entirely distinct. http://www.nytimes.com/2008/01/02/world/africa/02sudan.html.

24. Power, *A Problem from Hell*, 351–52.

25. Power, *A Problem from Hell*, 508. A good example of what Power is talking about is available on George Washington University's National Security Archive Website: "The U.S. and the Genocide in Rwanda 1994: Information, Intelligence and the U.S. Response," William Ferroggiaro, March 24, 2004 (www.gwu.edu/~nsarchiv/NSAEBB/NSAEBB117/index.htm).

26. Mark Levine, *Genocide in the Age of the Nation State: The Meaning of Genocide* (vol. 1) (New York: I. B.Taurus, 2005); and *Genocide in the Age of the Nation State: The Rise of the West and the Coming of Genocide* (vol. 2) (New York: I. B.Taurus, 2005).

27. Levine, *Genocide in the Age of the Nation State*, 2:8.

28. See also Robert Meister, *After Evil: A Politics of Human Rights* (New York: Columbia University Press, 2010).

29. Levine, *Genocide in the Age of the Nation State*, 1:176; *Genocide in the Age of the Nation State,*, 2:216. Notwithstanding important critical differences, Levine's reading resonates in interesting ways with the account Arendt adopted in *The Origins of Totalitarianism*. Looking to imperialism of the late nineteenth and early twentieth century—and, specifically, to the continental imperialism of the Pan-German and Pan-Slavic moments that sought conquests in Europe rather than Africa—Arendt sees the transformation of the modern (nation-)state into an instrument of capital as a critical component in creating totalitarianism's conditions. It is the shift from landed property to mobile wealth, with all its attendant social disruptions, the single-minded pursuit of profit, the competition for new markets and resources, and the violence that is brought to bear in securing these markets and resources, both natural and human, that destabilizes extant political institutions and fosters a new kind of administrative politics and political identity, organized principally around ethnic bonds. The story Arendt tells is obviously considerably more complicated than this, but what I find especially interesting are her efforts to contain and mute the role and consequences of capitalist expansion, even after she notes that what gets institutionalized at this historical moment and politicized is an economic rationality. Following Margaret Canovan, "although in Arendt's account imperialism started from the subordination of politics to bourgeois economics, it culminated in the abandonment of economic imperatives, and the adoption instead of sheer violence by men who had discovered a new form of community, a chosen race." It seems to me a more convincing account would be to track that constellation of practices that allowed economic imperatives to be naturalized rather than abandoned. See Margaret Canovan, *Hannah Arendt: A Reinterpretation of Her Political Thought* (Cambridge: Cambridge University Press, 1992), 39.

30. Levine, *Genocide in the Age of the Nation State*, 2:217–18, 221. Emphasis in the original.

31. On the production and distribution of suffering, see Adi Ophir, *The Order of Evils: Toward an Ontology of Morals* (Cambridge, MA: Zone Books, 2005), 296: "Systems that regularly produce suffering tend to naturalize it, to represent it as a result of bad luck, an uncontrollable and unpredictable coincidence, which is moreover impossible to prevent: 'fate,' 'God's hand,' 'natural disaster.' A critical discourse will try to describe the suffering, its production, spreading, and distribution, in order to denaturalize the socially produced suffering (or the suffering that is not prevented or alleviated). . . . Such a discourse will try to reconstruct the historicality of suffering, the unique sociology of the institutions that produce, distribute, and legitimate it. In order to do this, one need not concentrate on the phenomenology of suffering or its typology. It is enough to identify the social conditions that prevent or make it very difficult to disengage from various forms of encounter (physical pain, hunger, yearning, boredom, humiliation). The conditions that prevent disengagement—the law, a brick wall, false consciousness, fear, guilt—are enslaving conditions. Increasing the ability to disengage is liberation."

32. "We began . . . by critiquing the standard assumption that genocide is extrinsic to Western liberalism, proposing in its place that actually it is the latter's global system that provides the key to understanding how genocides can develop out of modern state-building agendas. And we conclude by noting that when such regime efforts impinge directly on Western interests that it is only then that the West absolutely demands their eradication. The blind spot however remains. Even when it comes to Iraq, the inability to acknowledge that 'our' direct or indirect long-term responsibility for the processes by which such a regime formed, shaped and perpetuated and in turn became thoroughly toxic seems to be beyond the ken of mainstream Western analysis." Mark Levine, "A Dissenting Voice: Or How Current Assumptions of Deterring and Preventing Genocide May Be Looking through the Wrong End of the Telescope, Part II," *Journal of Genocide Research* 6.3 (2004): 437–38.

33. Mark Levine, "A Dissenting Voice: Or How Current Assumptions of Deterring and Preventing Genocide May Be Looking at the Problem through the Wrong End of the Telescope, Part I," *Journal of Genocide Research* 6.2 (2004): 155, 156. Levine continues: "Where reference is made to specific Western acts of genocide it is usually (and arguably rather conveniently) related to the quite distant past with racial prejudice or xenophobia the usual—if aberrant—culprits rather than mainstream state building agendas themselves. This does not mean that there is no wringing of hands over Western failures in a contemporary frame. In fact, there is rather a lot of this. But it is mostly treated as a failure of omission. Rwanda 1994 has been the classic, recent reference point for this approach, vast reams of print being expended on the Western inability or unwillingness to pronounce genocide after April 6, 1994 or do anything to activate the UN to halt it. By contrast, studies which have suggested that Western *commission* (by which I mean post-colonial actions rather than simply the egregious nature of a racially-informed German or Belgian colonialism) may have been central to the outcome, either in terms of specifically aggravating the localized post-1990 crisis of more generally determining economic and political conditions which may have destabilized Rwanda in the first place, are few and far between" (156).

34. Robert Jackson, cited in Lawrence Douglas, *The Memory of Judgment: Making Law and History in the Trials of the Holocaust* (New Haven: Yale University Press, 2001), 50. Douglas continues: "As Jackson acknowledged, 'We have some regrettable circumstances at times in our own country in which minorities are unfairly treated.' He was loath, then, to create a precedent that would permit these 'regrettable circumstances' to be condemned in international law as crimes against humanity for which, say, the president could be held personally responsible. . . . Along with Jackson's political concerns, however, were formal legal considerations. For, as one expert in international law put it, 'Even if the acts of nationals of one state against citizens of the same state amounted to the most flagrant violations of fundamental principles of civilized behavior as recognized by most nations, it is not certain that this fact alone would constitute sufficient legal basis for holding individuals criminally responsible for them.'" Similar issues have emerged with respect to prosecuting members of the Bush administration who authorized the use of torture. See Austin Sarat and Nasser Hussain, eds., *When Governments Break the Law: The Rule of Law and the Prosecution of the Bush Administration* (New York: New York University Press, 2010).

35. An analysis of Germany and the rise of National Socialism within a framework resonant with Levine's is developed by the political economist Guido Giacomo Preparata in his decidedly unconventional and provocative history, *Conjuring Hitler: How Britain and America Made the Third Reich* (London: Pluto Press, 2005). What Preparata offers, as the title suggests, is a close reading of international markets in the early twentieth century and over

approximately a thirty-year period in order to foreground the ways in which these markets were manipulated primarily by Britain and to a lesser degree the United States, especially between 1919 and 1933, to drive Germany into the arms of a reactionary force that would in turn eventually move against the Soviet Union. According to Preparata, this was part of a master geopolitical scheme first devised by Halford Mackinder and more or less executed by Montagu Norman, governor of the Bank of England. And the rationale behind this strategy? To prevent an alliance between Germany and Russia that would "fuse into a Eurasian embrace" two powers whose combined resources of men, knowledge, and military capability would threaten, certainly, what was left of the British Empire but more generally endanger Anglo-Saxon dominance. Preparata explains: "In standard textbooks, the economics behind the rise of Nazism suffers a dreadful treatment at best, or, most often, is not treated at all, and the reader is customarily defrauded by being hastily assured that Hitler came 'because of the crisis,' no further explanation being forthcoming. What of the 'crisis'? Unless an effort is made to unveil the mechanics of this spectral collapse, Hitler remains an effect of chance, the social by-product of a silly financial season gone awry. And such a view is absurd. . . . Without properly comprehending the functioning of traditional banking systems and the nature of money, the key to Hitler's rise to power may never be held. And it is the lack of such comprehension that is chiefly to blame for discarding the decisive passage in the promotion of Nazism as the fruit of bad luck in times of crisis" (140–41).

36. David Caroll, cited in Friedländer, Introduction to *Probing the Limits of Representation*, 6.

37. Des Pres, cited in Ernst van Alphen, "Deadly Historians: Boltanski's Intervention in Holocaust Historiography," in *Visual Culture and the Holocaust*, ed. Barbie Zelizer (New Brunswick, NJ: Rutgers University Press, 2001), 46. For a more exhaustive account of the stakes of these claims, see Alan S. Rosenbaum, ed., *Is the Holocaust Unique? Perspectives on Comparative Genocide* (Boulder, CO: Westview Press, 1996).

38. Hannah Arendt certainly foregrounds these links in *The Origins of Totalitarianism*; for a study that develops them both in terms of Arendt's account and the contemporary literature, see Owens, *Between War and Politics*.

39. A controversial exhibition of mostly amateur photographs taken by soldiers from the *Wehrmacht*—the German Armed Forces—in the course of actions in the East raises precisely such questions of what it is one sees when one looks. See Hamburg Institute for Social Research, *The German Army and Genocide: Crimes Against War Prisoners, Jews, and Other Civilians, 1939–1944* (New York: New Press, 1999).

40. Mario Biagioli, "Science, Modernity, and the Final Solution," in Friedländer, *Probing the Limits of Representation*, 185–205.

41. David Fraser, *Law after Auschwitz: Towards a Jurisprudence of the Holocaust* (Durham, NC: Carolina Academic Press, 2005), 127. See also Telford Taylor, *The Anatomy of the Nuremberg Trials* (New York: Alfred A. Knopf, 1992), 61: "Symbolically the city was quite appropriate for a trial of the Nazi leaders, as it was here that the Nazi party had staged its annual mass demonstrations and where the anti-Semitic 'Nuremberg Laws' had been decreed in 1935."

42. Edwin Black, *IBM and the Holocaust: The Strategic Alliance between Nazi Germany and America's Most Powerful Corporation* (Washington, DC: Dialog Press, 2001), 10: "People and asset registration was only one of the many uses Nazi Germany found for high speed data sorters. Food allocation was organized around databases, allowing Germany to starve the Jews. Slave labor was identified, tracked, and managed largely through punch cards. Punch cards even made the trains run on time and cataloged their human cargo." On the importance of IBM's punch card and sorting system for the Nazi census, see Götz Aly and Karl Heinz

Roth, *The Nazi Census: Identification and Control in the Third Reich* (Philadelphia: Temple University Press, 2004).

43. Biagioli, "Science, Modernity, and the Final Solution," 186.

44. Hannah Arendt, *The Origins of Totalitarianism* (New York: Meridian Press, 1972), 459.

45. "The camps are meant not only to exterminate people and degrade human beings, but also to serve the ghastly experiment of eliminating, under scientifically controlled conditions, spontaneity itself as an expression of human behavior and transforming the human personality into a mere thing, into something even animals are not." Arendt, *Origins of Totalitarianism*, 438.

46. Dana Villa, *Politics, Philosophy, Terror: Essays on the Thought of Hannah Arendt* (Princeton: Princeton University Press, 1999), 20, 34–35.

47. Alan Milchman and Alan Rosenberg, "Foucault, Auschwitz, and the Destruction of the Body," in *Postmodernism and the Holocaust*, ed. Alan Milchman and Alan Rosenberg (Atlanta: Rodopi, 1998), 220.

48. Arendt, *Eichmann*, 287–88; emphasis in the original.

49. Jeffrey Shandler, *While America Watches: Televising the Holocaust* (Oxford: Oxford University Press, 1999), 83.

50. Soshana Felman, *The Juridical Unconscious: Trials and Traumas in the Twentieth Century* (Cambridge, MA: Harvard University Press, 2002), 126.

51. Gidean Hausner, *Justice in Jerusalem* (New York: Harper & Row, 1966), 292.

52. Felman, *The Juridical Unconscious*, 127.

53. State of Israel Ministry of Justice, *The Trial of Adolf Eichmann, Volume I: Record of the Proceedings in the District Court of Jerusalem* (Jerusalem: Israel State Archives, 1992), 62.

54. On Woodrow Wilson's vision of establishing racially homogeneous territories (as opposed to strictly strategic ones) in Europe in the aftermath of World War I, see Jeremy W. Crampton, "Maps, Race and Foucault: Eugenics and Territorialization Following World War I," in *Space, Knowledge, and Power: Foucault and Geography*, ed. Jeremy W. Crampton and Stuart Elden (Burlington, VT: Ashgate, 2007). Wilson's vision was informed by the work of a secret research group called the "Inquiry." Established by presidential order to rationalize the redrawing of borders on the war-torn continent, the group was headquartered at Isaiah Bowman's American Geographical Society and called on the critical skills of a variety of intellectuals, journalist Walter Lippmann and eugenicist Charles Davenport among them.

55. Sheila Faith Weiss, *The Nazi Symbiosis: Human Genetics and Politics in the Third Reich* (Chicago: University of Chicago Press, 2010), 32–35. While noting the global nature of state programs and practices during the early to mid-twentieth century that sought to regulate, ensure, and enhance the health and quality of populations, Weiss makes the especially important observation that often what regulation and enhancement meant and/or entailed varied widely.

56. Crampton, "Maps, Race, and Foucault," 233.

57. Illustrating precisely what Arendt seemed to be reaching for with the notion of "thoughtlessness" is the figure of the Bosnian Serb military leader and war crimes fugitive Ratko Mladic. Accused of overseeing the 1995 Srebenica massacre, or what is considered the "worst ethnically motivated mass murder on the Continent since World War II," Mladic was finally arrested in May 2011. During an extradition hearing to transfer him to the Hague to face charges for crimes against humanity, Mladic's foremost concern, apparently, was having the freeze on his military pension lifted. As the *New York Times* reports, "He asked for his pension three times: 'I need my pension. I need my pension.'" Doreen Carvajal and Steven Erlanger, "Serb Fugitive Slowly Starved of Friends and Cash," *New York Times*, May 30, 2011, A1.

58. Rony Brauman and Eyal Sivan, *The Specialist: Portrait of a Modern Criminal* (France, Momento! 1999) (128 min.). The video footage used in the making of *The Specialist* was originally shot by the American filmmaker Leo Hurwitz, working for American Cities Broadcasting Company. As Rebecka Thor notes, "Hurwitz . . . placed four concealed cameras in the courtroom and connected them to a control booth across the street, from which he could instruct the camera operators and edit the footage in real time. He had four monitors screening the camera images and in accordance with his instructions one camera was recorded on videotape, while the other three were not recorded at all. Hurwitz had to make instant decisions and, since he could only understand what was said when the trial was conducted in English since he spoke neither German nor Hebrew, his editing was dependent not on what was said but on his understanding of the situation based on visual information. He shot up to 600 hours in this manner." "Representing the Eichmann Trial: Ten Years of Controversy around *The Specialist*" (M.A. thesis, New School, 2009), 13.

59. Hillel Tryster, "We Have Ways of Making You Believe: The Eichmann Trial as Seen in *The Specialist*," *Antisemitism International* (2004): 34–44. See also Hillel Tryster, "Eyal Sivan Eichmann, Lies, and Videotape," *Indymedia*, 2007, http://no666.wordpress.com/2007/05/18/eyal-sivan-eichmann-lies-and-videotape/.

60. Fraser, *Law after Auschwitz*, 27.

61. On the visual rhetoric of Holocaust imagery and its disruption, see Norman L. Kleeblatt, ed., *Mirroring Evil: Nazi Imagery/Recent Art* (New Brunswick, NJ: Rutgers University Press, 2001).

62. Elisabeth Young-Bruehl, *Why Arendt Matters* (New Haven: Yale University Press, 2006), 198.

63. Giorgio Agamben, *Means without End: Notes on Politics* (Minneapolis: University of Minnesota Press, 2000), 124–25. On the media practices and pressures that readily exchange sentiment and high drama (or the look and feel of crisis) for political analysis, see Susan D. Moeller, *Compassion Fatigue: How the Media Sell Disease, Famine, War, and Death* (New York: Routledge, 1999); Lilie Chouliaraki, *The Spectatorship of Suffering* (Thousand Oaks, CA: Sage, 2006); Luc Boltanski, *Distant Suffering: Morality, Media, and Politics* (Cambridge: Cambridge University Press, 1999); Carolyn J. Dean, *The Fragility of Empathy after the Holocaust* (Ithaca: Cornell University Press, 2004).

NOTES TO CHAPTER 1

1. Gideon Hausner, *Justice in Jerusalem* (New York: Herzl Press, 1977), 300, 90–97.

2. As at Nuremberg, establishing a *direct* link between the defendant's actions and the suffering of those brought to testify was especially challenging for the prosecution. Much of the lengthy survivor testimony rarely mentioned Eichmann in a legally reliable or authoritative way, leading presiding Judge Landau to describe the evidentiary value of such testimony as being "next to nothing." Lawrence Douglas, *The Memory of Judgment: Making Law and History in the Trials of the Holocaust* (New Haven: Yale University Press, 2001), 134, 140–49.

3. Douglas, *Memory of Judgment*, 179.

4. Elaine Scarry, *The Body in Pain: The Making and Unmaking of the World* (New York: Oxford University Press, 1985), 58–59.

5. Hannah Arendt, *Eichmann in Jerusalem: A Report on the Banality of Evil* (New York: Penguin, 1964), 287–88; emphasis in the original.

6. Hannah Arendt, "Thinking and Moral Considerations: A Lecture," *Social Research* 38.3 (1971): 417.

7. Lawrence Douglas makes a similar point and offers a provocative discussion of the dramatically different ways in which the documentary *Nazi Concentration Camps* signified when it was screened at Nuremberg in 1946 and fifteen years later in Jerusalem. See *Memory of Judgment*, chaps. 1 and 3, esp. 97–103.

8. Arendt, *Eichmann*, 276.

9. Arendt, *Eichmann*, 117, 125–26.

10. Douglas, *Memory of Judgment*, 154.

11. Arendt, *Eichmann*, 125

12. Douglas, *Memory of Judgment*, 156.

13. Peter Novick, *The Holocaust in American Life* (Boston: Houghton Mifflin, 1999), 133; Pnina Lahav, *Judgment in Jerusalem: Chief Justice Simon Agranat and the Zionist Century* (Berkeley: University of California Press, 1997), 147.

14. David Ben-Gurion, *Israel: A Personal History* (New York: New English Library, 1972), 599.

15. See, for example, Hausner, *Justice in Jerusalem*, 291–92: "I wanted our people at home to know as many of the facts of the great disaster as could be legitimately conveyed through these proceedings. It was imperative for the stability of our youth that they should learn the full truth of what had happened, for only through knowledge could understanding and reconciliation with the past be achieved. Our younger generation, absorbed as it was in the building and guarding of the new state, had far too little insight into events which ought to be a pivotal point in its education. The teenagers of Israel, most of them born into statehood or during the struggle for it, had no real knowledge, and therefore no appreciation of the way in which their own flesh and blood had perished. There was here a breach between generations, a possible source of an abhorrence of the nation's yesterday. This could be removed only by factual enlightenment. Then there was also the world at large, which had so lightly and happily forgotten the horrors that had occurred before its eyes, to such a degree that it even begrudged it the trial of their perpetrator. It was imperative, for its own good, that the world should be reminded, with as much detail as possible of the gigantic human tragedy, which is an ineradicable part of a century with unlimited possibilities of both good and evil."

16. For a compelling discussion of the ways in which telecasts of the trial shaped public response to the case and its depiction of the Holocaust, see Jeffrey Shandler, *While America Watches: Televising the Holocaust* (New York: Oxford University Press, 1999), esp. chap. 4, "The Man in the Glass Box." As Shandler observes: "Televised presentations of the Eichmann trial . . . invok[ed] the trope of witnessing as a morally charged act. At the same time, the Eichmann case provided the occasion for the first extended contention over the significance of the Holocaust as a moral paradigm in America, and television figured strategically in the debate" (84–85).

17. Novick takes critical aim at the view, now part of accepted lore and institutionalized at the U.S. Holocaust Memorial Museum, that the American and British governments failed to pursue an energetic rescue policy during the war to save European Jewry that might have included (1) relaxing immigration quotas, (2) negotiating on behalf of Jews in custody, and (3) bombing the rail lines that led to Auschwitz. Such a view, he contends, is "a comfortable morality tale that has passed for history" and not supported by scholarly consensus. Novick, *Holocaust in American Life*, 54–55. For a more detailed discussion, see chap. 2.

18. Douglas, *Memory of Judgment*, 109.

19. ADL, writing on the Eichmann trial, cited in Novick, *Holocaust in American Life*, 139.

20. Hausner, *Justice in Jerusalem*, 453, 454. See also Haim Gouri, "Facing the Glass Booth," in *Holocaust Remembrance: The Shapes of Memory*, ed. Geoffrey H. Hartman (Cambridge, MA: Blackwell, 1994), 153–60.

21. Douglas, *Memory of Judgment*, 154.

22. Jennifer Ring, *The Political Consequences of Thinking: Gender and Judaism in the Work of Hannah Arendt* (New York: State University of New York Press, 1997), 80. See also Tom Segev, *The Seventh Million: The Israelis and the Holocaust* (New York: Henry Holt, 1993), 259.

23. Lahav, *Judgment in Jerusalem*, 132, 146; also see 121–44.

24. Hausner, *Justice in Jerusalem*, 294–95. Zuckerman himself would indict the Jewish leadership years later in his autobiography: "We didn't figure that the Germans would put in the Jewish element, that Jews would lead Jews to death." Yitzhak Zuckerman, *A Surplus of Memory: Chronicle of the Warsaw Ghetto Uprising* (Berkeley: University of California Press, 1993), 210; see also 208–9.

25. Raul Hilberg, *The Politics of Memory: The Journey of a Holocaust Historian* (Chicago: Ivan R. Dee, 1996), see esp. 147–57. It should be said that Hilberg, too, was originally thought to have gone too far in writing about the role of the Jewish Councils in carrying out Nazi directives and had difficulty finding a publisher for his work. Indeed, in 1958 his work was rejected outright by "expert critics" of the history of the Nazi catastrophe at Yad Vashem, Israel's official "Remembrance Authority of the Disaster and Heroism," because of its use of German sources, its appraisal of the Jewish resistance, and its findings—and this is only one notable item from a long list of intellectual and professional abuses he suffered (110–11). At the same time, the reception of his book once it was published provides an interesting contrast to the response that greeted Arendt's. As Jennifer Ring points out, "Hilberg [was] applauded for his scholarship [even when reviewers took issue with his conclusions] while Arendt, who makes a similar argument . . . , is excoriated for betraying the Jews, and for relying on Hilberg's 'superior' scholarship to do it." Ring, *The Political Consequences of Thinking*, 27.

26. Gershom Scholem and Hannah Arendt, "An Exchange of Letters," in *The Jew as Pariah*, ed. Ron H. Feldman (New York: Grove Press, 1978), 241, 242.

27. Walter A. Laqueur, "A Reply to Hannah Arendt," in Feldman, *The Jew as Pariah*, 277.

28. Scholem and Arendt, "An Exchange of Letters," 243.

29. Jules Steinberg, *Hannah Arendt on the Holocaust: A Study in the Suppression of Truth* (New York: Edwin Mellen Press, 2000), 223, 220. Steinberg's book is probably best characterized as an extended rant against the "fascist pattern of political thinking" that he believes runs through Arendt's work. According to Steinberg, she emerges from and defends "the same philosophical tradition that helped lead to Hitlerism" and has managed to deceive academic audiences for decades about the "true" nature of her intellectual orientation and commitments. Be that as it may, at least with respect to her work on Eichmann, Steinberg is here echoing only what other critics similarly maintained—consider, for example, Walter Laqueur in his review of Jacob Robinson's rebuttal of Arendt, *And the Crooked Shall Be Made Straight: The Eichmann Trial, The Jewish Catastrophe, and Hannah Arendt's Narrative.* "Footnotes to the Holocaust" in Feldman, *The Jew as Pariah*, 252–59.

30. Mosez Torcyzner, in the *American Zionist*, quoted in Novick, *Holocaust in American Life*, 141.

31. Ring, *Political Consequences of Thinking*, 110, 111; emphasis in the original.

32. In a superbly crafted reading of contemporary Holocaust literature, Gary Weissman draws attention to the utterly decisive place gender occupies in what has come to be regarded

as the "real story" and meaning of Auschwitz: "The story of boy-meets-Auschwitz is a form of existential romance, suggesting that the magnitude of the Holocaust and its implications for humanity are most dramatically and effectively conveyed through a lone male figure's existential crisis." *Fantasies of Witnessing: Postwar Efforts to Experience the Holocaust* (Ithaca: Cornell University Press, 2004), 83, 86–87.

33. Gary Jonathan Bass reports that both Churchill and Roosevelt recommended castrating the defeated Nazi leadership as punishment in lieu of putting them on trial. See Bass, *Stay the Hand of Vengeance: The Politics of War Crimes Tribunals* (Princeton: Princeton University Press, 2000), 7.

34. G. M. Gilbert, *Nuremberg Diary* (New York: Da Capo Press, 1995), 11.

35 Gilbert, *Nuremberg Diary*, 145. For a provocative discussion of the persistent impulse to equate homosexuality and Nazism—and, in particular, the many incarnations of the view that "the Holocaust was essentially perpetrated by a group of homosexuals" and, further, that a pathological sexuality was at the root of a pathological politics—see Carolyn Dean, *The Fragility of Empathy: After the Holocaust* (Ithaca: Cornell University Press, 2004), 110, but esp. chap. 4. Along these same lines, consider as well the observations of reporter Rebecca West, *A Train of Powder: Six Reports on the Problem of Guilt and Punishment in Our Time* (Chicago: Ivan R. Dee, 1955), 5–6: "Streicher was pitiable. . . . He was a dirty old man of the sort that gives trouble in parks, and a sane Germany would have sent him to an asylum long before. Baulder von Schirach, the [Hitler] youth Leader [who was eventually sentenced to twenty years' imprisonment], startled because he was like a woman in a way not common among men who looked like women. It was as if a neat and mousey governess sat there, not pretty, but with never a hair out of place, and always to be trusted never to intrude when there were visitors: as it might be Jane Eyre. And though one had read surprising news of Göring for years, he still surprised. He was so very soft. Sometimes he wore a German Air Force uniform, and sometimes a light beach suit in the worst of playful taste, and both hung loosely on him, giving him an air of pregnancy. . . . He did not look like any recognized type of homosexual, yet he was feminine. Sometimes, particularly when his humor was good, he recalled the madame of a brothel. His like are to be seen in the late morning in doorways along the steep streets of Marseille, the professional mask of geniality still hard on their faces though they stand in relaxed leisure, their fat cats rubbing against their spread skirts. Certainly there had been a concentration on appetite and on elaborate schemes for gratifying it; and yet there was a sense of desert thirst."

36. *The Trial of Adolf Eichmann*, Devillier Donegan Enterprises, a coproduction of ABC News Productions and Great Projects Film Co. (VHS, PBS Home Video, 1997); Shandler, *While America Watches*, 110. See also Zvi Aharoni and William Dietl, *Operation Eichmann: The Truth about the Pursuit, Capture, and Trial* (New York: Wiley, 1996), 171: "Simon Wiesenthal arrived on the first day of the [trial] and saw a 'weak, colorless, shabby fellow in a glass cell between two Israeli police officers; they looked more interesting and remarkable than he did. . . . There was nothing demonic about him; he looked like an accountant who was afraid to ask for a raise. . . . He wore a cheap dark suit and presented the picture of an empty, two-dimensional cardboard figure.' He lacked the black uniform with the death's-head insignia. Wiesenthal suggested to the prosecutor, Senior District Attorney Gidion Hausner, that Eichmann be dressed in an authentic uniform. [To his credit,] Hausner refused."

37. Shandler, *While America Watches*, 113.

38. Amit Pinchevski and Roy Brand note that circulating at the time of the Eichmann trial was a pulp fiction series, The Stalags, especially popular with Israeli teenagers. Written by native

Israelis in Hebrew, these paperbacks depicted the brutality of concentration camp captivity largely in terms of the relationships between sexually insatiable SS female guards— "wearing tight pants, shining boots, and vests from cloth that stretched across tall and upright breasts"— and primarily Allied servicemen whose dominance, humiliation, and sexual servitude form the erotic core of the stories. Pinchevski and Brand argue that the Stalags functioned "as a fictional counterpart of the Eichmann trial." On the one hand, they "reiterated, sometimes almost verbatim, the vocabulary and rhetoric heard inside the Eichmann courtroom." On the other hand, they were a vehicle for negotiating a contradiction brought to the cultural foreground by the trial between "the new Jew—the native Israeli or Sabra—[who] was deemed strong, courageous, and masculine, capable of defending his land and his people—[and his] complete antithesis . . . the old Diaspora Jew, who was deemed weak, servile, cowardly and feminine. . . . Seen against the gendered metaphors of Israeli identity politics of that period . . . the Stalags offered a singularly compact repository for rehearsing the question of 'what would we have done in their place,' using the fictional camp as a displaced arena for role-play. Through the erotization of power relations, captivity was no longer about servile Jews assailed by Nazi perpetrators but about virile Allied soldiers sexually abused by Aryan women. Servitude and powerlessness were dissociated from victimhood and infused with pleasurable, exciting potential" (401, 402). Amit Pinchevski and Roy Brand, "Holocaust Perversions: The Stalags Pulp Fiction and the Eichmann Trial," *Critical Studies in Media Communication* 24.5 (2007): 387–407.

39. Ring, *Political Consequences of Thinking*, 49.

40. Segev, *The Seventh Million*, 76, 97; see also Novick, *Holocaust in American Life*.

41. On the careful crafting of this story, see Ruth Linn, *Escaping Auschwitz: A Culture of Forgetting* (Ithaca: Cornell University Press, 2004). Linn examines why and how it is that the escape from Auschwitz of Rudolf Vrba and Alfred Wetzler in April 1944 has been almost universally ignored and/or discredited in Israeli historiography and until recently "kept" (her word) from the Israeli Hebrew-reading public. On escaping, Vrba and Wetzler successfully returned to their native country, Slovakia, and provided the first credible account of the systematic extermination procedures and processes in place at the camp. They "conveyed in detail to the members of the Jewish Council the geographic plan of Auschwitz-Bikenau, the specifics of the Germans' method of mass murder—tattooing, gassing, and cremation—and the course of events they had witnessed. . . . They warned that preparations were being made for the murder of nearly 800,000 Jews from Hungary. They also suspected that 3,000 Czech Jews, in Auschwitz-Birkenau 'family camp' would be gassed within a few months. . . . [Although] the Vrba-Wetzler report was the first document about the Auschwitz death camp to reach the free world . . . [i]t is doubtful that its content reached more than a small number of prospective victims, though [their] critical and alarming assessment was in the hands of Hungarian Jewish Leaders as early as April 28. . . . Between mid-May and early July 1944, about 437,000 Hungarian Jews boarded in good faith the 'resettlement trains' that carried them to the Auschwitz death camps, where most were immediately gassed. . . . [M]emoirs by a handful of surviving Hungarian deportees, even those who arrived in Auschwitz as late as July 8, 1944, reveal their absolute ignorance of their impending fate at the death camp. Elie Wiesel summarized it as follows: 'We were taken just two weeks before D-Day, and we did not know that Auschwitz existed. . . . [E]veryone knew except the victims'" (4, 5).

42. Novick, *Holocaust in American Life*, 141. Novick is generally sympathetic to the ways in which Arendt insisted on the complexity and ambiguity of the issues conjured by the trial. However, he too notes that her tone and lack of caution in issuing judgment very much worked against the otherwise significant questions her analysis sought to raise.

43. Robinson, 1962 draft in the Yad Vashem Library (247), cited in Elisabeth Young-Bruehl, *Hannah Arendt: For Love of the World* (New Haven: Yale University Press, 1982), 356.

44. Haim Gouri, *Facing the Glass Booth: The Jerusalem Trial of Adolf Eichmann* (Detroit: Wayne State University Press, 2004), 84.

45. Gouri, *Facing the Glass Booth*, 81, 82.

46. As Gouri puts it, "We shall not at this point call ourselves, too, to account, although someday, heaven help us, we shall have to do so." Even so, let me be clear: although Gouri appears, at least in my reading, to have discerned a landscape not unlike the one Arendt described, I do not also mean to suggest that he reached similar conclusions about it. *Facing the Glass Booth*, 103.

47. Arendt, *Eichmann*, 125–26.

48. This point is explored in considerable detail in Richard Bernstein, "'The Banality of Evil' Reconsidered," in *Hannah Arendt and the Meaning of Politics*, ed. Craig Calhoun and John McGowan, (Minneapolis: University of Minnesota Press, 1997), 297–322. See also the letters Arendt exchanged with Gershom Scholem on the publication of *Eichmann in Jerusalem* in Feldman's edited volume, *The Jew as Pariah*. Arendt explains: "There was no people and no group in Europe which reacted differently under the immediate pressure of terror. The question I raised was that of the cooperation of Jewish functionaries during the 'Final Solution,' and this question is so very uncomfortable because one cannot claim that they were traitors. (There were traitors too, but that is irrelevant.) In other words, until 1939 and even until 1941, whatever Jewish functionaries did or did not do is understandable and excusable. Only later does it become highly problematical. The issue came up during the trial and it was of course my duty to report it. This constitutes our part of the so-called 'unmastered past,' and although you may be right that it is too early for a 'balanced judgment' (though I doubt this), I do believe that we shall only come to terms with this past if we begin to judge and to be frank about it. I have made my own position plain, and yet it is obvious that you did not understand it. I said that there was no possibility of resistance, but there existed the possibility of *doing nothing*. And in order to do nothing, one did not need to be a saint, one needed only to say: 'I am just a simple Jew, and I have no desire to play any other role.'" Feldman, *The Jew as Pariah*, 248; emphasis in the original.

49. Novick, *Holocaust in American Life*, 141.

50. Elie Wiesel is most often identified as the exemplar of such claims.

51. Carol Brightman, ed., *Between Friends: The Correspondence of Hannah Arendt and Mary McCarthy, 1949–1975* (New York: Harcourt Brace, 1995), 148.

52. Arendt, *Eichmann*, 269. I return to this in chap. 5. Arendt elaborates on this appeal to the idea of "humanity" as a guarantor against deadly global danger in *The Origins of Totalitarianism*, 378–79. For a systematic reading of this theme in Arendt's work, see Peg Birmingham, *Hannah Arendt and Human Rights: The Predicament of Common Responsibility* (Bloomington: Indiana University Press, 2006).

53. Arendt, *Eichmann*, 269, 272.

54. Arendt, *Eichmann*, 5.

55. See, for example, Douglas, *Memory of Judgment*; and Hanna Yoblonka, *The State of Israel vs. Adolf Eichmann* (New York: Schocken Books, 2004). Both Douglas and Yablonka reject Arendt's characterization of the trial. First, Douglas: "Arendt was aiming not to describe but to vilify" (111). And Yablonka: "The Eichmann trial certainly contained elements that could cause it to be seen as a show trial . . . , but [it] was not a show trial . . . [if by show trial we understand] . . . a theater production . . . planned by the state in order to reinforce its

regime from within, and to achieve various external political objectives" (238). But both then go on to explain—Yablonka to a greater extent than Douglas—that the trial necessarily and legitimately served a host of historical, political, and nationalist imperatives, ulterior to the principal task of rendering judgment on the particular actions of a particular individual in the dock.

56. Arendt, *Eichmann*, 276.

57. Significantly, as Lars Svendsen notes in *A Philosophy of Evil* (London: Dalkey Archive Press, 2010), the expression "crimes against humanity" was first invoked by the historian George Washington Williams to describe violence in the Belgian Congo employed as a matter of course to facilitate the imperialist endeavors of European powers. Svendsen elaborates: "It's difficult to say how many died as a direct result of Belgium's policies, but the most common estimate is that the population was reduced from twenty million to just under ten million during the years (1880–1920) that the land was officially ruled by Belgium. Belgium's involvement in the Congo was almost exclusively economic. That is, Belgium's goal wasn't simply to exterminate the populace. . . . [T]he violence was essentially instrumental in nature, based on a concept of how land could best be ruled with an eye toward turning the maximum profit" (34).

58. Arendt, *Eichmann*, 272. See also Hannah Arendt, "Auschwitz on Trial," in *Responsibility and Judgment*, ed. Jerome Kohn (New York: Schocken Books, 2003), 242–43.

59. Lotte Kohler and Hans Saner, eds., *Hannah Arendt / Karl Jaspers Correspondence: 1926–1969* (New York: Harcourt Brace Jovanovich, 1992), 413.

60. Arendt's assumption is that justice in the form of law presents a viable elsewhere from which to begin to think state-sponsored slaughter. As David Fraser notes, this ignores the critical role of law in facilitating such slaughter: "If Auschwitz was fundamentally a legal phenomenon, if almost all modern atrocities are committed in the name of a nation state, or of a people, with a claim to legality, legitimacy, and sovereignty, what business has law in any of this?" *Law after Auschwitz: Towards a Jurisprudence of the Holocaust* (Durham, NC: Carolina Academic Press, 2005), 192.

61. For a comprehensive discussion, see Samantha Power, *A Problem from Hell: America and the Age of Genocide* (New York: Basic Books, 2002). More succinct accounts of precisely this tension regularly appear in the op-ed section of the *New York Times*. By way of example, see Nicholas D. Kristof's meditation on Darfur, "Uncover Your Eyes," June 7, 2005, A23.

62. Power, *A Problem from Hell*, xxi.

63. David Rieff, cited in Power, *A Problem from Hell*, 504.

NOTES TO CHAPTER 2

1. Hannah Arendt, *The Origins of Totalitarianism* (New York: Meridian, 1958), 446.

2. Jürgen Habermas, cited in Saul Freidländer, ed., *Probing the Limits of Representation: Nazism and the "Final Solution"* (Cambridge, MA: Harvard University Press, 1992), 3.

3. Lotte Kohler and Hans Saner, eds., *Hannah Arendt / Karl Jaspers Correspondence: 1926–1969*, (New York: Harcourt Brace Jovanovich, 1992), 54.

4. Kohler and Saner, *Hannah Arendt / Karl Jaspers Correspondence*, 62.

5. Gershom Scholem and Hannah Arendt, "An Exchange of Letters," in *The Jew as Pariah*, ed. Ron Feldman (New York: Grove Press, 1978), 251.

6. Kohler and Saner, *Hannah Arendt / Karl Jaspers Correspondence*, 69.

7. *Trial of Adolph Eichmann in Jerusalem: Judgment Part I* (www.nikor.org, accessed October 18, 1999), 3.

8. Barbie Zelizer, *Remembering to Forget: Holocaust Memory through the Camera's Eye* (Chicago: University of Chicago Press, 1998).

9. Hannah Arendt, "The Image of Hell," in *Essays in Understanding: 1930–1954* (New York: Harcourt Brace, 1994), 198.

10. And the conditions for Stalinism as well, but many commentators regard Arendt's considerations on this front more of an afterthought.

11. "The various national governments looked with misgiving upon the tendency to transform business into a political issue and to identify the economic interests of a relatively small group with national interests as such. But it seemed that the only alternative to export of power was the deliberate sacrifice of a great deal of national wealth. Only through the expansion of the national instruments of violence could the foreign-investment movement be rationalized, and the wild speculations with superfluous capital . . . be reintegrated into the economic system of the nation. The state expanded its power because, given the choice between greater loses than the economic body of any country could sustain and greater gains than any people left to its own devices would have dreamed, it could only choose the later. . . . Only the unlimited accumulation of power could bring about the unlimited accumulation of capital." Arendt, *Origins of Totalitarianism*, 136.

12. Arendt, *Origins of Totalitarianism*, 240. See also p. 242: "That the pan-movements' fanaticism hit upon the Jews as the ideological center, which was the beginning of the end of European Jewry, constitutes one of the most logical and bitter revenges history has ever taken. For of course there is some truth in 'enlightened' assertions from Voltaire to Renan and Taine that the Jews' concept of chosenness, their identification of religion and nationality, their claim to an absolute position in history and singled-out relationship with God, brought into Western civilization an otherwise unknown element of fanaticism (inherited by Christianity with its claim to exclusive possession of Truth) on one side, and on the other an element of pride that was dangerously close to its racial perversion. Politically, it was of no consequence that Judaism and an intact Jewish piety always were notably free of, and even hostile to, the heretical immanence of the Divine. . . . The hatred of the racists against the Jews sprang from a superstitious apprehension that it actually might be the Jews, and not themselves, whom God had chosen, to whom success was granted by divine providence. There was an element of feeble-minded resentment against a people who, it was feared, had received a rationally incomprehensible guarantee that they would emerge eventually, and in spite of appearances, as the final victors in world history."

13. Hannah Arendt, "On the Nature of Totalitarianism," in *Essays in Understanding*, 342–43: "Terror, the obedient servant of Nature or History and the omnipresent executor of their predestined movement . . . mercilessly presses men, such as they are, against each other so that the very space of free action—and this is the reality of freedom—disappears."

14. Arendt, "On the Nature of Totalitarianism," 342.

15. Hannah Arendt, "Social Science and Concentration Camps," in *Essays in Understanding*, 235: "Neither the fate of European Jewry nor the establishment of death factories can be fully explained and grasped in terms of anti-Semitism. Both transcend anti-Semitic reasoning as well as the political, social, and economic motives behind the propaganda of anti-Semitic movements. Anti-Semitism only prepared the ground to make it easier to start the extermination of peoples with the Jewish people. We know now that this extermination program of Hitler's did not stop short of planning the liquidation of large sections of the German people."

16. Arendt, *Origins of Totalitarianism*, 426. See also, Hannah Arendt, "Mankind and Terror," in *Essays in Understanding*, 304–5.

17. Dana Villa, *Politics, Philosophy, Terror: Essays on the Thought of Hannah Arendt* (Princeton: Princeton University Press, 1999), 20, 34–35.

18. Arendt, *Origins of Totalitarianism*, ix.

19. Götz Aly, "The Planning Intelligentsia and the Final Solution," in *The Holocaust: Origins, Implementation, Aftermath*, ed. Omer Bartov (New York: Routledge, 2000), 99.

20. Götz Aly, *Final Solution: Nazi Population Policy and the Murder of European Jews* (London: Arnold, 1999), 246, 245.

21. Götz Aly and Susanne Heim, *Architects of Annihilation: Auschwitz and the Logic of Destruction* (Princeton: Princeton University Press, 2002), 5.

22. Consider, for example, the following mathematical exercise that appeared in a 1935 high school textbook: "Based on a number of calculations, a mentally ill person costs the state about 1,500 RM [Reichmarks] annually, a student in special education about 300 RM, a student in elementary schools about 250 RM annually. Illustrate the above figures as a curve on a graph." Note that students are being taught to think about and solve a number of different kinds of problems with this exercise. Götz Aly and Karl Heinz Roth, *The Nazi Census: Identification and Control in the Third Reich* (Philadelphia: Temple University Press, 2004), 95.

23. Henry Friedlander, "Step by Step: Expansion of Murder 1939–1941," in Bartov, *The Holocaust: Origins, Implementation, Aftermath*, 65.

24. 1939: Poland and parts of Czechoslovakia; April–June 1940: Norway, Denmark, Netherlands, Belgium, Luxemburg, and France; 1940/41: Rumania, Hungary, Yugoslavia; June 1941: invasion of Russia.

25. Götz Aly, "'Jewish Resettlement': Reflections on the Political Prehistory of the Holocaust," in *National Socialist Extermination Policies: Contemporary German Perspectives and Controversies*, ed. Ulrich Herbert (New York: Berghahn Books, 2000), 59.

26. Aly, *Final Solution*, 59.

27. [Heydrich's] special responsibility for the 'Jewish question' is well known and has been described many times. Less well researched are his dual jurisdictions for the Main Office for Immigrants (*Einwandererzentralstelle*; EWZ) and the Main Office for Resettlers (*Umwandererzentralstelle*; UWZ). On the one hand, Heydrich was active in the "Home into the Reich" resettlement of the ethnic Germans from eastern and southern Europe; on the other, he organized the "deportations" necessary for their settlement. Aly, "'Jewish Resettlement,'" 60.

28. Aly, "'Jewish Resettlement,'" 60.

29. Aly, "'Jewish Resettlement,'" 67, 69. As Robert Proctor observes, "Doctors were never *ordered* to murder psychiatric patients and handicapped children. They were *empowered* to do so, and fulfilled their task without protest, often on their own initiative" (emphasis in the original). *Racial Hygiene: Medicine under the Nazis* (Cambridge, MA: Harvard University Press, 1988), 193.

30. Aly, "'Jewish Resettlement,'" 69. See also Aly, *Final Solution*, 76: "Even for these initial mass murders, it is indicative that no concrete order existed to murder the mentally ill. Although the forced resettlements at the time are well documented, there are no documents explicitly proving the linkage between the murder of thousands of German and Polish patients and the resettlement of Baltic and Volhynian Germans."

31. As Aly and Heim note, "Germanization" was not primarily organized by a sentimental nationalism. "[It] was about dividing the subjugated peoples into 'useful' and 'useless' groups[,] . . . 'creaming-off' 'human resources' for the social and economic 'rebuilding of the Reich' and the conduct of the war. . . . The mentally ill, social misfits, active Communists, persons living in so-called mixed marriages and other maladjusted types could not become Germans. To

qualify for this 'privilege,' candidates must be given a clean bill of health—medically, geneti-cally and politically. Without this such persons were classed as 'racially undesirable'—even if they were ethnic German." Aly and Heim, *Architects of Annihilation*, 82–83.

32. Martin Borman described the arrangement this way: "[Cheap labor would] be an advantage to every German, to every German worker. The General government is not to become a closed economic area producing its own necessary industrial goods in part or entirely; the General government is a reservoir of labor for menial work (brick-making, street building, etc. etc). . . . The lending agency for unskilled laborers . . . a great Polish work camp." Cited in Aly, *Final Solution*, 117. The historian Christopher Browning elaborates: "The ethnic identity of the leftovers, deprived of their racially valuable stock and dumped together in the General Government along with those from Germany 'of the same racial and human type,' would gradually disappear. The non-descript, denationalized population would then serve as a reservoir for migrant labor to Germany." *The Path to Genocide* (New York: Oxford University Press, 1992), 16.

33. Dieter Pohl, "The Murder of the Jews in the General Government," in Herbert, *National Socialist Extermination Policies*, 94. Aly elaborates: "In total, more than five mil-lion people, deprived beforehand of all their means of survival, were to be deported into an economically truncated area that already contained twelve million inhabitants and was about as big as Bavaria and Baden-Württemberg together." Aly, *Final Solution*, 61.

34. Aly, *Final Solution*, 245. In the words of one commentator, echoing this view, "Setting mass murder in motion in no way required any peculiar anti-Jewish sentiment." Ulrich Her-bert, "Extermination Policy: New Answers and Questions about the History of the 'Holo-caust' in German Historiography," in Herbert, *National Socialist Extermination Policies*, 32. Or the words of another: "The murder of Jews functioned increasingly as a reaction to various problems—from housing shortages to inadequate food supplies and epidemics." Pohl, "The Murder of the Jews in the General Government," 92.

35. Aly, *Final Solution*, 9; emphasis added.

36.. Aly and Heim, *Architects of Annihilation*, 50

37. Aly and Heim, *Architects of Annihilation*, 51. See also Laurence Rees, *Auschwitz: A New History* (New York: Public Affairs/Perseus Books, 2005), 37: "Planners [in Poland] note[d] how Stalin had dealt with similar overpopulation in the Soviet Union. In the Ukraine during the 1930s, a policy of deportation of the kulak (rich peasant) class and collectivization of the remainder had led to the deaths of about nine million people."

38. It is perhaps no small irony that Paul Mombert was a professor of political economy at Giessen University until 1933, when he was identified as a "non-Aryan" and forced to retire.

39. Aly and Heim, *Architects of Annihilation*: "The annexation of western Poland was an 'extension of feeding capacity' for the German Reich, the campaigns of mass murder were a 'reduction of population numbers' and the plundering of food in the German-occupied areas of Europe was a 'lowering of living standards' that served to offset the growing restrictions on Germany's own 'feeding capacity.' The recruitment of forced labor brought about the desired 'lowering of population numbers' in occupied Poland. More than that: it also compensated temporarily for the departure from 'optimum population size' within the Reich that resulted from the conscription of German males for military service" (61).

40. Aly, "The Planning Intelligentsia and the 'Final Solution,'" 99–100.

41. Aly, "The Planning Intelligentsia and the 'Final Solution,'" 99.

42. Aly, "The Planning Intelligentsia and the 'Final Solution,'" 101, 100. Consider the following guidelines set out by planners: "Many tens of millions of people will become

superfluous to requirements in these areas [i.e., the forests and industrial towns of the north] and will die or have to move to Siberia. Attempts to prevent the population there from starving by moving food supplies from the black earth zone can only be done at the cost of supplying Europe. This would undermine Germany's capacity to prevail during the war and would undermine Germany and Europe's capacity to resist blockade." As Himmler saw it, the purpose of the Russian campaign was to decimate the Slavic population by 30 million.

43. Aly, "The Planning Intelligentsia and the 'Final Solution,'" 17.

44. Rees, *Auschwitz*, 17.

45. "As a rule, two or three Polish and Jewish families had to make way for one German family." By winter 1940–41, those awaiting placement included approximately 200,000 in 1,500 camps. Aly, "The Planning Intelligentsia and the 'Final Solution,'" 80, 113.

46. About this, see Christopher Browning, with Jürgen Matthäus, *The Origins of the Final Solution: The Evolution of Nazi Jewish Policy, September 1939–1942* (Lincoln: University of Nebraska Press, 2004), 167: "German occupation policy and anti-Jewish measures had indeed created a 'self-fulfilling prophecy' in which the appearance and behavior of Polish Jewry confirmed the Nazi anti-Semitic stereotype. Ruthless expropriation and exploitation of labor combined with a totally inadequate food supply, terrible overcrowding in poor housing, and utterly inadequate sanitation and medical care turned Polish Jewry into a starving, disease-ridden, impoverished community desperately struggling for survival through 'illegal' smuggling, bribery, and black market activities. . . . As is evident in their documents, as least some of the ghetto managers understood that this 'vicious circle' had been set in motion by German policy."

47. There were 356 ghettos established throughout Poland, the Soviet Union and Balkan states, Czechoslovakia, Romania, and Hungary between 1939 and 1945. Of these ghettos, Warsaw and Lódz were the largest (400,000 and 160,000 respectively).

48. Cited in Aly and Heim, *Architects of Annihilation*, 164–65.

49. See Browning and Matthäus, *The Origins of the Final Solution*, 88: "The Madagascar Plan was born and died of military circumstances. The defeat of France and seemingly imminent victory over Great Britain promised both the colonial territory and the merchant fleet necessary for a massive oversees expulsion of the European Jews. Just as quickly, the failure to defeat Great Britain, fully apparent in September 1940, made realization of this plan impossible."

50. Aly and Heim, *Architects of Annihilation*, 195–96.

51. See Browning and Matthäus, *The Origins of the Final Solution*, 296. As they note elsewhere: "The Polish ghettos in this period should not be seen as some covert scheme cynically perpetrated by local German authorities to carry out gradual extermination although Jews within the ghettos understandably drew such conclusions. The local Germans in fact had every inducement to maximize ghetto productivity and drew the obvious conclusion that starving Jews did not make the most productive workers. The starvation rations were maintained in spite of, not because of their efforts" (152)

52. Aly and Heim, *Architects of Annihilation*, 168: "While the murderers subsequently defended their actions with the argument that they had 'granted death as a blessed release' to 'seriously ill patients' who were 'at death's door' anyway, [the statistician, Edmund] Brandt [later employed by the postwar Federal Ministry of the Interior] sat down in 1942 to work out the projected savings—in food, accommodation, coats, shirts—over a ten-year period (to 1951 inclusive). Based on the average daily needs of an institutional inmate, this calculation indicated that the killing of sick persons unfit for work would yield more than 880 million

Reichmarks in savings by 1951." See also Michael Burleigh, "Psychiatry, German Society and the Nazi 'Euthanasia' Programme," in Bartov, *The Holocaust: Origins, Implementation, Aftermath*; Friedlander, "Step by Step," 67; Rees, *Auschwitz*, 110–64.

53. The killing centers began operation at the end of 1941: Chelmno received its first transport from the Lodz ghetto in December 1941; Belzec, initially a labor camp, was operating as a death camp in March 1942; Sobibor, in May 1942; and Treblinka, in July 1942. It was only in 1943, when it became clear that Germany was losing the war, that Auschwitz would begin to play a prominent role in the mass killings for which it is today infamous.

54. Aly and Heim, *Architects of Annihilation*, 210–11: "It is frequently claimed that systematic murder of the Polish Jews from the spring of 1942 onwards damaged the German war economy, which was short of manpower at the time. The economists who were then in charge in the Government General saw things very differently, and for sound economic reasons. In 1942 and 1943 the civilian and military administrations closed down hundreds of unprofitable firms in the Government General in a bid to make industry 'leaner and meaner', concentrating resources in a number of highly efficient' firms. . . . [T]he theoretical labor cost advantage over the Reich, which derived from the low standard of living, was effectively cancelled out by the supply shortages, high absenteeism due to sickness and the obsolete equipment and organization of existing firms. In fact, unit wage costs in the Government General were generally quite a bit higher than in the Reich—even though wages and employers' contributions were substantially lower."

55. Christian Gerlach, "The Wannsee Conference, the Fate of German Jews, and Hitler's Decision in Principle to Exterminate All European Jews," in Bartov, *The Holocaust: Origins, Implementation, Aftermath*, 110.

56. Matthäus and Browning, *The Origins of the Final Solution*, 258.

57. Arno Mayer, *Why Did the Heavens Not Darken? The 'Final Solution' in History* (New York: Pantheon Books, 1990), 312. Mayer's thesis has been the subject of considerable critical review among Holocaust scholars in part for his claim that the genocide of European Jewry was a by-product of the regime's anti-Bolshevik crusade and the economic imperatives of total war. See, for example, Christopher Browning's review of Mayer's book in *The Path to Genocide*, 77–85.

58. Daniel Jonah Goldhagen, *Hitler's Willing Executioners: Ordinary Germans and the Holocaust* (New York: Vintage, 1996), 157–58.

59. Mark Roseman, *The Wannsee Conference and the Final Solution: A Reconsideration* (New York: Henry Holt, 2002), 114, 116.

60. For a discussion of the ostensibly new but still inconclusive definition that was generated as a consequence of this meeting and the debate this new definition precipitated, see Bernhard Loesener's memoirs, Karl A. Schleunes, ed., *Legislating the Holocaust: The Bernard Leosener Memoirs and Supporting Documents* (Boulder, CO: Westview Press, 2001); and David Cesarani, *Eichmann: His Life and Crimes* (New York:Vintage, 2004), 123–58. As Cesarani observes: "The men in charge of the deportation and murder apparatus were never able to reach a satisfactory definition of who was a Jew, nor were they able to entirely curb the practice of shielding certain categories. It runs contrary to common sense, but Eichmann expended much time and energy refining the definition of who was and was not subject to the 'Final Solution'. The issue was not simply a pseudo-'scientific' or quasi-legal matter. In the Third Reich and the areas it controlled, a person's national, ethnic, religious and above all ascribed 'racial' identity determined which agencies might exercise jurisdiction over them and to what ends. Consequently, the scope (and income) of an agency expanded or shrank according to the generosity of the definition of those over whom it exerted control" (122).

61. "Protocol," cited in Roseman, *The Wannsee Conference and the Final Solution*, 101. For a somewhat different translation, see Browning and Matthäus, *The Origins of the Final Solution*, 412.

62. See Browning and Matthäus, *The Origins of the Final Solution*, 412.

63. Arendt, *Eichmann*, 113.

64. Arendt, *Eichmann*, 114.

65. Jochen Von Lang, with Claus Sibyll, ed., *Eichmann Interrogated: Transcripts from the Archives of the Israeli Police* (New York: Da Capo Press, 1999), 68; Arendt, *Eichmann*, 84.

66. Arendt, *Eichmann*, 114. See also David Cesarani, *Eichmann*, 115: "There is reason to believe [Eichmann's] statements in captivity that he was uncomfortable with the policy of 'physical annihilation', and not only the messy business of shooting. Eichmann initially balked at the prospect of industrialized mass murder using poison gas, too. . . . [A] 'territorial solution', after all, offered him more chance of prestige and promotion than mass murder."

67. Omer Bartov, *Germany's War and the Holocaust: Disputed Histories* (Ithaca: Cornell University Press, 2003), 93.

68. Bartov, *Germany's War and the Holocaust*, 92.

69. Bartov, *Germany's War and the Holocaust*, 98.

70. Saul Friedländer, "The Extermination of the European Jews in Historiography: Fifty Years Later," in Bartov, *The Holocaust: Origins, Implementation, Aftermath*, 88. In an interview with Amos Goldberg and Amos Morris-Reich at Yad Vashem (January 28, 1998), Susanne Heim made a gesture toward countering such criticisms: "You can't explain the deportation of every single Jew solely by economic criteria. Why for example, in the farthest Greek island did they search for Jews in order to deport them? However, the general consideration was economic. Most parts of the Eastern European economy—and what they saw as the Jewish sector of the economy or even the production of the ghettos—was inefficient compared to German criteria. They could have used the same raw material in a more efficient way using machinery, with fewer people to maintain, whereas in the ghettos, they employed many more workers but on a very low level. It was slave labor that didn't cost anything, but still they had to maintain the workers, and maybe up to a certain point, their families as well. Another point is . . . that the development of the Final Solution was not made when the Germans faced the 'Jewish Question' in Western Europe, but rather when they faced the 'Jewish Question' in Eastern Europe, in Poland, after the beginning of the war. In Poland, there were millions of Jews, not hundreds of thousands as in Germany. They didn't try to force Polish Jews to emigrate, even though beforehand they had forced German Jews to do so. In Western Europe, they tried to profit from expropriating the Jews and to reinforce either the Germany economy or the economy in the occupied Western European countries mainly in favor of the Germans, of course, but also to a certain degree in favor of the local population." Susanne Heim, "The Role of Academics and Professionals in the Final Solution," www.yadvashem.org.

71. Browning, *The Path to Genocide*, 69, 76.

72. Dan Diner, *Beyond the Conceivable: Studies on Germany, Nazism, and the Holocaust* (Berkeley: University of California Press, 2000), 140.

73. Diner, *Beyond the Conceivable*, 140.

74. See also Yehuda Bauer, *Rethinking the Holocaust* (New Haven: Yale University Press, 2001), esp. 86–92. "For Aly, ideology, including antisemitism, exists as a necessary backdrop against which the various Nazi extermination plans were developed. But the very plans he so persuasively describes were not motivated by pragmatic considerations. They were the practical result or the practical translation, of a racist ideology. The thesis holds true: when you

want something badly, you try to translate your desire into reality. That is precisely what the Germans did: they were possessed by a racist ideology, and they enacted it, which is why they tried to restructure the ethnic and national map of Eastern Europe" (92).

75. Michel Foucault, *Society Must Be Defended: Lectures at the Collège de France, 1975–1976* (New York: Picador Press, 1997), 254.

76. Omer Bartov, *Mirrors of Destruction: War Genocide, and Modern Identity* (Cambridge: Oxford University Press, 2000), 111. See also Aly and Heim, *Architects of Annihilation*, 112: "In 1943, when millions of European Jews had already become victims of mass murder, the planners were still working on the assumption that [Auschwitz] would remain in existence as an integral part of the industrial region for another ten to twenty years at least." The concentration camp was to provide labor and an efficient means for killing "useless persons unfit for work."

77. Cited in Aly and Roth, *The Nazi Census*, 9–10. See also Claudia Koonz, *The Nazi Conscience* (Cambridge, MA: Harvard University Press, 2003), 103–30. As Koonz notes, "imperfect" Aryans were as much the object of demographic and racial policy as "people from alien backgrounds." For a comprehensive discussion of racial policy and the proliferation of confused racial schemes and taxonomies, see Michael Burleigh and Wolfgang Wippermann, *The Racial State: Germany, 1933–1945* (Cambridge: Cambridge University Press, 1991) and Christopher M. Hutton, *Race and the Third Reich*, (Malden, MA: Polity Press, 2005).

78. See Foucault, *Society Must Be Defended*: Giving the name "biopower" to the logic Arendt and Bartov, among others, partially and certainly more narrowly render, Foucault describes the Nazi state as one that "makes the field of the life it manages, protects, guarantees, and cultivates in biological terms absolutely co-extensive with the sovereign right to kill anyone, meaning not only other people, but also its own people" (260).

79. Diner, *Beyond the Conceivable*, 154. This is not entirely the case. The extermination centers—Chelmno, Belzec, Sobibor, and Treblinka—were shut down for the most part by 1943 (Sobibor and Treblinka, because of prisoner uprisings; Chelmno, because its killing technology—death by carbon monoxide—was deemed inefficient) with the conclusion of Operation Rheinhard. However, what took their place as part of the evolving apparatus of genocide was Auschwitz-Birkenau. An enormous labor installation (housing an estimated 100,000 slave laborers) combined with facilities for extermination, Auschwitz became the largest and most efficient killing center in Poland, with plans for expansion interrupted only by the war's end. Auschwitz was not exclusively dedicated to extermination or the extermination of European Jewry (even while 9 out of 10 of some 2 million victims who died at Auschwitz were Jews). Nevertheless, it was very clearly considered the model for the future administration of subject populations in a new ethnically and economically reorganized Europe. On the development of the town and camp, see Debórah Dwork and Robert Jan Van Pelt, *Auschwitz: 1270 to the Present* (New York: Norton, 1996); and Rees, *Auschwitz: A New History*. On the operation of the camp from the perspective of the interned, see Filip Müller, *Eyewitness Auschwitz: Three Years in the Gas Chambers* (Chicago: Ivan R. Dee, 1979); and Dr. Miklos Nyiszli, *Auschwitz: A Doctor's Eyewitness Account* (New York: Arcade, 1960). On the operation of the camp from the perspective of its commandant, see Rudolf Höss, *Death Dealer: The Memoirs of the SS Kommandant at Auschwitz*, ed. Steven Paskuly (New York: Prometheus Books, 1992).

80. Diner, *Beyond the Conceivable*, 185.

81. Diner, *Beyond the Conceivable*, 175.

82. Shoshanna Felma, "Theaters of Justice: Arendt in Jerusalem, the Eichmann Trial, and the Redefinition of Legal Meaning in the Wake of the Holocaust," *Critical Inquiry* 27.2 (2001): 236–37: "The Eichmann trial was a singular event of law that, through its monumental legal

record and its monumental legal chorus of testimonies of the persecuted, unwittingly became creative of a canonical or *sacred narrative*. This new born sacred narrative was, and could not but be, at once a tale of jurisdiction and a collective tale of mourning" (emphasis in the original).

83. Diner, *Beyond the Conceivable*, 185.

84. Diner, *Beyond the Conceivable*, 140.

85. Aly and Heim, *Architects of Annihilation*, 294.

86. David Carr, "Place and Time: On the Interplay of Historical Points of View," Agency after Postmodernism, *History and Theory* 40.4(December 2001): 159, 160.

87. Interview with Susanne Heim, "The Role of Academics and Professionals in the Final Solution," 1–2. See also Michael Thad Allen, *The Business of Genocide: The SS, Slave Labor, and the Concentration Camps* (Chapel Hill: University of North Carolina Press, 2002). As Allen observes: "Ideology and 'rational' management did not contradict but reinforced each other" (49).

88. See Proctor, *Racial Hygiene*, 125. Thus, for example, "in 1933 Professor G. A. Wagner, director of the women's clinic of Berlin's Charité Hospital and editor of the *Archiv für Gynäkologie*, declared the nation's stock of ovaries a national resource and property of the German state. Wagner called for "mandatory care for these vital organs, vital not only for the individual, but for the health and future of the entire Volk."

89. Proctor, *Racial Hygiene*, 38. See also Aly, "The Planning Intelligentsia and the 'Final Solution,'" 105.

90. I will take this up in considerably more detail in chapter 4. A detailed description of the process is available in Stephan Landsman, *Crimes of the Holocaust: The Law Confronts Hard Cases* (Philadelphia: University of Pennsylvania Press, 2005), 15–16.

91. Aly and Heim, *Architects of Annihilation*, 112–14. See also Aly and Roth, *The Nazi Census*, 22–33.

92. Aly and Roth, *The Nazi Census*, 148–49.

93. See James C. Scott, *Seeing Like a State: How Certain Schemes to Improve the Human Condition Have Failed* (New Haven: Yale University Press, 1998).

94. Aly and Roth, *The Nazi Census*, 92–93.

95. Aly and Roth, *The Nazi Census*, 1.

96. Adi Ophir, *The Order of Evils: Toward an Ontology of Morals* (Cambridge, MA: MIT Press, 2005), 529.

NOTES TO CHAPTER 3

1. Arendt, quoted in Elisabeth Young-Bruehl, *Hannah Arendt: For Love of the World* (New Haven: Yale University Press, 1984), 452–53.

2. The conference was recorded over a three-day period. Heavily edited portions of the discussions were rearranged for thematic coherence—"to make Arendt's thinking apparent"—and reproduced in "Hannah Arendt: On Hannah Arendt," in Melvin A. Hill, ed., *Hannah Arendt: The Recovery of the Public World* (New York: St. Martin's Press, 1979), 301–2.

3. Hill, *Hannah Arendt,*, 301–39.

4. Hill, *Hannah Arendt*, 305.

5. Hill, *Hannah Arendt*, 307.

6. Hill, *Hannah Arendt*, 308.

7. Hill, *Hannah Arendt*, 308.

8. Or elsewhere for that matter. See, for example, Hannah Arendt, "Personal Responsibility under Dictatorship," in Kohn, *Responsibility and Judgment*, 17–48; also, Hannah Arendt, *Eichmann in Jerusalem: A Report on the Banality of Evil* (New York: Penguin, 1964), Postscript.

9. For a cautious meditation on Vietnam and German war crimes, see Telford Taylor, *Nuremberg and Vietnam: An American Tragedy* (New York: Random House, 1970). Milgram's study continues to have a certain traction in the context of efforts to explain how "ordinary men" could become apparently uncoerced participants in crimes of mass murder. Christopher Browning's widely respected, much-cited study, *Ordinary Men: Reserve Police Battalion 101 and the Final Solution in Poland* (New York: HarperCollins, 1992), is a good example of a contemporary inquiry that turns to Milgram's findings to account for how otherwise "normal" individuals are transformed into killers. Browning argues that the transformation of the men of Reserve Police Battalion 101 had less to do with belief, indoctrination, or ideology than circumstance: "Everywhere society conditions people to respect and defer to authority.... Everywhere people seek career advancement.... [B]ureaucratization and specialization attenuate the sense of personal responsibility. Within virtually any social collective, the peer group exerts tremendous pressures on behavior and sets moral norms. If the men of Reserve Police Battalion 101 could have become killers under such circumstances, what group of men cannot?" (189).

10. Stanley Milgram, *Obedience to Authority* (New York: HarperPerennial, 1983), 5–6. The extent to which Milgram's study both captivated and disturbed the public imagination is evidenced in the 1976 production of *The Tenth Level*. This movie (which enlisted Milgram as a consultant) was a prime-time dramatization of the experiments he performed at Yale in 1961–62. It aired on CBS (August 1976) and starred William Shatner.

11. Daniel Jonah Goldhagen, *Hitler's Willing Executioners: Ordinary Germans and the Holocaust* (New York: Basic Books, 1996).

12. Goldhagen, *Hitler's Willing Executioners*, 597 n. 74. "The moment that aspects, especially the social aspects, of the perpetrators' lives come into focus other than the simple act of killing, the false images of the Germans as one-dimensional men in situations that abstract them away from their social relations become harder to maintain. Even the full character of the perpetrators' social and cultural existence is hard to recover, the unreal images of them as isolated, frightened, thoughtless beings performing their tasks reluctantly are erroneous. The German executioners, like other people, consistently made choices about how they would act, choices that consistently produced immense Jewish suffering and mortality. They individually made those choices as contented members of an assenting genocidal community, in which the killing of Jews was normative and often celebrated" (406).

13. Michael Thad Allen, *The Business of Genocide: The SS, Slave Labor, and the Concentration Camps* (Chapel Hill: University of North Carolina Press, 2002), 2–3.

14. Allen, *The Business of Genocide*, 3.

15. Yaacov Lozowick, *Hitler's Bureaucrats: The Nazi Security Police and the Banality of Evil* (New York: Continuum, 2000), 8

16. Lozowick, *Hitler's Bureaucrats*, 8.

17. Lozowick, *Hitler's Bureaucrats*, 4, 8.

18. Arendt, "Personal Responsibility under Dictatorship," 17.

19. Consider an alternative interpretation of Milgram's findings proffered by the philosopher C. Fred Alford based on a rereading of the film Milgram made of his experiment. Alford insists that conventional opinion of the past forty years regarding what the experiment means—that a large majority of individuals will inflict pain on unknown others when ordered

or compelled to do so by a credible authority figure— misses a critical feature of participants' responses in the context of the lab. This critical feature is the affect of participants; the embarrassed pleasure they expressed through "grotesque laughter and giggling fits" as they delivered ever more severe shocks to victims who failed to successfully complete a task or correctly answer a question. In Alford's view, what this affect reveals is not only or even primarily an anxious compliance, deference, loss of agency, or longing to please authority. Rather, what it reveals is sadism, a nervous relief in being *given permission* to hurt someone: "The structure of the Milgram experiment protects them from knowledge of their own sadism, while allowing them to express it." Alford links sadistic behavior to what he describes as the existentially given condition of contemporary life and argues that when bound to institutional forms— when organized by and for the state—it is virtually invisible. Thus he asks: "Could it be the psychological function of leaders to provide plausible psychological deniability to their followers, as well as to shelter them from the consequences of their desires?" C. Fred Alford, "Hitler's Willing Executioners: What Does 'Willing' Mean?" *Theory and Society* 26 (1997): 732. See also Arne Johan Vetlesen's discussion of Alford's argument, in *Evil and Human Agency: Understanding Collective Evildoing* (New York: Cambridge University Press, 2005), 105.

20. As Tim Cole notes (*Selling the Holocaust: From Auschwitz to Schindler. How the Holocaust is Bought Packaged and Sold* [New York: Routledge, 1999]), 33: Very early on in the postwar period Anne Frank emerged as "the patron Saint of Liberalism." Said to offer "a testament of hope," to represent moral triumph in the face of adversity, or to embody, as Eleanor Roosevelt put it, "the ultimate shining nobility of the [human] spirit," her universalized, dehistoricized story has since become the principal curricular vehicle through which secondary school children in the United States encounter the Holocaust or some version of it in the form, as Alvin H. Rosenfeld describes it, "of a young girl's gaiety and moral gallantry." Rosenfeld, "Popularization and Memory: The Case of Anne Frank," in *Lessons and Legacies: The Meaning of the Holocaust in a Changing World*, ed. Peter Hayes (Evanston, IL: Northwestern University Press, 1991), 254.

21. Benjamin Robinson, "*The Specialist* on the Eichmann Precedent: Morality, Law, and Military Sovereignty," *Critical Inquiry* 30 (Autumn 2003): 75.

22. Zygmunt Bauman, "The Holocaust's Life as a Ghost," in *Social Theory after the Holocaust*, ed. Robert Fine and Charles Turner (London: Liverpool University Press, 2000), 12.

23. Bauman, "The Holocaust's Life as a Ghost," 15. See also Peter Novick, *The Holocaust in American Life* (Boston: Houghton Mifflin, 1999); and Norman G. Finkelstein, *The Holocaust Industry: Reflections on the Exploitation of Jewish Suffering* (New York: Verso, 2000).

24. Rabbi David Polish, cited by Mark Krupnick, "'Walking in Our Sleep': Bitburg and the Post-1939 Generation" (originally published by in *Christian Century*, June 5–12), in *Bitburg in Moral and Political Perspective*, ed. Geoffrey Hartman (Bloomington: Indiana University Press, 1986), 190.

25. Martin E. Marty, "'Storycide' and the Meaning of History' (originally published in the *Los Angeles Times*, May 12, 1985), included in Hartman, *Bitburg in Moral and Political Perspective*, 225–26.

26. On the other hand, the Simon Wiesenthal Center, one of the preeminent Holocaust institutions on the West Coast, honored Reagan in 1988 for his staunch support of Israel with the Humanitarian of the Year award; and Reagan was similarly honored by the Anti-Defamation League in 1994 with the Torch of Liberty award. Finkelstein, *The Holocaust Industry*, 30–31.

27. Bauman, "The Holocaust's Life as a Ghost," 16.

28. Arendt, "Personal Responsibility under Dictatorship," 18. Critical readers of her work have seen it differently. Richard Bernstein points out that the "facts of the case," which Arendt insists are self-evident and beyond dispute, are precisely what are at stake and being contested. See Richard J. Bernstein, *Hannah Arendt and the Jewish Question* (Cambridge, MA: The MIT Press, 1996), 167; emphasis in the original.

29. Villa, *Politics, Philosophy, Terror*, 56. See also Jean Bethke Elsthain's provocative discussion of Arendt's reformulation, following Augustine, of "the problem of evil," in *Augustine and the Limits of Politics* (Notre Dame: Notre Dame University Press, 1995), 69–87.

30. On this, see Jeffrey Shandler, *While America Watches: Televising the Holocaust* (New York: Oxford University Press, 1999), esp. chap. 3, "The Man in the Glass Booth," 83–132; and Cole, *Selling the Holocaust*, esp. chap. 2, "Adolf Eichmann," 47–72.

31. Arendt, *Eichmann*, 276.

32. Harry Mulisch, *Criminal Case 40/61: The Trial of Adolf Eichmann* (Philadelphia: University of Pennsylvania Press, 2005), 50. Like Arendt, Mulisch went to Jerusalem as a journalist for the weekly magazine *Elseviers Weekblad*.

33. Here Arendt is describing the prosecution's characterization of Eichmann during the trial. *Eichmann*, 276.

34. This is how she framed the matter in 1969 in a letter to the Rockefeller Foundation. Arendt, cited in Villa, *Politics, Philosophy, Terror*, 57.

35. Arendt, *Eichmann*, 26.

36. It bears mentioning—in part because it shows up in various critical accounts of Arendt's work and was invoked by the prosecution during the trial—that a psychological diagnosis was submitted that saw in Eichmann "a perverted, sadistic personality" and characterized him, in contrast to the conclusions reached by six other psychiatrists, as "a man possessed by a dangerous and insatiable urge to kill, arising out of a desire for power" (cited in Gideon Hausner, *Justice in Jerusalem* [New York: Herzl Press, 1977]), 6–7; Cornelis Van Hattem, *Superfluous People: A Reflection on Hannah Arendt and Evil* [Lanham, MD: University Press of America, 2005], 73; and Cesarani, *Eichmann*, 358). This diagnosis was made by the Hungarian psychiatrist Leopold Szondi who did not know the identity of the subject (Eichmann) whose test results he was reading. When shown the results of the test he devised, called the "Szondi Test," Szondi is said to have been shocked and "to have never seen such convincing results," leading former concentration camp survivor and writer, Imre Kértesz, among others, to conclude as recently as 2004 that with Szondi's expert diagnosis "all theories about a 'desk-murderer' have been refuted" (cited in Van Hattem, *Superfluous People*, 73).

The Leopold Szondi test works from the assumption that personality traits are genetic and links specific traits to specific physical appearances. It also assumes that people with similar genetics/personality traits will be attracted to each other. In the Szondi Test, subjects are shown forty-eight photographs of various people and asked to identify two images they like and two they dislike. The photographs represent what Szondi considered were "extreme and pure illustrations" of individuals diagnosed with various psychiatric ailments, including mental derangement, homosexuality, sadism, epilepsy, hysteria, and paranoid-schizophrenia. By Szondi's reasoning, the images to which a given subject was attracted reflected the drives dominant in his or her personality. While popular in the 1950s and 1960s, especially in Europe, Szondi's test has come to be regarded since as an ineffective diagnostic tool for personality disorders. Still, given the density of assumptions that shape, for example, the very categories that Szondi identifies as "criminal disorders"—in what sense are homosexuality, epilepsy, and "hysteria" evidence of antisocial or criminal tendencies?—one wonders how or why his assessment continues to be regarded as anything approaching credible in the context of discussions about Eichmann.

37. Arendt, *Eichmann*, 48–49.

38. Arendt, *Eichmann*, 48.

39. Arendt, *Eichmann*, 48.

40. Arendt, *Eichmann*, 48.

41. As Vetlesen argues, "The call for empathy can be met because we are all human beings, principally sharing the same access to the experience of pain." Arne Johan Vetlesen, *Perception, Empathy, and Judgment: An Inquiry into the Precondition of Moral Performance* (University Park: Pennsylvania State University Press, 1994), 120, 119.

42. Vetlesen, *Evil and Human Agency*, 101.

43. Arendt, *Eichmann*, 101.

44. Eichmann, cited in Arendt, *Eichmann*, 136.

45. Vetlesen, *Perception, Empathy, and Judgment*, 105.

46. Hannah Arendt, *On Revolution* (New York: Viking, 1963), 69.

47. Arendt, *On Revolution*, 69.

48. Arendt understands these terms as follows: Passion she defines as the capacity for suffering, while compassion is the capacity for suffering with others. *On Revolution*, 76.

49. Arendt, *On Revolution*, 82.

50. Arendt, *On Revolution*, 85, 86.

51. "Thinking, existentially speaking, is a solitary but not a lonely business; solitude is the human situation in which I keep myself company. Loneliness comes about when I am alone without being able to keep myself company, when, as Jaspers used to say, 'I am in default of myself' (*ich bleibe mir aus*), or, to put it differently, when I am one and without company." Hannah Arendt, *Life of the Mind: Thinking* (vol. 1) (New York: Harcourt Brace Jovanovich, 1977), 185.

52. Hannah Arendt, "Truth and Politics," in *Between Past and Future: Eight Exercises in Political Thought* (New York: Penguin Books, 1977), 241 (emphasis added); and *Essays in Understanding, 1930–1954*, ed. Jerome Kohn (New York: Harcourt Brace, 1994), 323.

53. Norma Moruzzi, *Speaking through the Mask: Hannah Arendt and the Politics of Social Identity* (Ithaca: Cornell University Press, 2000), 126.

54. Arendt, *Life of the Mind* (vol. 1), 181. As she explains in *On Revolution* (102): "The Socratic agent, because he was capable of thought, carried within himself a witness from whom he could not escape; wherever he went and whatever he did, he had his audience, which, like any other audience, would automatically constitute itself into a court of justice, that is, into a tribunal which later ages have called conscience."

55. Arendt, "Thinking and Moral Considerations," in *Responsibility and Judgment*, ed. Jerome Kohn (New York: Schocken Books, 2003), 177.

56. Arendt, *Life of the Mind* (vol. 1), 88.

57. Arendt, *Life of the Mind* (vol. 1), 192.

58. Arendt, "Thinking and Moral Considerations," 177.

59. Arendt, *Life of the Mind* (vol. 1), 192.

60. An example here would be the approach of Gitta Sereny, a journalist who interviewed numerous high-placed former Nazis in an attempt to determine, in her words, "some new truth which would contribute to the understanding of things that had never yet been understood." Sereny, *Into That Darkness: An Examination of Conscience* (New York: Vintage, 1974), 23. See also Gitta Sereny, *Albert Speer: His Battle with Truth* (New York: Vintage, 1996).

61. Arendt, *Life of the Mind* (vol. 1), 191.

62. Arendt, *Eichmann*, 114.

63. Cesarani, *Eichmann*, 106.

64. Cesarani, *Eichmann*, 106, 107.

65. Arendt, *Eichmann*, 51.

66. Arendt, *Eichmann*, 51–52.

67. Arendt, *Essays in Understanding*, 323.

68. Arendt, *Eichmann*, 25.

69. Arendt, *Life of the Mind* (vol. 1), 190–91.

70. Arendt, *Eichmann*, 52.

71. Jochen Von Lang, with Claus Sibyll, eds., *Eichmann Interrogated: Transcripts from the Archives of the Israeli Police* (New York: Da Capo Press, 1999), 197, 199–200.

72. Arendt, *Eichmann*, 231.

73. Arendt, *Eichmann*, 230.

74. Von Lang and Sibyll, *Eichmann Interrogated*, 157.

75. Morruzi, *Speaking through the Mask*, 133.

76. Arendt, *Eichmann*, 233. Alongside Schmidt's story, Arendt juxtaposes another, drawn from the memoirs of army physician, Peter Bamm. Bamm writes of witnessing the collection and gassing (by mobile van) of Jews near the Russian front and notes that while it was unmistakably clear that a massacre was transpiring, no one in his unit moved to intervene. He offers the plausible explanation, echoed by many others after the war, that serious protest was simply not possible: "It belongs among the refinements of totalitarian governments in our century that they don't permit their opponents to die a great, dramatic martyr's death for their convictions. A good many of us might have accepted such a death. The totalitarian state lets its opponents disappear in silent anonymity. It is certain that anyone who had dared to suffer death rather than silently tolerate the crime would have sacrificed his life in vain. This is not to say that such a sacrifice would have been morally meaningless. It would only have been practically useless. None of us had a conviction so deeply rooted that we could have taken upon ourselves a practically useless sacrifice for the sake of a higher moral meaning." A similar sentiment was echoed by Franz Strangl, former *Kommandant* of the extermination camp Treblinka and, briefly, Sobibor, in a series of interviews conducted by Gitta Sereny in 1971. Strangl described himself as having been horrified and sickened when he first arrived at Treblinka and witnessed the killing process and to have been stricken subsequently by inner doubt and conflict. Sereny asked him why he had not expressed his doubt, and he, like Bamm, claimed it would have been the end for him: "'Supposing for a moment, [she replied], it would have been the end as you say. There were people in Germany who stood up for their principles: not many, it is true, but some. Yours was a very special position. There can't have been more than a dozen men like you in all of the Third Reich. Don't you think, if you had found that extraordinary courage, it would have had an effect on people who served under you?' He shook his head. 'If I had sacrificed myself. . . . If I had made public what I felt and had died . . . it would have made no difference. Not an iota. It would have gone on just the same, as if it and I had never happened." *Into That Darkness*, 231–32. Arendt does not speak to Stangl's account specifically, but her reflections with respect to Bamm's failure to act have some bearing: "It is true totalitarian domination tried to establish these holes of oblivion into which all deeds, good and evil, would disappear, but just as the Nazis' feverish attempts, from June, 1942, on, to erase all traces of the massacres . . . were doomed to failure, so all efforts to let their opponents 'disappear in silent anonymity' were in vain. Holes of oblivion do not exist. Nothing human is

that perfect, and there are simply too many people in the world to make oblivion possible. One man will always be left alive to tell the story. Hence, nothing can ever be 'practically useless,' at least not in the long run" (233).

77. Vetlesen, *Perception, Empathy, and Judgment,* 106–7.

78. Vetlesen, *Perception, Empathy, and Judgment,* 119. See also Carolyn J. Dean, *The Fragility of Empathy: After the Holocaust* (Ithaca: Cornell University Press, 2004), esp. chap. 1.

79. Arendt, *Life of the Mind* (vol. 1), 4.

80. The filmmakers found some 500 hours of video of which only 350 hours were "usable." On the impact of the trial on the development of television, see Jeffrey Shandler, *While America Watches: Televising the Holocaust* (New York: Oxford Unviersity Press, 1999), esp. chap. 4. Shandler notes that daily broadcasts of the trial had an especially profound impact on American Holocaust consciousness. In his words: "The Eichmann case provided the first opportunity for television networks to deal with the Holocaust in the context of reporting a major news story. In fact, American television audiences are most likely to have first heard the word *Holocaust* used to describe the Nazi persecution of European Jewry during broadcasts of the trial" (83).

81. Siven, cited in Goel Pinto, "Update to the 'Forgery Accusation," www.Haaretz.com (February 5, 2005), 5.

82. *The Specialist: Portrait of a Modern Criminal,* Special Features: Post-production interview (60 min.), 2002.

83. *The Specialist: Portrait of a Modern Criminal,* Special Features: Post-production interview (60 min.), 2002. *The Specialist* avoids some of the common strategies of documentary filmmaking—it is not guided, for example, by the voice-over of an invisible narrator, nor does it incorporate additional, contextualizing footage—while adopting others. The conventions introduced anew include selective editing, the laying over of a complex nondiegetic music and vocal sound track—a post-Shoenberg modernist composition that weaves music and bits of phrases in various tones and languages—as well as special effects in the form of sharpening the contours and contrasts of the images, thus making them "more acceptable to late twentieth-century viewers." Though it could be described as spare in its technical interventions, the film was criticized by Hillel Tryster, former director of the Spielberg archive, as a text that falsifies the trial by splicing together segments that produce a dialog and a cumulative story that never happened. See Hillel Tryster, "We Have Ways of Making You Believe: The Eichmann Trial as Seen in *The Specialist,*" *Antisemitism International* (2004): 34–44. See also Tryster, "Eyal Sivan Eichmann, Lies, and Videotape," *Indymedia,* 2007, http://no0666. wordpress.com/2007/05/18/eyal-sivan-eichmann-lies-and-videotape/.

84. Hausner, *Justice in Jerusalem,* 347.

85. Hausner's claim that it is *necessary* to look at such images seems at first blush, especially to contemporary audiences, entirely self-evident. But their use in a legal context, however compelling, is—rather than necessary—problematic at best: such images are highly prejudicial and do not clearly establish a link between those on trial for such brutality and the actual (or aftermath of) brutality captured on film (Stephan Landsman, *Crimes of the Holocaust: The Law Confronts Hard Cases* [Philadelphia: University of Pennsylvania Press, 2005], 28). What, then, are they evidence of? On the other hand, viewing these images has been said to be "morally necessary." As Novick observes (*Holocaust in American Life,* 260), "The push behind teaching the Holocaust in the schools is the conviction that an encounter with the Holocaust, particularly an emotional encounter [as is provoked by viewing atrocity imagery], is bound to be productive of lessons. The same conviction was held by those who built the Washington

Holocaust Museum." And it informs, in part, the move by the prosecution in Jerusalem as well. But in what respects does looking at such imagery make sense of atrocity and, more specifically, of what happened over the course of approximately a decade? As Janina Struk puts it, "If acts of atrocity are beyond the comprehension of most of us, then little can be achieved by looking at images of them. So why display them? *Are the effusive display of photographs really teaching us something?*" *Photographing the Holocaust: Interpretations of the Evidence* (New York: I. B. Tauris, 2004), 214; emphasis in the original.

86. Joseph Kessel, quoted in *Nuremberg: The Nazis Facing Their Crimes*, directed by Christian Delage (Compagnie des Phares et Balises, France, 2006).

87. Homer Bigart, *New York Times*, June 9, 1961, 16.

88. Hausner, *Justice in Jerusalem*, 348.

89. Gideon Hausner, opening address to the Court, in *The Specialist* (3:40).

90. It is the documentary-like format of the film and the particular didactic, truth-telling functions of this genre that have led critics to describe *The Specialist* as a "forgery"—historically deceptive and intentionally designed to manipulate "memory" while also misleading audiences on behalf of an anti-Zionist agenda. I will have more to say about documentary's "rhetoric of appeal" in chapter 4. On the medium's knowledge-producing strategies, see John Tagg, *The Disciplinary Frame: Photographic Truths and the Capture of Meaning* (Minneapolis: University of Minnesota Press, 2009).

NOTES TO CHAPTER 4

1. Hannah Yablonka, *The State of Israel vs. Adolf Eichmann* (New York: Schocken Books, 2004), 233.

2. Mark Osiel, *Mass Atrocity, Collective Memory, and the Law* (New Brunswick, NJ: Transaction, 2000), 117.

3. Gary Jonathan Bass, *Stay the Hand of Vengeance: The Politics of War Crimes Tribunals* (Princeton: Princeton University Press, 2000), 148. By "self-serving," Bass means to suggest that each of the prosecuting parties sought redress for crimes against their military and civilian populations and pursued the Nazis in only the most anemic fashion for crimes against humanity.

4. Shoshanna Felman, "Theaters of Justice: Arendt in Jerusalem, the Eichmann Trial, and the Redefinition of Legal Meaning in the Wake of the Holocaust," *Critical Inquiry* 27.2 (2001): 231 n. 5.

5. David Ben-Gurion, *Israel: A Personal Story* (New York: New English Library, 1972), p. 599, cited in Felman, "Theaters of Justice," 222, and elsewhere: "We are not out to punish Eichmann; there is no fit punishment. . . . [O]ne of our motives in bringing [him] to trial is to make the details of his case known to the generation of Israelis who have grown up since the Holocaust. It is necessary that our youth remember what happened to the Jewish people. . . . They should be taught the lesson that Jews are not sheep to be slaughtered but a people who can hit back—as Jews did in the War of Independence."

6. Tony Judt, "The Past Is Another Country: Myth and Memory in Postwar Europe," in *The Politics of Retribution in Europe: World War II and Its Aftermath*, ed. István Deák, Jan T. Gross, and Tony Judt (Princeton: Princeton University Press, 2000), 296.

7. See Tony Judt, *Postwar: A History of Europe since 1945* (New York: Penguin, 2005), 24–25, 26. Judt explains: "What was taking place in 1945, and had been underway for at least a year, was . . . an unprecedented exercise in ethnic cleansing and population transfer. In part

this was the outcome of 'voluntary' ethnic separation: Jewish survivors leaving a Poland where they were unsafe and unwanted, for example, or Italians departing the Istrian peninsula rather than live under Yugoslav rule. . . . Bulgaria transferred 160,000 Turks to Turkey; Czechoslovakia, under a February 1946 agreement with Hungary, exchanged 120,000 Slovaks living in Hungary for an equivalent number of Hungarians from communities north of the Danube, in Slovakia. Other transfers of this kind took place between Poland and Lithuania and between Czechoslovakia and the Soviet Union; 400,000 people from southern Yugoslavia were moved to land in the north to take the place of 600,000 departed Germans and Italians. Here as elsewhere, the populations concerned were not consulted. But the largest affected group was the Germans. . . . Between the popular desire to punish local Germans for the ravages of war and occupation, and the exploitation of this mood by post-war governments, the German-speaking communities of Yugoslavia, Hungary, Czechoslovakia, Poland, the Baltic region and the western Soviet Union were doomed. . . . Some western observers were shocked at the treatment of the German communities. Ann O'Hare, a *New York Times* correspondent, recorded her impressions on October 23rd 1946: 'The scale of this resettlement, and the conditions in which it takes place, are without precedent in history. No one seeing its horrors first hand can doubt that it is a crime against humanity for which history will exact a terrible retribution.' . . . History has exacted no such retribution."

On the issue of population transfers and the forcible clearing of Germans from Eastern Europe, see also Giles MacDonogh, *After the Reich: The Brutal History of the Allied Occupation* (New York: Basic Books, 2007), esp. chaps. 4 and 5.

8. S. M. Plokhy, *Yalta: The Price of Peace* (New York: Viking, 2010), 252. While twenty-four individuals were originally indicted, only twenty-two stood trial one of whom, Martin Bormann, was tried, convicted, and sentenced to death in absentia.

9. Richard Overy (*Interrogations: The Nazi Elite in Allied Hands, 1945* [New York: Viking Press, 2001]) suggests that while considered the most important of the four charges, a "conspiracy to wage aggressive war" was perhaps the least convincing. "The idea that Nazi policy at home and abroad could be reduced to a single pattern of action compelled the American prosecutors to bend historical reality. The idea that 'the Nazis' conspired together to conquer the world was scarcely credible, even in 1945, yet it was the centerpiece of the prosecution case" (48).

10. The Kellogg-Briand Pact was invoked to counter charges that the Allies had simply invented law to try the accused at Nuremberg. The pact, reached after World War I, was signed by the United States, Britain, France, Germany, Italy, and Japan, among other powers, and in effect renounced war as a strategy of national policy.

11. In response to questions raised in the early weeks of negotiation over what was to become the London Charter, Justice Jackson insisted that establishing the illegality and criminal nature of key groups or organizations was critical, indeed, the only sure way to avoid a situation in which, as Sir David Maxwell-Fyfe put it, "thousands of members of the Gestapo and SS would be walking free in Germany because we could not prove a specific crime against the member." Jackson elaborated: "The organizations that we think should be included would be only voluntary organizations . . . which have played a cruel and controlling part in subjugating first the German people and then their neighbors . . . [and] where the membership was in itself significant of an adherence to the purposes of the organization and where the organization was sufficiently close knit so the responsibility of the member would be a reasonable conclusion." The organizations identified for possible criminal indictment were the SS, the SD, the Gestapo, the SA, the Reich Cabinet, the Leadership Corps of the Nazi Party, and the

General Staff and High Command. Of these organizations, the SS, the SD, the Gestapo, and the Leadership Corps of the Nazi Party were found to be criminal, thereby implicating over a million individuals. Drexel A. Sprecher, *Inside the Nuremberg Trial: A Prosecutor's Comprehensive Account*, 2 vols. (Lanham, MD: University Press of America, 1999), 1:424–25; 2:1370.

12. Stephan Landsman, *Crimes of the Holocaust: The Law Confronts Hard Cases* (Philadelphia: University of Pennsylvania Press, 2005), 10. Howard Ball explains the architecture of the charge of criminal conspiracy: "If a Nazi organization—political, military, or police—'contemplated illegal methods or illegal ends,' each member of the organization was liable for the acts of all other knowing members. Collective criminality, the crime of membership was at the core of [this] plan. As developed by the IMT [International Military Tribunal] . . . there were five questions that had to [be] asked by prosecutors before indicting a detainee: (1) Did the Nazi organization have a common plan of criminal action? (2) Was a group's actions criminal? (3) Was a person's membership in such a group voluntary? (4) Was a person's membership a knowing one, that is, did the person have some knowledge of the criminal aims of the organization? (5) Was there evidence that the person was such a member and that he or she acted to achieve the organization's criminal goals?" Howard Ball, *Prosecuting War Crimes and Genocide: The Twentieth-Century Experience* (Lawrence: University Press of Kansas, 1999), 46–47. The prosecution of organizations—and of individuals based on their membership in an organization whose operation was held to be criminal according to one or more of the four counts set out in the London Charter—is variously described by commentators as "untested and simplistic" (Landsman, 11); "far-reaching and novel" (Sprecher); "a mistaken and dangerous juridical course of action" (David Fraser, *Law after Auschwitz: Toward a Jurisprudence of the Holocaust* [Durham, NC: Carolina Academic Press, 2005], 7). Significantly, it is the brainchild—albeit several iterations removed—of Raphel Lemkin, tireless lobbyist for and coauthor of the UN genocide convention, passed in 1948. See Robert E. Conot, *Justice at Nuremberg* (New York: Caroll & Graf, 1983), 11–13.

This was an especially blunt and ineffective strategy of "guilt by association." A case in point regarding the notorious SS: "Despite the Nuremberg trials stating that the SS was a 'criminal' organization in its entirety, no attempt was ever made to enforce the view that the mere act of working in the SS at Auschwitz was a war crime—a view that popular opinion would have surely supported. A conviction and sentence—however minimal—for every SS man who was there would have sent a clear message for the future. It did not happen. About 85 percent of the SS membership who served at Auschwitz and survived the war escaped scot-free. When Himmler began the development of the gas chambers in order to distance the SS men from the psychological 'burden' of shooting people in cold blood, he could scarcely have predicted that it would have this additional benefit for the Nazis. This method of murder meant that the vast majority of the SS members who served at Auschwitz could escape punishment after the war by claiming to not have been directly involved in the extermination process." Laurence Rees, *Auschwitz: A New History* (New York: Public Affairs/Perseus Books, 2005), 296.

13. This would include, for example, the bombing of Dresden (February 1945); the mistreatment of German prisoners of war who were often housed in the Reich's own concentration camps where they were deliberately starved, systematically robbed, and in some sectors worked to death; the mass rape of German women and girls by Soviet troops as well as the Soviet action at Katyn in 1940 where the Soviet secret police oversaw the murder of approximately 22,000 members of the Polish officer corps. The slaughter was captured on film and described at Nuremberg as the work of the German army. See MacDonogh, *After the Reich*, esp. chap. 15, "Where Are Our Men?"

14. Fraser, *Law after Auschwitz*, 27.

15. Telford Taylor, *Nuremberg and Vietnam: An American Tragedy* (New York: Random House, 1970), 13–14: "Today, 'Nuremberg' is both what actually happened there and what people think happened, and the second is more important than the first. To set the record straight is, no doubt, a useful historical exercise, but sea change is itself a reality, and it is not the bare record, but the ethos of Nuremberg with which we must reckon today.... Put another way, Nuremberg is not only what was said and done there, but also what was said about it, then and subsequently."

16. As the film studies scholar Thomas Doherty muses, "Imagine how sparse would be the programming options of the History Channel and the Arts & Entertainment Network without the grain black-and-white footage in the public domain, from Universal Newsreel and military photographic units." "World War II in Film: What Is the Color of Reality?" *Chronicle Review: The Chronicle of Higher Education*, October 9, 1998, B4 (accessed November 21, 2007, from http://chronicle.com/weekley/v45/i07/ 07b00401.htm).

17. Thomas Doherty, *Projections of War: Hollywood, American Culture, and World War II* (New York: Columbia University Press, 1993).

18. Lawrence Douglas, *The Memory of Judgment: Making Law and History in the Trials of the Holocaust* (New Haven: Yale University Press, 2001), 37.

19. On the other hand, as Marouf Hasian points out, in my view rightly: "Scholars today often complain that the Nuremberg tribunals focused too much attention on crimes of 'aggression' and avoided tackling the issue of the 'uniqueness' of the Judeocide. These scholars have a point, but they may underestimate the number of times the Allied prosecutors talked or wrote about the 'extermination' of Europe's Jews in the establishment of their case against ranking Nazis." *Rhetorical Vectors of Memory in National and International Holocaust Trials* (East Lansing: Michigan State University Press, 2006), 35.

20. Douglas, *Memory of Judgment*, 29.

21. Telford Taylor, *The Anatomy of The Nuremberg Trials: A Personal Memoir* (New York: Alfred A. Knopf, 1992), 186.

22. IMT transcript, 264–65.

23. Landsman, *Crimes of the Holocaust*, 26.

24. Landsman, *Crimes of the Holocaust*, 26.

25. Donald Bloxham, *Genocide on Trial: War Crimes Trials and the Formation of Holocaust History and Memory* (Oxford: Oxford University Press, 2003), 61: "With regard to the potential use of four witnesses who had been involved to varying degrees with resistance movements in the Third Reich, one of [Jackson's] peculiar objections was that 'they . . . had a strong bias against the Hitler regime.'"

26. When at least one member of the legal staff suggested that eyewitness testimony might provide the trial with "an affirmative human aspect," thus making the prosecution's case more effective, Jackson unceremoniously removed him from counsel and ordered him back to the United States. On this issue and others that plagued the prosecution, see Whitney R. Harris, *Tyranny on Trial: The Trial of the Major German War Criminals at the End of World War II at Nuremberg, Germany, 1945–1946* (Dallas: Southern Methodist University Press, 1999); Conot, *Justice at Nuremberg*; G. M. Gilbert, *Nuremberg Diary*, (New York: Da Capo Press, 1995).

27. William J. Bosch, *Judgment On Nuremberg: American Attitudes toward the Major German War-Crime Trials* (Chapel Hill: University of North Carolina Press, 1970), 94, 95.

28. Rebecca West, "Greenhouse with Cyclamens I," in *A Train of Powder: Six Reports on the Problem of Guilt and Punishment in Our Time* (Chicago: Ivan R. Dee, 1955), 11, 17.

29. *Nuremberg: The Nazis Facing Their Crimes*, dir. Christian Delage (France, 2006, 3.5 hr.). The performance of justice at Nuremberg was as much an object lesson for Americans as it was for Germans. In the spring of 1945, public sentiment in the United States leaned toward swift, sharp justice, with mass executions of members of the SS and Nazi leadership. As Giles MacDonogh notes, Joseph Pulitzer of the *St. Louis Post-Dispatch* put the number to be shot at about 150,000; others set the number still higher, at 450,000. Secretary of the Treasury Henry J. Morgenthau Jr. argued that trials would simply "reap a crop of martyrs"; but then Morgenthau had also advocated for a "hard" peace that would divide Germany into four autonomous agrarian regions. Roosevelt was apparently taken with the idea through 1943, and so too Stalin who saw in a much reduced, divided, and dependent postwar Germany the source of slave labor for the rebuilding of Russia. However, by the time Churchill, Roosevelt, and Stalin met at Yalta (February 1945) to reconfigure the map of postwar Europe and redistribute postwar populations, the Western Allies had grown increasingly wary of Stalin's ever-expanding geostrategic ambitions and thus increasingly less enamored of a dismembered Germany. See MacDonogh, *After the Reich*; Plokhy, *Yalta*; and Bosch, *Judgment on Nuremberg*.

30. *New York Times*, December 6, 1945; cited in Bosch, *Judgment on Nuremberg*, 99.

31. IMT trial transcript, 2, 22, 3. For a compelling account of Jackson's opening address, see Douglas, *The Memory of Judgment*, esp. chap. 2, "The Idiom of Judgment: Crimes Against Humanity."

32. Robert Jackson, opening address, cited in Harris, *Tyranny on Trial*, 35.

33. *Nazi Concentration Camps* was screened on November 29, 1945; *The Nazi Plan*, December 11, 1945; and *The Atrocities Committed by the German-Fascists in the USSR*, February 9, 1946.

34. *Nuremberg: The Nazis Facing Their Crimes*, 35:42. See also Specher, *Inside the Nuremberg Trial*, vol 1. Sprecher, a member of the American prosecution, notes that this film was designed to illustrate the prosecution's case as presented under Count 1 (conspiracy) and Count 2 (aggressive war). The film consisted of four parts: (1) "The Rise of the NSDAP, 1921–1933"; (2) "Acquiring Control of Germany, 1933–1935"; (3) "Preparation for Wars of Aggression, 1935–1939"; (4) "Wars of Aggression, 1939–1944." The accused were reported to have relished this screening: "Von Ribbentrop is said to have wept saying, 'Can't you feel the strength of [Hitler's] personality?'"; "Goring stated that the film was so inspiring that Justice Jackson would now wish to join the Nazi party" (292–93). On the intimate partnership that developed during this period between the Hollywood studios (War Activities Committee of the Motion Picture Industry) and the U.S. War Department (Office of War Information), see Doherty, *Projections of War*.

35. Depicting the Germans as a victimized people marked a shift in the approach of the U.S. whose first impulse early in the occupation was to generalize and distribute guilt for war crimes across the population. The Soviets, on the other hand, had adopted a somewhat less punitive rhetoric that attributed the war to international monopoly capitalism, German militarism, and German big industry while depicting the German population as innocent victims of class thugs. Understanding themselves to be in an only slightly muted competition for the "hearts and minds" of the population and already anxious about Soviet ambitions for further western expansion, the U.S. occupying forces assumed a more moderate stance with respect to questions of responsibility at the urging of the Psychological Warfare Division of the Supreme Headquarters of the Allied Expeditionary Force. This shift then was reflected in and publicized through the prosecution's presentation at Nuremberg. In Jackson's words, "We have no purpose to incriminate the whole German people. We know that the Party was not put in power by a majority of the German vote. We know it came to power by an evil alliance between the most extreme of Nazi revolutionists, the most unrestrained of the German reactionaries and the most aggressive of the German militarists. If the German populace had willingly accepted the Nazi program, no Storm-troopers would have been needed in the early days of the Party and there would have been no need for concentration camps or the Gestapo, both of which institutions were inaugurated as soon as the Nazis gained control of the German State" (*Trial of the Major War Criminals before the International Military Tribunal*, 2:102).

36. The Soviet witnesses included a survivor of the German pogrom in Vilna, a survivor of Treblinka, and former inmates of Auschwitz and Majdanek.

37. Gilbert, *Nuremberg Diary*, 161.

38. Unlike the camps encountered by the American and British forces, Auschwitz had been shut down and for the most part evacuated by camp personnel—the inmates taken on the infamous death marches to points west—when Soviet troops overtook the site in January 1945. Next to the graphic images shot by the Army Signal Corps of concentration camps "still in operation," then, the Soviet footage appears considerably less "spectacular" even while nearly six thousand prisoners remained in and around the camp premises. Still, inmates who did survive and were brought back to health or were at least strong enough to stand performed their liberation for the camera weeks after the original arrival of troops: they are shown cheering and happily greeting soldiers as they streamed through the camp's gates. The scene was not scripted, but it was certainly staged. Majdanek, on the other hand, was still in operation when Soviet troops arrived in July 1944, and the film taken by Soviet crews is every bit as horrendous as the footage gathered by American and British troops. Soviet film of the liberation of both camps has only recently been made available for distribution: *Holocaust: The Liberation of Majdanek* (2006, 60 min.), Irmgard Von Zur Mühlen, director; *Holocaust: The Liberation of Auschwitz* (2005, 53 min.), Irmgard Von Zur Mühlen, director.

39. Taylor, *The Anatomy of the Nuremberg Trials*, 187.

40. Landsman, *Crimes of the Holocaust*, 28. See also Jessica M. Silbey, "Judges as Film Critics: New Approaches to Filmic Evidence," *Suffolk University Law School: Faculty Publications*, http://lsr.nellco.org/suffolk/fp/papers/17 2004. One of the issues here is the blurred line between "illustration" and "proof": Donovan presented the films at Nuremberg as a "demonstrative aid" marshaled to explain other evidence of the prosecution's case. However, in the context of the court—and for the public at large, clearly—the footage was treated as evidence or proof, even while the claims it advanced and the point of view it occupied escaped interrogation. This is where the court's confidence (and the public's as well) in the presumed objectivity and factual transparency of the camera comes into play. Does it matter, for example, that the Soviet film presented a reenacted liberation of Auschwitz or attributed a depicted massacre to German soldiers that had actually been committed by Soviet forces? Is it relevant that U.S. troops had rearranged bodies and artifacts in the camps for filmic and didactic effect?

41. Cited in Sprecher, *Inside the Nuremberg Trial*, 1:621.

42. John Tagg, *The Disciplinary Frame: Photographic Truths and the Capture of Meaning* (Minneapolis: University of Minnesota Press, 2009), 90.

43. See Robert Hariman and John Louis Lucaites, *No Caption Needed: Iconic Photographs, Public Culture, and Liberal Democracy* (Chicago: University of Chicago Press, 2007), 55.

44. Tagg, *The Disciplinary Frame*, 93.

45. It bears mentioning that many of the films produced under the authority of various New Deal agencies were translated into German and shown in theaters, schools, and town meetings across Germany to "highlight the virtues of grassroots democracy and social

cooperation, introduce civic and equalitarian values, and stress the virtues of tolerance, cooperation, and solidarity." Cora Sol Goldstein, *Capturing the German Eye: American Visual Propaganda in Occupied Germany* (Chicago: University of Chicago Press, 2009), 49.

46. "German civilians living near the camps were . . . guided by GIs in combat gear, to follow a fixed path through barracks and open mass graves. An aspect of the museum as an educational institution was nonetheless evident in the arrangement of the relics of Nazi atrocities according to a plan. At Buchenwald, for instance, SS mementos of obscene gruesomeness—pickled human organs, remnants of human skin, shrunken heads—were placed together on a table and displayed to viewers—be they American delegations or German civilians. A mannequin was hung in a noose to demonstrate how one common torture device functioned. . . . Corpses were central elements in the visual displays. The piles of bodies on carts were not always those left by the SS. One of the most famous photographs of Buchenwald—a wagon overflowing with emaciated corpses—belonged to an exhibit in preparation. Since the bodies withered and disintegrated, every few days GIs replaced older corpses with newer bodies, reconstructing the pile for the new confrontation tours. The evidence was restaged to create a visual narrative of Nazi atrocity." Goldstein, *Capturing the German Eye*, 31. See also Robert H. Abzug, *Inside the Vicious Heart: Americans and the Liberation of Nazi Concentration Camps* (New York: Oxford University Press, 1985), 130: The bipartisan congressional committee that visited the sites issued a sixteen-page report on its return that endorsed the war crimes trial and expressed hope that the spectacle of the camps would incite "a firmer realization that men of all nations and all tongues must resist encroachments of every theory and every ideology that debases mankind and that a more just and enduring peace may arise upon the ruins and from the sacrifices which the human race has endured through one of the most crucial periods of its history."

47. The films circulated as a vehicle for argument and explanation. Consider in this regard Eisenhower's justification: "We are told the American soldier does not know what he is fighting for. Now at least he will know what he is fighting against." Cited in Abzug, *Inside the Vicious Heart*, 30.

48. Film exit interview of a German citizen included in the confidential report issued by the Psychological Warfare Division of the Supreme Headquarters of the Allied Expeditionary Force assessing the impact of atrocity films and photographs on German civilians, cited in Goldstein, *Capturing the German Eye*, 33. As a member of the military observed, watching German citizens watch the camp footage: "They didn't accept responsibility and the only sadness they showed was horror at what they saw." Cited in Abzug, *Inside the Vicious Heart*, 67.

49. Cornelia Brink, "Secular Icons: Looking at Photographs from Nazi Concentration Camps," *History and Memory* 12.1 (Spring–Summer 2000); 147. See also Goldstein's discussion, *Capturing the German Eye*, 28–44.

50. Judt, *Postwar*, 57.

51. Stephan Landsman, "Review: Those Who Remember the Past May Not Be Condemned to Repeat It," *Michigan Law Review* 100.6 (May 2002): 1571; and Landsman, *Crimes of the Holocaust*, 28. See also Jessica M. Silbey, "Judge as Film Critics: New Approaches to Filmic Evidence," *Suffolk University Law School Faculty Publications* (2004), http://lsr.nellco.org/suffolk/fp/papers/17, September 22, 2006.

52. In the immediate aftermath of the war, there perhaps were no words to describe the carnage. But to insist across the decades and in the wake of considerable scholarship since the war that this remains the case, as many do and, moreover, that the images demand such

silence in order to be both heard and understood works largely to mythify and mystify what is now a densely constructed discursive field.

53. Rebecca West took a decidedly skeptical view of the Allies' deployment of psychiatrists and psychologists to manage the accused during the trial in part because of the deception the staff perpetrated (i.e., their clearly duplicitous concern for the mental well-being of their "patients") and because for all their surveillance and close scrutiny the prisoners were hung without the world having learned "why they had done what they did." "All the Nazis . . . had been plagued by the attentions of the psychiatrists who haunted Nuremberg Jail, exercising a triple function of priest, doctor and warder hard to approve. They visited the men in the cells and offered themselves as confidants, but performed duties at the behest of the court authorities. When some of the defendants seemed to be taking an unrepentant pro-Nazi stand in their line of defense, one of the psychiatrists [Gilbert] worked out, at the comman-dant's request, a plan for a new seating arrangement at the lunch table in order to break up this group and expose them to other influences. It is not easy to think of an accused person on trial before an international tribunal being subjected to such manipulation by prison officials. There was no silver lining to this cloud. One of these psychiatrists has related, without humor-ous intention, that when Göring asked him what a certain psychological test had revealed about his character, he replied that it had shown that he lacked the guts to face responsibility." West, *A Train of Powder*, 60, 68.

54. Twenty-five hours of the ten-month trial—or what was presented at the time as its "key moments"—were filmed by members of the OSS Field Photographic Branch under the direction of John Ford, then a captain in the U.S. Navy. Novelist and screenwriter Bud Schul-berg was a member of Ford's Nuremberg film crew. Among other tasks, Schulberg gathered footage for and assembled *The Nazi Plan* with the editing assistance of Leni Riefenstahl, who he had brought to Nuremberg and held as a material witness.

55. Tagg, *The Disciplinary Frame*, 82.

56. Gilbert, *Nuremberg Diary*, 45–46. The ellipses are Gilbert's own unless enclosed in brackets.

57. Joseph Kessel, quoted in *Nuremberg: The Nazis Facing Their Crimes*.

58. "German Who Ruled Poland Gags at Buchenwald Horror Pictures," *New York Times*, July 23, 1945, A6.

59. The defendants apparently had no difficulty recognizing themselves when *The Nazi Plan* was screened over the course of two days in December. Gilbert reports that most were delighted with an interlude that enabled them to relive "good old times." Gilbert, *Nuremberg Diary*, 65–68. See also Taylor, *Anatomy of the Nuremberg Trials*, 200.

60. Quoted in Leon Goldensohn, *The Nuremberg Interviews: An American Psychiatrist's Conversations with the Defendants and Witnesses* (New York: Alfred A. Knopf, 2004), 91.

61. Cited in Gilbert, *Nuremberg Diary*, 49.

62. Fraser, *Law after Auschwitz*, 25.

63. *Trial of the Major War Criminals before the International Military Tribunal*, 2:100.

64. Fraser, *Life after Auschwitz*, 163.

65. For a fuller discussion on history of eugenics, see Daniel J. Kevles, *In the Name of Eugenics: Genetics and the Uses of Human Heredity* (Berkeley: University of California Press, 1985); and Edwin Black, *War against the Weak: Eugenics and America's Campaign to Create a Master Race* (New York: Four Walls Eight Windows, 2003). On the particular iteration of eugenics in Germany, see Robert N. Proctor, *Racial Hygiene: Medicine under the Nazis*

(Cambridge, MA: Harvard University Press, 1988); and Sheila Faith Weiss, *The Nazi Symbiosis: Human Genetics and Politics in the Third Reich* (Chicago: University of Chicago Press, 2010).

66. Fraser, *Life after Auschwitz*, 23. Mario Biagioli notes a similar impulse to quarantine "Nazi science and medicine" as incommensurable with proper medical practice and scientific research. Such a move works to preserve the objective, value-free, "truth-finding character" of scientific disciplines and rescues "'normal' medical science from being seen as implicated in the Final Solution." Biagioli, like Fraser with respect to law, resists this move as dangerously naive and urges instead an approach that tracks the ways in which the possibility of Auschwitz was (and continues to be) embedded in the legitimating cultural assumptions and practices of "normal science and medicine." See Biagioli, "Science, Modernity, and the Final Solution," in *Probing the Limits of Representation: Nazism and the "Final Solution,"* ed. Saul Friedländer (Cambridge, MA: Harvard University Press), 185–205. See also Simon Enoch, "The Contagion of Difference: Identity, Bio-politics, and National Socialism," *Foucault Studies*, no. 1 (December 2004): 53–70.

67. Robert H. Jackson, "Justice Jackson Weighs Nuremberg's Lessons," *New York Times*, June 16, 1946, SM7. See also Taylor, *Anatomy of the Nuremberg Trials*, 527.

68. Fraser, *Life after Auschwitz*, 25.

69. Consider in this regard the trajectory of the category "asocial"—attached to homosexuals, for example, as well as Gypsies. With the liberation of the camps many individuals so designated were simply reincarcerated as "common criminals"; being distinguished from among the regime's real "victims"—those groups victimized for "no reason" in the course of the regime's ever-expanding conspiracy against the peace—they were also considered ineligible for compensation. In Fraser's view, this clearly underscores the continuity of classificatory schemes across political and legal regimes that Nuremberg is complicit in naturalizing and/or obscuring: "Claims that Nazi law was not law because it singled out specific groups and members of those groups for criminalization and exclusion on the basis of a theory of racial inferiority and/or in order to protect the physical and social well-being of the body politic from outsiders . . . simply cannot stand up to critical examination." Fraser, *Law after Auschwitz*, 45.

70. Actually, it entailed many changes in definition. Hilberg is referring here to the Nuremberg Laws of 1935 and efforts within Germany to determine what constituted a "Jew." But these efforts followed a decades-long interest in Germany and other scientifically advanced countries to devise classificatory systems that might enable states to sort populations according to "hereditary burdens." And one of the promising vectors for implementing such systems was the criminal code. When the International Federation of Eugenic Organizations met in September 1929 at the Statistical Institute in Italy, grand designs were set out for ridding the world of the unfit, continent and country by continent and country. The starting point was to be the American continent because "America was still the only country with years of experience in state-sanctioned sterilization and other eugenic legislation. . . . Changes in the German Criminal code were coming and these would soon enable widespread sterilization and other eugenic methods as well." Black, *War against the Weak*, 280; Raul Hilberg, *The Destruction of the European Jews* (New Haven: Yale University Press, 2003), 1:61. See also Saul Friedländer, *Nazi Germany and the Jews*, vol. 1: *The Years of Persecution* (New York: HarperPerennial, 1997), esp. chap. 5; Henry Friedländer, "German Law and German Crimes in the Nazi Era," in *The Holocaust's Ghost: Writing on Art, Politics, Law, and Education*, ed. F. C. Decoste and Bernard Schwartz (Edmonton: University of Alberta Press, 1997), 283–89; and Alan E. Steinweis, *Studying the Jew: Scholarly Antisemitism in Nazi Germany* (Cambridge,

MA: Harvard University Press, 2006), 41–46. On the Nuremberg Laws of 1935, see Karl A. Schleunes, ed., *Legislating the Holocaust: The Bernhard Loesener Memoirs and Supporting Documents* (Boulder, CO: Westview Press, 2001).

71. Fraser, *Law after Auschwitz*, 12.

72. Judt, "The Past Is Another Country," 296–98.

73. For an elaboration on this and related themes, see Janina Struk, *Photographing the Holocaust: Interpretations of the Evidence* (New York: I. B. Tauris, 2004); Barbie Zelizer, *Remembering to Forget: Holocaust Memory through the Camera's Eye* (Chicago: University of Chicago Press, 1998); Richard Raskin, *A Child at Gunpoint: A Case Study in the Life of a Photo* (Aarhus, Denmark: Aarhus University Press, 2004).

NOTES TO CHAPTER 5

1. Hannah Arendt, "On Hannah Arendt," in *The Recovery of the Public World*, ed. Melvyn A. Hill (New York: St. Martin's Press, 1979), 307.

2. "Non-thinking, which seems so recommended a state for political and moral affairs . . . has its dangers. By shielding people against the dangers of examination, it teaches them to hold fast to whatever the prescribed rules of conduct may be at a given time in a given society. What people then get used to is not so much the content of the rules, a close examination of which would always lead them into perplexity, as the possession of rules under which to subsume particulars. In other words, they get used to never making up their minds." Hannah Arendt, "Thinking and Moral Considerations," in *Responsibility and Judgment*, ed. Jerome Kohn (New York: Schocken Books, 2003), 178.

3. Arendt, "On Hannah Arendt," 309.

4. "So I think that this 'thinking,' about which I wrote and am writing now—thinking in the Socratic sense—is a maieutic function, a midwifery. That is, you bring out all your opinions, prejudices, what have you; and you know that never, in any of the [Platonic] dialogues did Socrates ever discover any child [of the mind] who was not a wind egg. That you remain in a way empty after thinking . . . [a]nd once you are empty, then, in a way which is difficult to say, you are prepared to judge. That is, without having any book of rules under which you can subsume the particular case, you have got to say 'this is good,' 'this is bad,' 'this is right,' 'this is wrong.'" Arendt, unpublished talk, cited in Elisabeth Young-Bruehl, *Hannah Arendt: For Love of the World* (New Haven: Yale University Press, 1982), 452.

5. Hannah Arendt, "Some Questions of Moral Philosophy," in *Responsibility and Judgment*, 78.

6. The problem Arendt subsequently set for herself was more generally to establish whether there was an "inner connection between the ability or inability to think and the problem of evil." Arendt, "Thinking and Moral Considerations," 160.

7. Peter Baehr, "Banality and Cleverness: Eichmann in Jerusalem Revisited," in *Thinking in Dark Times: Hannah Arendt on Ethics and Politics*, ed. Roger Berkowitz, Jeffrey Katz, and Thomas Keenan (New York: Fordham University Press, 2010), 142.

8. Hannah Arendt, "Eichmann in Jerusalem: An Exchange of Letters between Gershom Scholem and Hannah Arendt," in *The Jew as Pariah: Jewish Identity and Politics in the Modern Age*, ed. Ron H. Feldman (New York: Grove Press, 1978), 245.

9. Dana R. Villa, *Politics, Philosophy, Terror: Essays on the Thought of Hannah Arendt* (Princeton: Princeton University Press, 1999), 41.

10. Young-Bruehl, *Hannah Arendt*, 367. Young-Bruehl continues: "The banality of evil, [Arendt] said in the last sentence of her book, is 'fearsome, word-and-thought-defying.' But its

existence is not proof of an original evil element in human nature and hence not an indictment of mankind."

11. Margaret Canovan, *Hannah Arendt: A Reinterpretation of Her Political Thought* (Cambridge: Cambridge University Press, 1992), 24 n. 30. Richard J. Bernstein, *Hannah Arendt and the Jewish Question* (Cambridge, MA: MIT Press, 1996), 152: "Did Arendt ever believe that Nazi crimes could be adequately explained as the 'deeds of monsters and demons'? No! She explicitly and consistently 'totally rejects' such an understanding of Nazi criminality. Did Arendt ever think that anything like 'satanic greatness' was a relevant concept for understanding the evil of totalitarian domination? No! Already in 1946 she makes it perfectly clear that she rejects such a notion—and even criticizes those formulations she uses that suggest such an understanding of Nazi evil. Arendt resists all tendencies to mythologize or aestheticize the radical evil of totalitarianism."

12. Canovan, *Hannah Arendt*, 24 n. 30.

13. Hannah Arendt, *The Origins of Totalitarianism* (New York: Meridian Press, 1958), 441.

14. Lotte Kohler and Hans Saner, eds., *Hannah Arendt / Karl Jaspers Correspondence: 1926–1969*, (New York: Harcourt Brace Jovanovich, 1992), 62. How odd that Jaspers would marshal the language and imagery that the Nazis themselves deployed to great effect to describe enemies of the state and legitimize the "medical" actions that were then taken against them.

15. Hannah Arendt, "Eichmann in Jerusalem," in Feldman, *The Jew as Pariah*, 250–51; emphasis added.

16. Hannah Arendt, "Religion and Politics," in *Essays in Understanding, 1930–1954*, ed. Jerome Kohn (New York: Harcourt Brace, 1994), 383; see also Arendt, *Origins of Totalitarianism*, 446–77.

17. Hannah Arendt, "On the Nature of Totalitarianism," in Kohn, *Essays in Understanding*, 352–53.

18. Arendt's word was "overrated." Hannah Arendt, *Between Friends: The Correspondence of Hannah Arendt and Mary McCarthy, 1949–1975*, ed. Carol Brightman (New York: Harcourt Brace, 1995), 147–48. See also Arendt, *The Origins of Totalitarianism*, 440 .

19. Arendt, *The Origins of Totalitarianism*, 440.

20. Arendt, *Between Friends*, 147–48.

21. Arendt, *The Origins of Totalitarianism*, 441.

22. Elisabeth Young-Bruehl, *Why Arendt Matters* (New Haven: Yale University Press, 2006), 108.

23. State of Israel Ministry of Justice, *The Trial of Adolf Eichmann, Volume IV* (session 106), 1815, 1820. Eichmann was referring, specifically, to the failed assassination attempt of Hitler in July 1944, which was organized by high-ranking members of the army and their civilian allies. Elsewhere, in an interview conducted before his capture, Eichmann referred to those who broke their military oath to join the ranks of the conspirators as "despicable pigs." *Life Magazine*, November 28, 1960.

24. State of Israel Ministry of Justice, *The Trial of Adolf Eichmann, Volume IV* (session 106), 1820.

25. State of Israel Ministry of Justice, *The Trial of Adolf Eichmann, Volume IV* (session 106), 1813; see also 1805–23. It was not entirely clear whether Eichmann was actually interested in having the opportunity to set the record straight, as he claimed, or adding to his notoriety by having undergone a lengthy cross-examination. About the latter he clearly took some pride. Judge: "Do you want—are you sure you want the truth about you to be known?"; Eichmann:

"Yes, indeed, and above all I also wish—I also had an interest in my own family being able to say here, my own sons being able to say to any people who might or could come to them on the basis of the propaganda there has been: 'You see, he was cross-examined, in the longest known cross-examination ever, and he said the truth so-and-so,' that is why I was interested in their being a lengthy cross-examination."

26. State of Israel Ministry of Justice, *The Trial of Adolf Eichmann, Volume IV* (session 106), 1810–11.

27. Adi Ophir, *The Order of Evils: Toward an Ontology of Morals* (Brooklyn, NY: Zone Books, 2005), 444. See also Peg Birmingham's *Hannah Arendt and Human Rights: The Predicament of Common Responsibility* (Bloomington: Indiana University Press, 2006).

28. Tony Judt, *Postwar: A History of Europe since 1945* (New York: Penguin, 2005), 61. See also S. M. Plokhy, *Yalta: The Price of Peace* (New York: Viking, 2010).

29. On this, consider the following passage from an article that appeared in 1946 in the *Atlantic Monthly*, written by ambulance driver and war correspondent, Edgar L. Jones. Jones's article was published well before the cold war had heated up and before the constitutive components of the mid-twentieth-century iteration of American exceptionalism had fully congealed. His observations nevertheless suggest that the popular and political mythologies that would cement a particular set of stories about the benevolent/liberating nature of U.S. interventions abroad were already at work. Jones writes: "What kind of war do civilians suppose we fought, anyway? We shot prisoners in cold blood, wiped out hospitals, strafed lifeboats, killed or mistreated enemy civilians, finished off the enemy wounded, tossed the dying into a hole with the dead, and in the Pacific boiled the flesh off enemy skulls to make table ornaments for sweethearts or carved their bones into letter openers. . . . As victors we are privileged to try our defeated opponents for their crimes against humanity, but we should be realistic enough to appreciate that if we were on trial for breaking international law, we should be found guilty on a dozen counts." Cited in James J. Weingartner, *Americans, Germans, and War Crimes Justice: Law, Memory, and 'The Good War'* (Santa Barbara, CA: Praeger, 2011), ix. It speaks to the power of these myths that an American public could by and large excuse the My Lai massacre of the Vietnam War and later accept that Abu Ghraib was, as former President George W. Bush insisted, merely the disgraceful conduct of a renegade few—even while the genocide of the former and the torture of the latter were state-sanctioned techniques on behalf of national security. See Michael Belknap, *The Vietnam War on Trial: The My Lai Massacre and the Court-Martial of Lieutenant Calley* (Lawrence: University Press of Kansas, 2002); Mark Danner, *Tortue and Truth: America, Abu Ghraib, and the War on Terror* (New York: New York Review Books, 2004); Andrew J. Bacevich, *Washington Rules: America's Path to Permanent War* (New York: Henry Holt, 2010).

30. Ophir, *The Order of Evils*, 280–97.

31. Bacevich, *Washington Rules*, 101.

32. Zygmunt Bauman, "The Holocaust's Life as a Ghost," in *The Holocaust's Ghost: Writings on Art, Politics, Law, and Education*, ed. F. C. Decoste and Bernard Schwartz (Edmonton: University of Alberta Press, 1997), 13.

33. Ophir, *The Order of Evils*, 625.

Bibliography

Abel, Lionel. "The Aesthetics of Evil." *Partisan Review* 30.2 (1963): 211–30.

Abraham, David. "Truth, Law, and History: New Departures in Israeli Legal History, Part One: Where Hannah Arendt Went Wrong." *Law and History Review* 18 (Fall 2000): 607–12.

Abzug, Robert H. *Inside the Vicious Heart: Americans and the Liberation of Nazi Concentration Camps.* New York: Oxford University Press, 1985.

Adams, Paul C., Steven Hoelscher, and Karen E. Till, eds. *Textures of Place: Exploring Humanist Geographies.* Minneapolis: University of Minnesota Press, 2001.

Agamben, Giorgio. *Homo Sacer: Sovereign Power and Bare Life.* Stanford, CA: Stanford University Press, 1998.

———. *Means without End: Notes on Politics.* Minneapolis: University of Minnesota Press, 2000.

———. *Remnants of Auschwitz: The Witness and the Archive.* New York: Zone Books, 1999.

———. *State of Exception.* Chicago: University of Chicago Press, 2005.

Aharoni, Zvi, and William Dietl. *Operation Eichmann: The Truth about the Pursuit, Capture, and Trial.* New York: Wiley, 1996..

Alexander, Jeffrey C. "On the Social Construction of Moral Universals: The 'Holocaust' from War Crime to Trauma Drama." *European Journal of Social Theory* 5.1 (2002): 5–85.

Alford, C. Fred. "Hitler's Willing Executioners: What Does 'Willing' Mean?" *Theory and Society* 26 (1997): 719–38.

———. *Rethinking Freedom: Why Freedom Has Lost Its Meaning and What Can Be Done about It.* New York: Palgrave, 2005.

———. *The Self in Social Theory: A Psychoanalytic Account of Its Construction in Plato, Hobbes, Locke, Rawls, and Rousseau.* New Haven: Yale University Press, 1991.

———. *What Evil Means to Us.* Ithaca: Cornell University Press, 1997.

Allen, Jonathan. "Balancing Justice and Social Unity: Political Theory and the Idea of a Truth and Reconciliation Commission." *University of Toronto Law Journal* 49.3 (Summer 1999): 315–53.

Allen, Michael Thad. *The Business of Genocide: The SS, Slave Labor, and the Concentration Camps.* Chapel Hill: University of North Carolina Press, 2002.

Aly, Götz. *Final Solution: Nazi Population Policy and the Murder of European Jews.* New York: Arnold, 1999.

———. *Hitler's Beneficiaries: Plunder, Racial War, and the Nazi Welfare State.* New York: Henry Holt, 2006.

———. "'Jewish Resettlement': Reflections on the Political Prehistory of the Holocaust." In *National Socialist Extermination Policies: Contemporary German Perspectives and Controversies,* ed. Ulrich Herbert, 53–82. New York: Berghahn Books, 2000.

———. "The Planning Intelligentsia and the 'Final Solution.'" In *The Holocaust: Origins, Implementation, Aftermath,* ed. Omer Bartov, 92–105. New York: Routledge, 2000.

Aly, Götz, Peter Chroust, and Christian Pross. *Cleansing the Fatherland: Nazi Medicine and Racial Hygiene*. Trans. Belinder Cooper. Baltimore: Johns Hopkins University Press, 1994.

Aly, Götz, and Susanne Heim. *Architects of Annihilation: Auschwitz and the Logic of Destruction*. Trans. A.G. Blunden. Princeton: Princeton University Press, 2002.

Aly, Götz, and Karl Heinz Roth. *The Nazi Census: Identification and Control in the Third Reich*. Philadelphia: Temple University Press, 2004.

An-Na'im, Abdullahi Ahmed, ed. *Human Rights in Cross-Cultural Perspective: A Quest for Consensus*. Philadelphia: University of Pennsylvania Press, 1992.

Arendt, Hannah. *Between Friends: The Correspondence of Hannah Arendt and Mary McCarthy, 1949–1975*. Ed. Carol Brightman. New York: Harcourt Brace, 1995.

———. *Between Past and Future*. New York: Penguin, 1977.

———. *Crises of the Republic*. New York: Harcourt Brace, 1972.

———. *Eichmann in Jerusalem: A Report on the Banality of Evil*. New York: Penguin, 1964.

———. *Essays in Understanding, 1930–1954*. Ed. Jerome Kohn. New York: Harcourt Brace, 1994.

———. *Hannah Arendt and Martin Heidegger, Letters, 1925–1975*. New York: Harcourt, 2004.

———. *The Human Condition*. Chicago: University of Chicago Press, 1958.

———. *The Jewish Writings*. Ed. Jerome Kohn and Ron H. Feldman. New York: Schocken Books, 2007.

———. *Lectures on Kant's Political Philosophy*. Ed. Ronald Beiner. Chicago: University of Chicago Press, 1992.

———. *The Life of the Mind*. Vol. I: *Thinking*. New York: Harcourt Brace Jovanovich, 1977.

———. *On Revolution*. New York: Viking, 1965.

———. *The Origins of Totalitarianism*. New York: Meridian Press, 1958.

———. *The Promise of Politics*. Ed. Jerome Kohn. New York: Schocken Books, 2005.

———. *Responsibility and Judgment*. Ed. Jerome Kohn. New York: Schocken Books, 2004.

———. "Thinking and Moral Considerations." *Social Research* 38.3 (1971): 417–46.

———. *Within Four Walls: The Correspondence between Hannah Arendt and Heinrich Blücher, 1936–1968*. New York: Harcourt, 2000.

Aschheim, Steven, ed. *Hannah Arendt in Jerusalem*. Berkeley: University of California Press, 2001.

Azoulay, Ariella. *The Civil Contract of Photography*. New York: Zone Books, 2008.

Baade, Hans. "The Eichmann Trial: Some Legal Aspects." *Duke Law Journal* 3 (1961): 400–420.

Bacevich, Andrew J. *Washington Rules: America's Path to Permanent War*. New York: Henry Holt, 2010.

Baehr, Peter. "Banality and Cleverness: Eichmann in Jerusalem Revisited." In *Thinking in Dark Times: Hannah Arendt on Ethics and Politics*, ed. Roger Berkowitz, Jeffrey Katz, and Thomas Keenan, 139–44. New York: Fordham University Press, 2010.

Ball, Howard. *Prosecuting War Crimes and Genocide: The Twentieth-Century Experience*. Lawrence: University Press of Kansas, 1999.

Ballinger, Pamela. "The Culture of Survivors." *History and Memory* 10.1 (1998): 99–132.

Bankier, David. *The Germans and the Final Solution: Public Opinion under Nazism*. Cambridge, MA: Blackwell, 1996.

Barnouw, Dagmar. *Visible Spaces: Hannah Arendt and the German-Jewish Experience*. Baltimore: Johns Hopkins University Press, 1990.

Baron, Lawrence. *Projecting the Holocaust into the Present: The Changing Focus of Contemporary Holocaust Cinema*. New York: Rowman & Littlefield, 2005.

Barradori, Giovanna. *Philosophy in a Time of Terror: Dialogues with Jürgen Habermas and Jacques Derrida*. Chicago: University of Chicago Press, 2003.

Bartov, Omer. *Germany's War and the Holocaust: Disputed Histories*. Ithaca: Cornell University Press, 2003.

———. *Mirrors of Destruction: War, Genocide, and Modern Identity*. New York: Oxford University Press, 2000.

———. *Murder in Our Midst: The Holocaust, Industrial Killing, and Representation*. New York: Oxford University Press, 1996.

———, ed. *The Holocaust: Origins, Implementations, Aftermath*. New York: Routledge, 2000.

Bass, Gary Jonathan. *Stay the Hand of Vengeance: The Politics of War Crimes Tribunals*. Princeton: Princeton University Press, 2000.

Bathrick, David, Brad Prager, and Michael D. Richardson, eds. *Visualizing the Holocaust: Documents, Aesthetics, Memory*. Rochester, NY: Camden House, 2008.

Bauer, Yehuda. *Rethinking the Holocaust*. New Haven: Yale University Press, 2001.

Bauman, Zygmunt. "The Holocaust's Life as a Ghost." In *Social Theory after the Holocaust*, ed. Robert Fine and Charles Turner, 7–18. London: Liverpool University Press, 2000.

———. *Modernity and the Holocaust*. Ithaca, NY: Cornell University Press, 1989.

Beilharz, Peter, Gillian Robinson, and John Rundell, eds. *Between Totalitarianism and Postmodernity*. Cambridge, MA: MIT Press, 1992.

Beiner, Ronald. *Political Judgment*. London: Methuen, 1983.

———, ed. "Interpretive Essay." In *Hannah Arendt: Lectures on Kant's Political Philosophy*. Chicago: University of Chicago Press, 1992.

Belknap, Michael R. *The Vietnam War on Trial: The My Lai Massacre and the Court-Martial of Lieutenant Calley*. Lawrence: University Press of Kansas, 2002.

Ben-Gurion, David. *Israel: A Personal Story*. New York: New English Library, 1972.

Benhabib, Seyla. "Identity, Perspective, and Narrative in Hannah Arendt's Eichmann in Jerusalem." *History and Memory* 8.2 (1996): 35–59.

———. "Judgment and the Moral Foundations of Politics in Arendt's Thought." *Political Theory* 16.1 (1988): 29–51.

———. *The Reluctant Modernism of Hannah Arendt*. Thousand Oaks, CA: Sage, 1996.

Bennett, Tony. "Pedagogic Objects, Clean Eyes, and Popular Instruction: Sensory Regimes and Museum Didactics." *Configurations* 6.3 (1998): 345–71.

Bennett, William J. *Why We Fight: Moral Clarity and the War on Terrorism*. Washington, DC: Regnery, 2003.

Benton, Wilbourn E., and Georg Grimm. *Nuremberg: German Views of the War Trials*. Dallas: Southern Methodist University Press, 1955.

Berenbaum, Michael. *The World Must Know: The History of the Holocaust as Told through the United States Holocaust Memorial Museum*. New York: Little, Brown, 1993.

Bergen, Bernard J. *The Banality of Evil: Hannah Arendt and "the Final Solution."* New York: Rowman & Littlefield, 1998.

Berkowitz, Roger, Jeffrey Katz, and Thomas Keenan, eds. *Thinking in Dark Times: Hannah Arendt on Ethics and Politics*. New York: Fordham University Press, 2010.

Bernstein, Richard J. *The Abuse of Evil: The Corruption of Politics and Religion since 9/11*. Malden, MA: Polity Press, 2005.

———. *Hannah Arendt and the Jewish Question*. Cambridge, MA: MIT Press, 1996.

———. *Radical Evil: A Philosophical Interrogation*. Malden, MA: Polity Press, 2002.

Best, Steven. *The Politics of Historical Vision: Marx, Foucault, Habermas*. New York: Guilford Press, 1995.

Biagioli, Mario. "Science, Modernity, and the Final Solution." In *Probing the Limits of Representation*, ed. Saul Friedländer, 185–205. Cambridge, MA: Harvard University Press, 1992.

Bilsky, Leora Y. "Judgment in the Shadow of the Holocaust: Introduction." *Theoretical Inquiries in Law* 1 (July 2000): 237–43.

———. "Judgment in the Shadow of the Holocaust: Section 3: Arendt on Eichmann: A Reappraisal: In a Different Voice: Nathan Alterman and Hannah Arendt on the Kastner and Eichmann Trials." *Theoretical Inquiries in Law* 1 (July 2000): 509–47.

———. "When Actor and Spectator Meet in the Courtroom: Reflections on Hannah Arendt's Concept of Judgment." *History and Memory* 8.2 (1996): 137–73.

Birmingham, Peg. *Hannah Arendt and Human Rights: The Predicament of Common Responsibility*. Bloomington: Indiana University Press, 2006.

———. "Holes of Oblivion: The Banality of Radical Evil." *Hypatia* 18.1 (Winter 2003): 80–103.

———. "A Lying World Order: Political Deception and the Threat of Totalitarianism." In *Thinking in Dark Times: Hannah Arendt on Ethics and Politics*, ed. Roger Berkowitz, Jeffrey Katz, and Thomas Keenan, 73–77. New York: Fordham University Press, 2010.

Black, Edwin. *The Transfer Agreement: The Dramatic Story of the Pact between the Third Reich and Jewish Palestine*. New York: Carroll & Graf, 2001.

———. *War against the Weak: Eugenics and America's Campaign to Create a Master Race*. New York: Four Walls Eight Windows, 2003.

Bloxham, Donald. *Genocide on Trial: War Crimes Trials and the Formation of Holocaust History and Memory*. Oxford: Oxford University Press, 2001.

Boltanski, Luc. *Distant Suffering: Morality, Media, and Politics*. New York: Cambridge University Press, 1999.

Bosch, William J. *Judgment on Nuremberg: American Attitudes toward the Major German War-Crime Trials*. Chapel Hill: University of North Carolina Press, 1970.

Bowker, Geoffrey C., and Leigh Star. *Sorting Things Out: Classification and Its Consequences*. Cambridge, MA: MIT Press, 2000.

Brackman, Arnold C. *The Other Nuremberg: The Untold Story of the Tokyo War Crime Trials*. London: William Collins Sons & Co., 1989

Braiterman, Zachery. 2000. "Against Holocaust-Sublime: Naive Reference and the Generation of Memory." *History and Memory* 12.2 (2000): 7–28.

Braun, Kathrin. "Biopolitics and Temporality in Arendt and Foucault." *Time and Society* 16.5 (2007): 5–23.

Braun, Robert. "The Holocaust and Problems of Representation." *History and Theory* 33.2 (May 1994): 172–97.

Brayard, Florent. "Grasping the Spokes of the Wheel of History: Gerstein, Eichmann, and the Genocide of the Jews." *History and Memory* 20.1 (2008): 48–88.

Breitman, Richard. "Plans for the Final Solution in Early 1941." *German Studies Review* 17.3 (1994): 483–93.

Brennan, Teresa, and Martin Jay, eds. *Vision in Context: Historical and Contemporary Perspectives on Sight*. New York: Routledge, 1996.

Brink, Cornelia. "Secular Icons: Looking at Photographs from Nazi Concentration Camps." *History and Memory* 12.1 (2000): 135–50.

Brooks, Roy L. *Atonement and Forgiveness: A New Model for Black Reparations*. Berkeley: University of California Press, 2004.

Brower, Benjamin C. "The Preserving Machine: The 'New' Museum and Working through Trauma—The Musee Memorial pour la Paix of Caen." *History and Memory* 11.1 (1999): 77–103.

Browning, Christopher R. *Ordinary Men: Reserve Police Battalion 101 and the Final Solution in Poland*. New York: Penguin, 2005.

———. *The Path to Genocide*. New York: Oxford University Press, 1992.

Browning, Christopher R., with Jürgen Matthäus. *The Origins of the Final Solution: The Evolution of Nazi Jewish Policy, September 1939–March 1942*. Lincoln: University of Nebraska Press, 2004.

Brunner, Jose. "Judgment in the Shadow of the Holocaust: Section 3: Arendt on Eichmann: A Reappraisal: Eichmann's Mind: Psychological, Philosophical, and Legal Perspectives." *Theoretical Inquiries in Law* 1 (July 2000): 429–63.

Bryant, Michael S. *Confronting the "Good Death": Nazi Euthanasia on Trial, 1945–1953*. Boulder: University Press of Colorado, 2005.

Burchell, Graham, Colin Gordon, and Peter Miller, eds. *The Foucault Effect: Studies in Governmentality*. Chicago: University of Chicago Press, 1991.

Burleigh, Michael, ed. *Confronting the Nazi Past: New Debates in Modern German History*. New York: St. Martin's Press, 1996.

———. "Psychiatry, German Society, and the Nazi 'Euthanasia' Programme." In *The Holocaust: Origins, Implementations, Aftermath*, ed. Omer Bartov, 43–62. New York: Routledge, 2000.

Burleigh, Michael, and Wolfgang Wippermann. *The Racial State: Germany, 1933–1945*. Cambridge: Cambridge University Press, 1991.

Calhoun, Craig, and John McGowan, eds. *Hannah Arendt and the Meaning of Politics*. Minneapolis: University of Minnesota Press, 1997.

Cameron, Norman, and R. H. Stevens, trans. *Hitler's Table Talk: 1941–1944*. New York: Enigma Books, 2000.

Canovan, Margaret. *Hannah Arendt: A Reinterpretation of Her Political Thought*. Cambridge: Cambridge University Press, 1992.

Cargas, Harry James, ed. *Problems Unique to the Holocaust*. Lexington: University of Kentucky Press, 1999.

Carr, David. "Place and Time: On the Interplay of Historical Points of View." *History and Theory* 40.4 (2001): 153–67.

Caruth, Cathy. *Empirical Truths and Critical Fictions*. Baltimore: Johns Hopkins University Press, 1991.

———. "Lying and History." In *Thinking in Dark Times: Hannah Arendt on Ethics and Politics*, ed. Roger Berkowitz, Jeffrey Katz, and Thomas Keenan, 79–92. New York: Fordham University Press, 2010.

———, ed. *Trauma: Explorations in Memory*. Baltimore: Johns Hopkins University Press, 1995.

Cesarani, David. *Eichmann: His Life and Crimes*. New York: Vintage, 2005.

———, ed. *The Final Solution: Origins and Implementation*. New York: Routledge, 1996.

Childers, Thomas, and Jane Caplan, eds. *Reevaluating the Third Reich*. New York: Holmes and Meier, 1993.

Chouliaraki, Lilie. *The Spectatorship of Suffering*. Thousand Oaks, CA: Sage, 2006.

Clendinnen, Inga. *Reading the Holocaust.* Cambridge: Cambridge University Press, 1999.

Cohen, Josh. *Interrupting Auschwitz: Art, Religion, Philosophy.* New York: Continuum, 2005.

Cole, Tim. *Selling the Holocaust: From Auschwitz to Schindler. How History Is Bought, Packaged, and Sold.* New York: Routledge, 1999.

———. "Popularization and Memory: The Case of Anne Frank." In *Lessons and Legacies: The Meaning of the Holocaust in a Changing World,* ed. Peter Hayes. Evanston, IL: Northwestern University Press, 1991.

Conot, Robert E. *Justice at Nuremberg.* New York: Carroll & Graf, 1983.

Cooke, Lynne, and Peter Wollen, eds. *Visual Display: Culture beyond Appearances.* New York: New Press, 1998.

Cornwell, John. *Hitler's Scientists: Science, War, and the Devil's Pact.* New York: Penguin, 2004.

Crampton, Jeremy W., and Stuart Elden, eds. *Space, Knowledge, and Power: Foucault and Geography.* Burlington, VT: Ashgate, 2010.

Crowe, David M. *Oscar Schindler: The Untold Account of His Life, Wartime Activities, and the True Story Behind the List.* Boulder, CO: Westview Press, 2004.

Curren, Vivian Grosswald. Review of *The Memory of Judgment: Making Law and History in the Trials of the Holocaust,* by Lawrence Douglas. *University of Toronto Law Journal* 53.3 (Summer 2003): (3): 305–23.

Curtis, Kimberley. *Our Sense of the Real: Aesthetic Experience and Arendtian Politics.* Ithaca: Cornell University Press, 1999.

Danner, Mark. *Torture and Truth: America, Abu Ghraib, and the War on Terror.* New York: New York Books, 2004.

Deák, István, Jan T. Gross, and Tony Judt, eds. *The Politics of Retribution in Europe: World War II and Its Aftermath.* Princeton: Princeton University Press, 2000.

Dean, Carolyn J. *The Fragility of Empathy: After the Holocaust.* Ithaca: Cornell University Press, 2004.

De Brito, Alexandra Barahona, Carmen Gonzaléz-Enríquez, and Paloma Auilar. *The Politics of Memory: Transitional Justice in Democratizing Societies.* Oxford: Oxford University Press, 2001.

De Coste, F. C., and Bernard Schwartz, eds. *The Holocaust's Ghost: Writings on Art, Politics, Law, and Education.* Edmonton: University of Alberta Press, 2000.

Didion, Joan. *Fixed Ideas: America since 9.11.* New York: New York Review Books, 2003.

Diner, Dan. *Beyond the Conceivable: Studies on Germany, Nazism, and the Holocaust.* Berkeley: University of California Press, 2000.

———. "On Guilt Discourse and Other Narratives." *History and Memory* 8.2 (1996): 301–20.

Diner, Dan, and Rita Bashaw. "Hannah Arendt Reconsidered: On the Banal and the Evil in Her Holocaust Narrative." *New German Critique* 71 (Spring–Summer 1997): 177–90.

Disch, Lisa Jane. *Hannah Arendt and the Limits of Philosophy.* Ithaca: Cornell University Press, 1994.

Doherty, Thomas. *Projections of War: Hollywood, American Culture, and World War II.* New York: Columbia University Press, 1993.

———. "World War II in Film: What Is the Color of Reality?" In *Chronicle Review: The Chronicle of Higher Education,* October 9, 1998, B4 (accessed November 21, 2007, from http://chronicle.com/weekley/v45/i07/ 07b00401.htm).

Douglas, Lawrence. *The Memory of Judgment: Making Law and History in the Trials of the Holocaust.* New Haven: Yale University Press, 2001.

Dubin, Steven C. *Displays of Power: Controversy in the American Museum from the Enola Gay to Sensation.* New York: New York University Press, 1999.

Dwork, Debórah, and Robert Jan Van Pelt. *Auschwitz: 1270 to the Present.* New York: Norton, 1996.

Eaglestone, Robert. *Postmodernism and Holocaust Denial.* London: Icon Books, 2001.

Ehrenfreund, Norbert. *The Nuremberg Legacy: How the Nazi War Crimes Trials Changed the Course of History.* New York: Palgrave, 2007.

Eisenman, Stephen F. *The Abu Ghraib Effect.* London: Reaktion Books, 2007.

Eley, Geoff, ed. *The "Goldhagen Effect": History, Memory, Nazism—Facing the German Past.* Ann Arbor: University of Michigan Press, 2000.

Elshtain, Jean Bethke. *Augustine and the Limits of Politics.* Notre Dame: University of Notre Dame Press, 1995.

Engelking, Barbara. *Holocaust and Memory: The Experience of the Holocaust and Its Consequences: An Investigation Based on Personal Narratives.* London: Leicester University Press, 2001.

Enoch, Simon. "The Contagion of Difference: Identity, Bio-politics, and National Socialism." *Foucault Studies,* no. 1 (2004): 53–70.

Eskin, Blake. *A Life in Pieces: The Making and Unmaking of Binjamin Wilkomirski.* New York: Norton, 2002.

Etlin, Richard A., ed. *Art, Culture, and Media under the Third Reich.* Chicago: University of Chicago Press, 2002.

Evans, Richard. *Lying about Hitler: History, Holocaust, and the David Irving Trial.* New York: Basic Books, 2001.

Falk, Richard. 1999. "Telford Taylor and the Legacy of Nuremberg." *Columbia Journal of Transnational Law* 37 (1999): 693–723.

Feldman, Ron H., ed. *Hannah Arendt, The Jew as Pariah: Jewish Identity and Politics in the Modern Age.* New York: Grove Press, 1978.

Felman, Shoshana. "Ghosts in the House of Justice: Death and the Language of the Law." *Yale Journal of Law and the Humanities* 13.1 (2001): 241–82.

———. "In an Era of Testimony: Claude Lanzmann's Shoah." Literature and Ethical Questions. *Yale French Studies* 79 (1991): 39–81.

———. *The Juridical Unconscious: Trials and Traumas in the Twentieth Century.* Cambridge, MA: Harvard University Press, 2002.

———. "Theaters of Justice: Arendt in Jerusalem, the Eichmann Trial, and the Redefinition of Legal Meaning in the Wake of the Holocaust." *Critical Inquiry* 27.2 (2001): 201–38.

Fest, Joachim. *Speer: The Final Verdict.* New York: Harcourt, 1999.

Fine, Robert. "Understanding Evil: Arendt and the Final Solution." In *Rethinking Evil,* ed. Maria Pia Lara, 132–52. Berkeley: University of California Press, 2001.

Fine, Robert, and Charles Turner, eds. *Social Theory after the Holocaust.* London: Liverpool University Press, 2000.

Finkelstein, Norman G. *The Holocaust Industry.* New York: Verso, 2000.

Finkelstein, Norman G., and Ruth Bettina Birn. *A Nation on Trial: The Goldhagen Thesis and Historical Truth.* New York: Henry Holt, 1998.

Finkielkraut, Alain. *Remembering in Vain: The Klaus Barbie Trial and Crimes against Humanity.* New York: Columbia University Press, 1992.

Flanzbaum, Hilene, ed. *The Americanization of the Holocaust.* Baltimore: Johns Hopkins University Press, 1999.

Foucault, Michel. *Essential Works of Foucault*. Vol. 1: *Ethics, Subjectivity, and Truth*. Ed. Paul Rabinow. New York: New Press, 1997.

——. *Power/Knowledge: Selected Interviews and Other Writings, 1972–1977*. Ed. Colin Gordon. New York: Pantheon Books, 1980.

——. *Security, Territory, Population: Lectures at the Collège de France, 1977–1978*. New York: Palgrave, 1997.

——. *Society Must Be Defended: Lectures at the Collège de France, 1975–1976*. New York: Picador Press, 1997.

Fraser, David. *Law after Auschwitz: Towards a Jurisprudence of the Holocaust*. Durham, NC: Carolina Academic Press, 2005.

Friedlander, Henry. "Step by Step: Expansion of Murder 1939–1941." In *The Holocaust: Origins, Implementation, Aftermath*, ed. Omer Bartov, 63–76. New York: Routledge, 2000.

Friedländer, Saul. "The Extermination of the European Jews in Historiography: Fifty Years Later." In *The Holocaust: Origins, Implementation, Aftermath*, ed. Omer Bartov, 79–91. New York: Routledge, 2000.

——. *Memory, History, and the Extermination of the Jews of Europe*. Bloomington: Indiana University Press, 1993.

——. *Nazi Germany and the Jews, 1939–1945: The Years of Extermination*. New York: HarperCollins, 2007.

——. *Nazi Germany and the Jews, 1933–1939: The Years of Persecution*. New York: HarperCollins, 1997.

——, ed. *Probing the Limits of Representation: Nazism and the "Final Solution."* Cambridge, MA: Harvard University Press, 1992.

Fritzsche, Peter. *Germans into Nazis*. Cambridge, MA: Harvard University Press, 1998.

Fulbrook, Mary. *German National Identity after the Holocaust*. Cambridge, MA: Polity Press, 1999.

Garrard, Eve, and Geoffrey Scarre, eds. *Moral Philosophy and the Holocaust*. Burlington, VT: Ashgate, 2003.

Geddes, Jennifer L. "Banal Evil and Useless Knowledge: Hannah Arendt and Carlotte Delbo on Evil after the Holocaust." *Hypatia* 18.1 (Winter 2003): 104–15.

Gellately, Rober, and Ben Kiernan, eds. *The Specter of Genocide: Mass Murder in Historical Perspective*. New York: Cambridge University Press, 2003.

Gerlach, Christian. "The Wannsee Conference, the Fate of German Jews, and Hitler's Decision in Principle to Exterminate All European Jews." In *The Holocaust: Origins, Implementations, Aftermath*, ed. Omer Bartov, 106–61. New York: Routledge, 2000.

Gilbert, G. M. *Nuremberg Diary*. New York: Da Capo Press, 1995.

Glover, Jonathan. *Humanity: A Moral History of the Twentieth Century*. New Haven: Yale University Press, 1999.

Goldensohn, Leon. *Nuremberg Interviews: An American Psychiatrist's Conversations with the Defendants and Witnesses*. New York: Alfred A. Knopf, 2004.

Goldhagen, Daniel Jonah. *Hitler's Willing Executioners: Ordinary Germans and the Holocaust*. New York: Vintage, 1996.

Goldstein, Cora Sol. *Capturing the German Eye: American Visual Propaganda in Occupied Germany*. Chicago: University of Chicago Press, 2009.

Gottlieb, Roger S., ed. *Thinking the Unthinkable: Meanings of the Holocaust*. New York: Paulist Press, 1990.

Gouri, Haim. *Facing the Glass Booth: The Jerusalem Trial of Adolf Eichmann*. Detroit: Wayne State University Press, 2004.

Graver, Lawrence. *An Obsession with Anne Frank*. Berkeley: University of California Press, 1995.

Guttenplan, D. D. *The Holocaust on Trial*. New York: Norton, 2001.

Haggith, Toby, and Joanna Newman, eds. *Holocaust and the Moving Image: Representations in Film and Television since 1933*. New York: Wallflower Press, 2005.

Hamburg Institute for Social Research. *The German Army and Genocide: Crimes against War Prisoners, Jews, and Other Civilians, 1939–1944*. New York: New Press, 1999.

Hansen, Phillip. *Hannah Arendt: Politics, History, and Citizenship*. Stanford: Stanford University Press, 1993.

Harel, Isser. *The House on Garibaldi Street*. London: Frank Cass, 1997.

Hariman, Robert, and John Louis Lucaites. *No Caption Needed: Iconic Photographs, Public Culture, and Liberal Democracy*. Chicago: University of Chicago Press, 2007.

Harris, Whitney R. *Tyranny on Trial: The Trial of the Major German War Criminals at the End of World War II at Nuremberg, Germany, 1945–1946*. Dallas: Southern Methodist University Press, 1954.

Hartman, Geoffrey H., ed. *Bitburg in Moral and Political Perspective*. Bloomington: Indiana University Press, 1986.

———. *Holocaust Remembrance: The Shapes of Memory*. Cambridge, MA: Blackwell, 1994.

Hasian, Marouf, Jr. *Legal Memories and Amnesias in America's Rhetorical Culture*. Boulder, CO: Westview Press, 2000.

———. *The Rhetoric of Eugenics in Anglo-American Thought*. Athens: University of Georgia Press, 1996.

———. *Rhetorical Vectors of Memory in National and International Holocaust Trials*. East Lansing: Michigan State University Press, 2006.

Hass, Aaron. *The Aftermath: Living with the Holocaust*. Cambridge: Cambridge University Press, 1996.

Hausner, Gideon. *Justice in Jerusalem*. New York: Herzl Press, 1977.

Hayes, Peter, ed. *Lessons and Legacies: The Meaning of the Holocaust in a Changing World*. Evanston, IL: Northwestern University Press, 1991.

———. *Lessons and Legacies*. Vol. 3: *Memory, Memorialization, and Denial*. Evanston, IL: Northwestern University Press, 1999.

Hayner, Priscilla B. *Unspeakable Truths: The Challenge of Truth Commissions*. New York: Routledge, 2002.

Henderson, Amy, and Adrienne L. Kaeppler, eds. *Exhibiting Dilemmas: Issues of Representation at the Smithsonian*. Washington, DC: Smithsonian Institution Press, 1997.

Herbert, Ulrich, ed. *National Socialist Extermination Policies: Contemporary German Perspectives and Controversies*. New York: Berghahn Books, 2000.

Herf, Jeffrey. *Reactionary Modernism: Technology, Culture, and Politics in Weimar and the Third Reich*. New York: Cambridge University Press, 1984.

Hilberg, Raul. *The Destruction of the European Jews: Volumes I–III*. 3rd ed. New Haven: Yale University Press, 2003.

Hill, Melvyn A., ed. *Hannah Arendt: The Recovery of the Public World*. New York: St. Martin's Press, 1979.

Hinchman, Lewis P., and Sandra K. Hinchman, eds. *Hannah Arendt: Critical Essays*. Albany: State University of New York Press, 1994.

Hirsch, Joshua. *After Image: Film, Trauma, and the Holocaust*. Philadelphia: Temple University Press, 2004.

Hoffman, Eva. *After Such Knowledge: Memory, History, and the Legacy of the Holocaust*. New York: PublicAffairs/Perseus Books, 2004.

Honig, Bonnie. "Arendt, Identity, and Difference." *Political Theory* 16.1 (1988): 77–98.

———, ed. *Feminist Interpretations of Hannah Arendt*. University Park: Pennsylvania State University Press, 1995.

Hornstein, Shelley, Laura Levitt, and Laurence J. Silberstein, eds. *Impossible Images: Contemporary Art after the Holocaust*. New York: New York University Press, 2003.

Höss, Rudolph. *Death Dealer: The Memoirs of the SS Kommandant at Auschwitz*. New York: Prometheus Books, 1992.

Hutton, Christopher M. *Race and the Third Reich*. Malden, MA: Polity Press, 2005.

Ignatieff, Michael. *Human Rights as Politics and Idolatry*. Princeton: Princeton University Press, 2001.

———. *The Lesser Evil: Political Ethics in an Age of Terror*. Princeton: Princeton University Press, 2004.

———. *The Needs of Strangers: An Essay on Privacy, Solidarity, and the Politics of Being Human*. New York: Penguin, 1984.

Insdorf, Annette. *Indelible Shadows: Film and the Holocaust*. Cambridge: Cambridge University Press, 1989.

Jackson, Michael. "The Prose of Suffering and the Practice of Silence." *Spiritus* 4 (2004): 44–59.

Jay, Martin. *The Dialectical Imagination: A History of the Frankfurt School and the Institute of Social Research, 1923–1950*. Berkeley: University of California Press, 1973.

Johnson, Eric A. *Nazi Terror: The Gestapo, Jews, and Ordinary Germans*. New York: Basic Books, 2000.

Judt, Tony. "The Past Is Another Country: Myth and Memory in Postwar Europe." In *The Politics of Retribution in Europe: World War II and Its Aftermath*, ed. István Deák, Jan T. Gross, and Tony Judt, 293–324. Princeton: Princeton University Press, 2000.

———. *Postwar: A History of Europe since 1945*. New York: Penguin, 2005.

Kaplan, Alice. *The Collaborator: The Trial and Execution of Robert Brasillach*. Chicago: University of Chicago Press, 2000.

Kaplan, Gisela T., and Clive S. Kessler. *Hannah Arendt: Thinking, Judging, Freedom*. Boston: Allen & Unwin, 1989.

Karp, Ivan, and Steven D. Lavine, eds. *Exhibiting Cultures: The Poetics and Politics of Museum Display*. Washington, DC: Smithsonian Institution Press, 1991.

Katz, Adam. 1998. "The Closure of Auschwitz but Not Its End: Alterity, Testimony, and (Post)Modernity." *History and Memory* 10.1 (1998): 59–98.

Kellner, Hans. *Language and Historical Representation*. Madison: University of Wisconsin Press, 1989.

———. "'Never Again Is Now.'" *History and Theory* 33.2 (May 1994): 127–44.

Kershaw, Ian. *Hitler: 1889–1936, Hubris*. New York: Norton, 1998.

———. *Hitler: 1936–1945, Nemesis*. New York: Norton, 2000.

———. *The Nazi Dictatorship: Problems and Perspectives of Interpretation*. New York: Oxford University Press, 2000.

Kirshenblatt-Gimblett, Barbara. *Destination Culture: Tourism, Museums, and Heritage*. Berkeley: University of California Press, 1998.

Klee, Ernst, Willi Dressen, and Volker Riess, eds. *"The Good Old Days": The Holocaust as Seen by Perpetrators and Bystanders*. New York: Free Press, 1991.

Kleeblatt, Norman L., ed. *Mirroring Evil: Nazi Imagery/Recent Art*. New Brunswick, NJ: Rutgers University Press, 2002.

Klemperer, Victor. *I Will Bear Witness: 1933–1941*. New York: Modern Library, 1999.

———. *I Will Bear Witness: 1942–1945*. New York: Modern Library, 2001.

Kohler, Lotte, and Hans Saner, eds. *Hannah Arendt / Karl Jaspers Correspondence: 1926–1969*. New York: Harcourt Brace Jovanovich, 1992.

Koonz, Claudia. *The Nazi Conscience*. Cambridge, MA: Harvard University Press, 2003.

Kohn, Jerome. Introduction to *Responsibility and Judgment*. New York: Schocken Books, 2003.

Kozlovsky-Golan, Yvonne. "The Shaping of the Holocaust Visual Image by the Nuremberg Trials: The Impact of the Movie *Nazi Concentration Camps*." *Search and Research— Research Papers*. Jerusalem: Yad Vashem, 2006.

Kristeva, Julia. *Life Is a Narrative*. Toronto: University of Toronto Press, 2001.

Krupnick, Mark. "'Walking in Our Sleep': Bitburg and the Post-1939 Generation." In *Bitburg in Moral and Political Perspective*, ed. Geoffrey Hartman, 187–90. Bloomington: Indiana University Press, 1986.

Kushner, Tony. *The Holocaust and the Liberal Imagination: A Social and Cultural History*. Cambridge, MA: Blackwell, 1994.

LaCapra, Dominick. *History and Memory after Auschwitz*. Ithaca: Cornell University Press, 1998.

———. *Representing the Holocaust: History, Theory, Trauma*. Ithaca: Cornell University Press, 1994.

———. "Revisiting the Historians' Debate: Mourning and Genocide." *History and Memory* 9.1–2 (1997): 80–112.

Lahav, Pnina. "The Eichmann Trial, the Jewish Question, and the American-Jewish Intelligentsia." *Boston University Law Review* 72 (1992): 555–75.

———. *Judgment in Jerusalem: Chief Justice Simon Agranat and the Zionist Century*. Berkeley: University of California Press, 1997.

Landauer, Carl. "Deliberating Speed: Totalitarian Anxieties and Postwar Legal Thought." *Yale Journal of Law and the Humanities* 12.2 (Summer 2000): 171–218.

Landsman, Stephan. *Crimes of the Holocaust: The Law Confronts Hard Cases*. Philadelphia: University of Pennsylvania Press, 2005.

Lang, Berel. 2003. *Act and Idea in the Nazi Genocide*. New York: Syracuse University Press, 2003.

———. *The Future of the Holocaust: Between History and Memory*. Ithaca: Cornell University Press, 1999.

———. "Is It Possible to Misrepresent the Holocaust?" *History and Theory* 34.1 (February 1995): 84–89.

Langer, Lawrence L. *Holocaust Testimonies: The Ruins of Memory*. New Haven: Yale University Press, 1991.

———. *Preempting the Holocaust*. New Haven: Yale University Press, 1998.

Langer, Walter C. *A Psychological Profile of Adolf Hitler: His Life and Legend*. Washington, DC: Office of Strategic Services, 1942.

Lanzmann, Claude. *Shoah: The Complete Text of the Acclaimed Holocaust Film*. New York: Da Capo Press, 1995.

Lanzmann, Claude, Ruth Larson, and David Rodowick. "Seminar with Claude Lanzmann, 11 April 1990." Literature and Ethical Questions. *Yale French Studies* 79 (1991): 82–99.

Laqueur, Walter. "Footnotes to the Holocaust." In *Hannah Arendt, The Jew as Pariah: Jewish Identity and Politcs in the Modern Age*, ed. Ron H. Feldman 252–59. New York: Grove Press, 1978.

———. "A Reply To Hannah Arendt." In *Hannah Arendt, The Jew as Pariah: Jewish Identity and Politcs in the Modern Age*, ed. Ron H. Feldman 277–79. New York: Grove Press, 1978.

Lara, María Pía, ed. *Rethinking Evil: Contemporary Perspectives.* Berkeley: University of California Press, 2001.

Larson, Magali Sarfatti. "Reading Architecture in the Holocaust Memorial Museum: A Method and an Empirical Illustration." In *From Sociology to Cultural Studies: New Perspectives*, ed. Elizabeth Long, 62–91. Malden, MA: Blackwell, 1997.

Lee, Carol Ann. *The Hidden Life of Otto Frank.* New York: Perennial, 2003.

Leff, Laurel. "When Facts Didn't Speak for Themselves: The Holocaust in the *New York Times*, 1939–1945." *Harvard International Journal of Press/Politics* 5.52 (2000): 52–72.

Lerner, Richard M. *Final Solutions: Biology, Prejudice, and Genocide.* University Park: Pennsylvania State University Press, 1992.

Levine, Mark. "A Dissenting Voice: Or How Current Assumptions of Deterring and Preventing Genocide May Be Looking through the Wrong End of the Telescope, Part I." *Journal of Genocide Research* 6.2 (2004): 153–66.

———. "A Dissenting Voice: Or How Current Assumptions of Deterring and Preventing Genocide May Be Looking through The Wrong End of the Telescope, Part II." *Journal of Genocide Research* 6.3 (2004): 431–45.

———. *Genocide in the Age of the Nation State: The Meaning of Genocide.* Vol. 1. New York: I. B. Taurus, 2005.

———. *Genocide in the Age of the Nation State: The Rise of the West and the Coming of Genocide.* Vol. 2. New York: I. B. Taurus, 2005.

Levy, Daniel, and Natan Sznaider. 2002. "Memory Unbound: The Holocaust and the Formation of Cosmopolitan Memory." *European Journal of Social Theory* 5.1 (2002): 87–106.

Liberman, Benjamin. *Terrible Fate: Ethnic Cleansing in the Making of Modern Europe.* Chicago: Ivan R. Dee, 2006.

Lifton, Robert Jay. *The Nazi Doctors: Medical Killing and the Psychology of Genocide.* New York: Basic Books, 1986.

Linke, Uli. *German Bodies: Race and Representation after Hitler.* New York: Routledge, 1999.

Linn, Ruth. *Escaping Auschwitz: A Culture of Forgetting.* Ithaca: Cornell University Press, 2004.

Lippman, Matthew. "Fifty Years after Auschwitz: Prosecutions of Nazi Death Camp Defendants." *Connecticut Journal of International Law* 11 (Winter 1996): 199–278.

Liss, Andrea. *Trespassing through the Shadows: Memory, Photography, and the Holocaust.* Minneapolis: University of Minnesota Press, 1998.

Llewellyn, Jennifer J., and Robert Howse. 1999. "Institutions for Restorative Justice: The South African Truth and Reconciliation Commission." *University of Toronto Law Journal* 49 (Summer 1999): 355–89.

Loshitzky, Yosefa, ed. *Spielberg's Holocaust: Critical Perspectives on "Schindler's List."* Bloomington: Indiana University Press, 1997.

Lozowick, Yaacov. *Hitler's Bureaucrats: The Nazi Security Police and the Banality of Evil.* New York: Continuum, 2002.

Luban, David. "A Man Lost in the Gray Zone." *Law and History Review* 19.1 (Spring 2001): 161–76.

McClellan, Scott. 2008. *What Happened: Inside the Bush White House and Washington's Culture of Deception*. New York: Public Affairs.

McCullagh, C. Behan. "Bias in Historical Description, Interpretation, and Explanation." *History and Theory* 39.1 (February 2000): 39–66.

MacDonogh, Giles. *After the Reich: The Brutal History of the Allied Occupation*. New York: Basic Books, 2007.

Maechler, Stefan. *The Wilkomirski Affair: A Study in Biographical Truth*. New York: Schocken Books, 2001.

Maga, Tim. *Judgment at Tokyo: The Japanese War Crimes Trial*. Lexington: University of Kentucky Press, 2001.

Mahlendorf, Ursula. *The Shame of Survival: Working through a Nazi Childhood*. `University Park: Pennsylvania State University Press, 2009.

Mann, Michael. *The Dark Side of Democracy: Explaining Ethnic Cleansing*. New York: Cambridge University Press, 2005.

Maoz, Asher. "Historical Adjudication: Courts of Law, Commissions of Inquiry, and 'Historical Truth.'" *Law and History Review* 18.3 (Autumn 2000): 559–606.

Marcuse, Harold. *Legacies of Dachau: The Uses and Abuses of a Concentration Camp, 1933–2001*. New York: Cambridge University Press, 2001.

Marrus, Michael R. *The Nuremberg War Crimes Trial, 1945–46: A Documentary History*. Boston: St. Martin's Press, 1997.

Marty, Martin E. "'Storycide' and the Meaning of History." In *Bitburg in Moral and Political Perspective*, ed. Geoffrey Hartman, 225–26. Bloomington: Indiana University Press, 1986.

May, Larry, and Jerome Kohn, eds. *Hannah Arendt: Ten Years Later*. Cambridge, MA: MIT Press, 1996.

Mayer, Arno. *Why Did the Heavens Not Darken? The "Final Solution" in History*. New York: Pantheon Books, 1988.

Mercey, Arch A. "Social Uses of the Motion Picture." *Annals of the American Academy of Political and Social Science* 250, Communication and Social Action (1947): 98–104.

Milchman, Alan, and Alan Rosenberg, eds. *Postmodernism and the Holocaust*. Atlanta: Rodopi, 1998.

Milgram, Stanley. *Obedience to Authority*. New York: HarperPerennial, 1983.

Milton, Sybil. "The Context of the Holocaust." *German Studies Review* 13.2 (1990): 269–83.

———. "Images of the Holocaust—Part I." *Holocaust and Genocide Studies* 1.1 (1986): 27–61.

Milton, Sybil, and Ira Nowinski. *In Fitting Memory: The Art and Politics of Holocaust Memorials*. Detroit: Wayne State University Press, 1991.

Minnow, Martha. "The Work of Re-membering: After Genocide and Mass Atrocity." *Fordham International Law Journal* 23 (December 1999): 429–39.

Mintz, Alan. *Popular Culture and the Shaping of Holocaust Memory in America*. Seattle: University of Washington Press, 2001.

Mnookin, Jennifer L. "The Image of Truth: Photographic Evidence and the Power of Analogy." *Yale Journal of Law and the Humanities* 10 (Winter 1998): 1–74.

Moeller, Susan D. *Compassion Fatigue: How the Media Sell Disease, Famine, War, and Death*. New York: Routledge, 1999.

Morrow, Lance. *Evil: An Investigation*. New York: Basic Books, 2003.

Moruzzi, Norma Claire. *Speaking through the Mask: Hannah Arendt and the Politics of Social Identity*. Ithaca: Cornell University Press, 2000.

Moses, A. D. "Structure and Agency in the Holocaust: Daniel J. Goldhagen and His Critics." *History and Theory* 37.2 (May 1998): 194–219.

Mulisch, Harry. *Criminal Case 40/61, the Trial of Adolf Eichmann: An Eyewitness Account*. Philadelphia: University of Pennsylvania Press, 2005.

Müller, Filip. *Eyewitness Auschwitz: Three Years in the Gas Chambers*. Chicago: Ivan R. Dee, 1999.

Musmanno, Michael A. *The Eichmann Kommandos*. Philadelphia: Macrae Smith, 1961.

Nedelsky, Jennifer. "Judgment in the Shadow of the Holocaust: Section 1: Judging and the Holocaust: The Human Rights Legacy: Communities of Judgement and Human Rights." *Theoretical Inquiries in Law* 1 (2000): 245–81.

Neiman, Susan. *Evil in Modern Thought: An Alternative History of Philosophy*. Princeton: Princeton University Press, 2002.

Nino, Carlos Santiago. *Radical Evil on Trial*. New Haven: Yale University Press, 1996.

Ni Aolain, Fionnuala. "Sex-Based Violence and the Holocaust: A Reevaluation of Harms and Rights in International Law." *Yale Journal of Law and Feminism* 12 (2000): 43–84.

Norman, Andrew P. "Telling It Like It Was: Historical Narratives on Their Own Terms." *History and Theory* 30.2 (May 1991): 119–35.

Novick, Peter. *The Holocaust in American Life*. Boston: Houghton Mifflin, 1999.

Nyiszli, Dr. Miklos. 1993. *Auschwitz: A Doctor's Eyewitness Account*. New York: Arcade, 1993.

Ophir, Adi. "Between Eichmann and Kant: Thinking on Evil after Hannah Arendt." *History and Memory* 8.2 (1996): 89–136.

———. *The Order of Evils: Toward an Ontology of Morals*. Cambridge, MA: MIT Press, 2005.

Osiel, Mark J. "Ever Again: Legal Remembrance of Administrative Massacre." *University of Pennsylvania Law Review* 144 (December 1995): 463–566.

———. *Mass Atrocity, Collective Memory, and the Law*. New Brunswick, NJ: Transaction, 2000.

Overy, Richard. *Interrogations: The Nazi Elite in Allied Hands, 1945*. New York: Viking, 2001.

Owens, Patricia. *Between War and Politics: International Relations and the Thought of Hannah Arendt*. Oxford: Oxford University Press, 2007.

Patraka, Vivian M. *Spectacular Suffering: Theatre, Fascism, and the Holocaust*. Bloomington: Indiana University Press, 1999.

Pendas, Devin O. "'I Didn't Know What Auschwitz Was': The Frankfurt Auschwitz Trial and the German Press, 1963–1965." *Yale Journal of Law and the Humanities* 12 (Summer 2000): 397–446.

Persico, Joseph E. *Nuremberg: Infamy on Trial*. New York: Penguin, 1994.

Peukert, Detlev J. K. *Inside Nazi Germany: Conformity, Opposition, and Racism in Everyday Life*. New Haven: Yale University Press, 1987.

Pinchevski, Amit, and Roy Brand. "Holocaust Perversions: The Stalags Pulp Fiction and the Eichmann Trial." *Critical Studies in Media Communication* 24.5 (2007): 387–407.

Pinchevski, Amit, Tamar Liebes, and Ora Herman. "Eichmann on the Air: Radio and the Making of an Historic Trial." *Historical Journal of Film, Radio, and Television* 27.1 (2007): 1–25.

Pitkin, Hanna Fenichel. *The Attack of the Blob: Hannah Arendt's Concept of the Social*. Chicago: University of Chicago Press, 1998.

Plant, Richard. *The Pink Triangle: The Nazi War against Homosexuals*. New York: Henry Holt, 1986.

Platt, David, ed. *Celluloid Power: Social Film Criticism from "Birth of a Nation" to "Judgment at Nuremberg."* Metuchen, NJ: Scarecrow Press, 1992.

Plokhy, S. M. *Yalta: The Price of Peace*. New York: Viking, 2010.

Pohl, Dieter. "The Murder of the Jews in the General Government." In *National Socialist Extermination Policies: Contemporary German Perspectives and Controversies*, ed. Ulrich Herbert, 83–103. New York: Berghahn Books, 2000.

Pomper, Philip. "Historians and Individual Agency." *History and Theory* 35.3 (October 1996): 281–308.

Porter, Theodore M. *The Rise of Statistical Thinking: 1820–1900*. Princeton: Princeton University Press, 1986.

———. *Trust in Numbers: The Pursuit of Objectivity in Science and Public Life*. Princeton: Princeton University Press, 1995.

Power, Samantha. *"A Problem from Hell": America and the Age of Genocide*. New York: Basic Books, 2002.

Preparata, Guido Giacomo. *Conjuring Hitler: How Britain and American Made the Third Reich*. London: Pluto Press, 2005.

Primus, Richard A. *The American Language of Rights*. New York: Cambridge University Press, 1999.

Pringle, Heather. *The Master Plan: Himmler's Scholars and the Holocaust*. New York: Hyperion Press, 2006.

Proctor, Robert N. *Racial Hygiene: Medicine under the Nazis*. Cambridge, MA: Harvard University Press, 1988.

Rabinbach, Anson. "From Explosion to Erosion: Holocaust Memorialization in America since Bitburg." *History and Memory* 9.1–2 (1997): 226–55.

Rabinowitz, Paula. "Wreckage upon Wreckage: History, Documentary, and the Ruins of Memory." *History and Theory* 32.2 (May 1993): 119–37.

Raskin, Richard. *A Child at Gunpoint: A Case Study in the Life of a Photo*. Aarhus, Denmark: Aarhus University Press, 2004.

Raszelenberg, Patrick. 1999. "The Khmers Rouges and the Final Solution." *History and Memory* 11.2 (1999): 62–93.

Raz, Gal. "Actuality of Banality: Eyal Sivan's *The Specialist* in Context." *Shofar: An Interdisciplinary Journal of Jewish Studies* 24.1 (July 2005): 4–21.

Rees, Laurence. *Auschwitz: A New History*. New York: Public Affairs/Perseus Books, 2005.

Ring, Jennifer. *The Political Consequences of Thinking: Gender and Judaism in the Work of Hannah Arendt*. New York: State University of New York Press, 1997.

Robertson, Geoffrey. *Crimes against Humanity: The Struggle for Global Justice*. New York: New York University Press, 1999.

Robinson, Benjamin. "*The Specialist* on the Eichmann Precedent: Morality, Law, and Military Sovereignty." *Critical Inquiry* 30 (Autumn 2003): 63–97.

Robinson, Jacob. *And the Crooked Shall Be Made Straight: The Eichmann Trial, the Jewish Catastrophe, and Hannah Arendt's Narrative*. New York: Macmillan, 1965.

Rorty, Richard. *Contingency, Irony, and Solidarity*. New York: Oxford University Press, 1989.

Rose, Gillian. *Mourning Becomes the Law: Philosophy and Representation*. New York: Cambridge University Press, 1996.

Roseman, Mark. *The Wannsee Conference and the Final Solution: A Reconsideration*. New York: Henry Holt, 2002.

Rosenbaum, Alan S. 1993. *Prosecuting Nazi War Criminals*. Boulder, CO: Westview Press.

———, ed. *Is the Holocaust Unique? Perspectives on Comparative Genocide*. Boulder, CO: Westview Press, 1991.

Rosenberg, Alan, James R. Watson, and Detlef Linke, eds. *Contemporary Portrayals of Auschwitz: Philosophical Challenges*. New York: Humanity Books, 2000.

Rosenfeld, Alvin. *Imagining Hitler*. Bloomington: Indian University Press, 1985.

———. "Popularization and Memory: The Case of Anne Frank." In *Lessons and Legacies: The Meaning of the Holocaust in a Changing World*, ed. Peter Hayes, 243–78. Evanston, IL: Northwestern University Press, 1991.

Rosenfeld, Gavriel D. "Architectural Discourse and the Memory of Nazism in the Federal Republic of Germany, 1977–1997." *History and Memory* 9.1–2 (1997): 189–225.

Rothberg, Michael. *Traumatic Realism: The Demands of Holocaust Representation*. Minneapolis: University of Minnesota Press, 2000.

Rothberg, Robert I., and Dennis Thompson, eds. *Truth v. Justice: The Morality of Truth Commissions*. Princeton: Princeton University Press, 2000.

Russell, Lord Edward Frederick Langley. *The Record: The Trial of Adolf Eichmann for His Crimes against the Jewish People and against Humanity*. New York: Alfred A. Knopf, 1963.

Sands, Philippe, ed. *From Nuremberg to the Hague: The Future of International Criminal Justice*. New York: Cambridge University Press, 2003.

Sarat, Austin, ed. *The Killing State: Capital Punishment in Law, Politics, and Culture*. New York: Oxford University Press, 1999.

Scarry, Elaine. *The Body in Pain: The Making and Unmaking of the World*. New York: Oxford University Press, 1985.

Schleunes, Karl A., ed. *Legislating the Holocaust: The Bernard Loesener Memoirs and Supporting Documents*. Boulder, CO: Westview Press, 2001.

Schmidt, Ulf. *Karl Brandt the Nazi Doctor: Medicine and Power in the Third Reich*. New York: Continuum Books, 2007.

Scholem, Gershom, and Hannah Arendt. "Eichmann in Jerusalem: An Exchange of Letters between Gershom Scholem and Hannah Arendt." In *Hannah Arendt, The Jew as Pariah*, ed. Ron H. Feldman, 240–51. New York: Grove Press, 1978.

Schulte-Sasse, Linda. 1996. *Entertaining the Third Reich: Illusions of Wholeness in Nazi Cinema*. Durham, NC: Duke University Press, 1996.

Schweitzer, Frederick M. "In Pursuit of Guilt and Responsibility." *Journal of Genocide Research* 5.3 (2003): 451–61.

Scott, James C. *Seeing Like a State: How Certain Schemes to Improve the Human Condition Have Failed*. New Haven: Yale University Press, 1998.

Scribner, Charity. "From Documenta to the Document: A German Return to Truth and Reconciliation." *Rethinking Marxism* 16.1 (2004): 49–56.

Seabald, W. G. *On the Natural History of Destruction*. New York: Modern Library, 2004.

Segev, Tom. *The Seventh Million: The Israelis and the Holocaust*. Trans. Haim Watzman. New York: Henry Holt, 1991.

Sereny, Gitta. *Albert Spear: His Battle with Truth*. New York: Vintage Books, 1996.

———. *The Healing Wound: Experiences and Reflections on Germany, 1938–2001*. New York: Norton, 2001.

————. *Into That Darkness: An Examination of Conscience*. New York: Vintage Books, 1983.

Shale, Suzanne. "Conflicts of Law and the Character of Men: Writing Reversal of Fortune and Judgment at Nuremberg." *University of San Francisco Law Review* 30.4 (Summer 1996): 991–1022.

Shandler, Jeffrey. *While America Watches: Televising the Holocaust*. New York: Oxford University Press, 1999.

Shandley, Robert R., ed. *Unwilling Germans? The Goldhagen Debate*. Minneapolis: University of Minnesota Press, 1998.

Sharpe, Barry. *Modesty and Arrogance in Judgment: Hannah Arendt's "Eichmann in Jerusalem."* Westport, CT: Praeger, 1999.

Shaw, David Gary. "Happy in Our Chains? Agency and Language in the Postmodern Age." *History and Theory* 40.4 (December 2001): 1–9.

Shermer, Michael, and Alex Grobman. *Denying History: Who Says the Holocaust Never Happened and Why Do They Say It?* Berkeley: University of California Press, 2000.

Shklar, Judith N. *Legalism: Law, Morals and Political Trials*. Cambridge, MA: Harvard University Press, 1986.

Silbey, Jessica M. "Judge as Film Critics: New Approaches to Filmic Evidence." *Suffolk University Law School Faculty Publications* (2004). http://lsr.nellco.org/sufflok/fp/papers/17 (accessed September 22, 2006).

Sicher, Efraim. "The Furture of the Past: Counter Memory and Postmemory in Contemporary American Post-Holocaust Narratives." *History and Memory* 12.2 (2000): 56–91.

Smith, Bradley F. *The American Road to Nuremberg: The Documentary Record, 1944–45*. Stanford, CA: Hoover Institution Press, 1982.

Smith, Helmut Walser. "The Vanishing Point of German History: An Essay on Perspective." *History and Memory* 17.1–2 (2005): 269–95.

Sobchack, Vivian, ed. *The Persistence of History: Cinema, Television, and the Modern Event*. New York: Routledge, 1996.

Sofsky, Wolfgang. *The Order of Terror: The Concentration Camp*. Trans. William Templer. Princeton: Princeton University Press, 1997.

Sontag, Susan. *Regarding the Pain of Others*. New York: Farrar, Straus and Giroux, 2003.

Spiegelman, Art. *Maus I: A Survivor's Tale*. New York: Pantheon Books, 1986.

————. *Maus II: And Here My Troubles Began*. New York: Pantheon Books, 1991.

Speer, Albert. *Inside the Third Reich*. New York: Avon Books, 1970.

————. *Spandau: The Secret Diaries*. London: Phoenix Press, 1976.

Sprecher, Drexel A. *Inside the Nuremberg Trial: A Prosecutor's Comprehensive Account*. 2 vols. Lanham, MD: University Press of America, 1999.

State of Israel Ministry of Justice. *The Trial of Adolf Eichmann: Record of the Proceedings in the District Court of Jerusalem, Volumes 1–3*. Jerusalem: Israel State Archives, 1992.

Steinberg, Jules. *Hannah Arendt on the Holocaust: A Study in the Suppression of Truth*. New York: Edwin Mellen Press, 2000.

Steinweiss, Alan E. *Studying the Jew: Scholarly Anti-Semitism in Nazi Germany*. Cambridge, MA: Harvard University Press, 2006

Stern, Judith. "Judgment in the Shadow of the Holocaust: Section 2: New Perspectives on the Eichmann Trial: The Eichmann Trial and Its Influence on Psychiatry and Psychology." *Theoretical Inquiries in Law* 1 (July 2000): 393–428.

Stier, Oren Baruch. *Committed to Memory: Cultural Mediations of the Holocaust*. Amherst: University of Massachusetts Press, 2003.

Struk, Janina. *Photographing the Holocaust: Interpretations of the Evidence*. London: I. B. Tauris, 2004.

Sturken, Marita. *Tangled Memories: The Vietnam War, the AIDS Epidemic, and the Politics of Remembering*. Berkeley: University of California Press, 1997.

Suchesky, Bernard, and Madeleine Dobie. 1994. "The Carmelite Convent at Auschwitz: The Nature and Scope of a Failure." Discourses of Jewish Identity in Twentieth-Century France. *Yale French Studies* 85 (1994): 160–73.

Svendsen, Lars. *A Philosophy of Evil*. London: Dalkey Archive Press, 2001.

Syrkin, Marie, with Harold Weisberg, Irving Howe, et. al. "More on Eichmann." *Partisan Review* 31.2 (1964): 253–83.

Tagg, John. *The Burden of Representation: Essays on Photographies and Histories*. Minneapolis: University of Minnesota Press, 1993.

———. *The Disciplinary Frame: Photographic Truths and the Culture of Meaning*. Minneapolis: University of Minnesota Press, 2009.

Taylor, Telford. *The Anatomy of the Nuremberg Trials: A Personal Memoir*. New York: Alfred A. Knopf, 1992.

———. *Nuremberg and Vietnam: An American Tragedy*. New York: Random House, 1970.

The Holocaust Chronicle: A History in Words and Pictures. Lincolnwood, IL: Publications International, 2000.

Terada, Rei. *Feeling in Theory: Emotion after the "Death of the Subject."* Cambridge, MA: Harvard University Press, 2001.

———. "Thinking for Oneself: Realism and Defiance in Arendt." *ELH* 71 (2004): 839–65.

Thomas, Laurence Mordekhai. *Vessels of Evil: America Slavery and the Holocaust*. Philadelphia: Temple University Press, 1993.

Thor, Rebecka. "Representing the Eichmann Trial: Ten Years of Controversy around *The Specialist*." M.A. thesis, New School, 2009.

Thucydides. *History of the Peloponnesian War*. Ed. M. I. Finley. New York: Penguin, 1972.

Tilles, Stanley, with Jeffrey Denhart. *By the Neck until Dead: The Gallows of Nuremberg*. Bedford, IN: JoNa Books, 1999.

Todorov, Tzvetan. *The Fragility of Goodness: Why Bulgaria's Jews Survived the Holocaust*. Princeton: Princeton University Press, 1999.

Torgovnick, Marianna. *The War Complex: World War II in Our Time*. Chicago: University of Chicago Press, 2005.

Tryster, Hillel. "Eyal Sivan Eichmann, Lies, and Videotape." *Indymedia*, 2007, 1–5. http://no666.wordpress.com/2007/05/18/eyal-sivan-eichmann-lies-and-videotape.

———. "We Have Ways of Making You Believe: The Eichmann Trial as Seen in *The Specialist*." *Antisemitism International* (2004): 34–44. http://no666.wordpress.com/2007/05/18/eyal-sivan-eichmann.

Turley, Jonathan. "Transformative Justice and the Ethos of Nuremberg." *Loyola of Los Angeles Law Review* 33 (January 2000): 655–80.

Tutu, Desmond Mpilo. *No Future without Forgiveness*. New York: Doubleday, 1999.

Valentino, Benjamin A. *Final Solutions: Mass Killing and Genocide in the 20th Century*. Ithaca: Cornell University Press, 2004.

Van Alphen, Ernst. "Deadly Historians: Boltanski's Intervention in Holocaust Historiography." In *Visual Culture and the Holocaust*, ed. Barbie Zelizer, 45–73. New Brunswick, NJ: Rutgers University Press, 2001.

Van Der Vat, Dan. *The Good Nazi: The Life and Lies of Albert Spear.* New York: Houghton Mifflin, 1997.

Van Hattem, Cornelis. *Superfluous People: A Reflection on Hannah Arendt and Evil.* Lanham, MD: University Press of America, 2005.

Vetlesen, Arne Johan. *Evil and Human Agency: Understanding Collective Evildoing.* London: Cambridge University Press, 2005.

———. *Perception, Empathy, and Judgment: An Inquiry into the Preconditions of Moral Performance.* University Park: Pennsylvania State University Press, 1994.

Vice, Sue. *Holocaust Fiction.* London: Routledge, 2000.

Vidal-Naquet, Pierre. *Assassins of Memory: Essays on the Denial of the Holocaust.* New York: Columbia University Press, 1987.

Villa, Dana, ed. *The Cambridge Companion to Hannah Arendt.* New York: Cambridge University Press, 2000.

———. *Politics, Philosophy, Terror: Essays on the Thought of Hannah Arendt.* Princeton: Princeton University Press, 1999.

Von Lang, Jochen, with Claus Sibyll. *Eichmann Interrogated: Transcripts from the Archives of the Israeli Police.* New York: Da Capo Press, 1999.

Vulliet, Armand, and Madeleine Dobie. "Letters to Claude Lanzmann and to the Grand Larousse." Discourses of Jewish Identity in Twentieth-Century France. *Yale French Studies* 85 (1994): 152–59.

Waller, James. *Becoming Evil: How Ordinary People Commit Genocide and Mass Killing.* New York: Oxford University Press, 2002.

Warmbrunn, Werner. *The German Occupation of Belgium, 1940–1944.* New York: Peter Lang, 1993.

Weingartner, James J. *Americans, Germans, and War Crimes Justice: Law Memory and the "Good War."* Santa Barbara, CA: Praeger, 2011.

Weiss, Peter. 2005. *The Investigation: Oratorio in 11 Cantos.* London: Marion Boyars, 2005.

Weiss, Sheila Faith. *The Nazi Symbiosis: Human Genetics and Politics in the Third Reich.* Chicago: University of Chicago Press, 2010.

Weissman, Gary. *Fantasies of Witnessing: Postwar Efforts to Experience the Holocaust.* Ithaca: Cornell University Press, 2004.

Weitz, Eric D. *A Century of Genocide: Utopias of Race and Nation.* Princeton: Princeton University Press, 2003.

West, Rebecca. *A Train of Powder: Six Reports on the Problem of Guilt and Punishment in Our Time.* Chicago: Ivan R. Dee, 1955.

White, James Boyd. *When Words Lose Their Meanings: Constitutions and Reconstitutions of Language, Character, and Community.* Chicago: University of Chicago Press, 1984.

Williams, Bernard. *Truth and Truthfulness: An Essay in Genealogy.* Princeton: Princeton University Press, 2002.

Wittmann, Rebecca. *Beyond Justice: The Auschwitz Trial.* Cambridge, MA: Harvard University Press, 2005.

———. "The Wheels of Justice Turn Slowly: The Pretrial Investigations of the Frankfurt Auschwitz Trial, 1963–65." *Central European History* 35.3 (2002): 345–78.

Woetzel, Robert K. *The Nuremberg Trials in International Law with a Postlude on the Eichmann Case.* New Roek: Praeger, 1962.

Wolin, Richard. "The Ambivalence of German-Jewish Identity: Hannah Arendt in Jerusalem." *History and Memory* 8.2 (1996): 9–34.

Wolin, Sheldon S. *Democracy Inc.: Managed Democracy and the Specter of Inverted Totalitarianism.* Princeton: Princeton University Press, 2008.

Yablonka, Hanna. *The State of Israel vs. Adolf Eichmann.* New York: Schocken Books, 2004.

Yakira, Elhanan. "Hannah Arendt, the Holocaust and Zionism: A Story of Failure." *Israel Studies* 11.3 (2006): 31–61.

Young, James E. *At Memory's Edge: After-Images of the Holocaust in Contemporary Art and Architecture.* New Haven: Yale University Press, 2000.

———. "Between History and Memory: The Uncanny Voices of Historian and Survivor." *History and Memory* 9.1–2 (1997): 47–58.

———. *The Texture of Memory: Holocaust Memorials and Meaning.* New Haven: Yale University Press, 1993.

———. "Toward a Received History of the Holocaust." *History and Theory* 36.4 (December 1997): 21–43.

———. *Writing and Rewriting the Holocaust: Narrative and the Consequences of Interpretation.* Bloomington: Indiana University Press, 1990.

Young-Bruehl, Elisabeth. *Hannah Arendt: For Love of the World.* New Haven: Yale University Press, 1982.

———. *Why Arendt Matters.* New Haven: Yale University Press, 2006.

Zelizer, Barbie. *Remembering to Forget: Holocaust Memory through the Camera's Eye.* Chicago: University of Chicago Press, 1998.

———, ed. *Visual Culture and the Holocaust.* New Brunswick, NJ: Rutgers University Press, 2001.

Zagorin, Perez. "History, the Referent, and Narrative: Reflections on Postmodernism Now." *History and Theory* 38.1 (February 1999): 1–24.

Žižek, Slavoj. *Did Somebody Say Totalitarianism?* New York: Verso Press, 2001.

Zuckerman, Yitzhak. *A Surplus of Memory: Chronicle of the Warsaw Ghetto Uprising.* Berkeley: University of California Press, 1993.

VISUAL TEXTS

Auschwitz: Inside the Nazi State. Directed by Lawrence Rees. BBC, 2005 (DVD, 300 min.).

D-Day to Berlin. Written and produced by George Stevens Jr. New Liberty Productions—Warner Home Video, 1998 (DVD, 46 min.).

The Death Camps. CAV Video Productions, 1993 (VHS, 60 min.).

Historic Nuremberg Trials Newsreels. Quality Information Publishers, 2005 (DVD, 9 min.).

Holocaust: The Liberation of Majdanek. Directed by Irmgard Von Zur Mühlen. Artsmagic, LTD, 2006 (DVD, 60 min.).

Holocaust: Dachau and Sachsenhausen. Directed by Irmgard Von Zur Mühlen. Artsmagic, LTD, 2006 (DVD, 59 min.)

Holocaust: The Liberation of Auschwitz. Directed by Irmgard Von Zur Mühlen. Artsmagic, LTD, 2005 (DVD, 53 min.).

Holocaust: Ravensbruck and Buchenwald. Directed by Irmgard Von Zur Mühlen. Artsmagic, LTD, 2005 (DVD, 60 min.).

Holocaust: Theresienstadt. Directed by Irmgard Von Zur Mühlen with Simon Wiesenthal. Artsmagic, LTD, 2005 (DVD, 53 min.).

Memory of the Camps. Directed by Alfred Hitchcock. Produced by Sidney Bernstein, Sergei Nobandov, Stephanie Tepper, and David Fanning. Frontline WGBH, 2005 (DVD, 60 min.).

Nazi Concentration and Death Camps Film Collection. Historical Archive Corporation, 2006 (DVD, 74 min.).

Night and Fog. Directed by Alain Resnais. Janus Films, 1955 (DVD, 31 min.).

Nuremberg: The Nazis Facing Their Crimes. Directed by Christian Delage. Compagnie des Phares et Balises, Delphis Films, 2007 (DVD, 3.5 hr.).

Television under the Swastika. Directed by Michael Kloft. FirstRunFeatures, 1999 (DVD, 52 min.).

The Trial of Adolf Eichmann. PBS, ABC News Production, 1997 (VHS, 120 min.).

Shoah. Directed by Claude Lanzmann. Les Films Aleph, 1985/New York Films Artwork, 1999 (VHS, 4 hr., 34 min.).

The Sorrow and the Pity. Directed by Marcel Ophuls. Milestone Film and Video (restored edition), 2000 (DVD, 251 min.).

The Specialist: Portrait of a Modern Criminal. Directed by Eyal Sivan. Momento!, 1999 (DVD, 123 min.).

Verdict on Auschwitz: The Frankfurt Auschwitz Trial, 1963–1965. Directed by Rolf Bickel and Dietrich Wagner. FirstRunFeatures, 2005 (DVD, 180 min.).

Index

Page numbers in italics refer to illustrations

absolutes, universal, 3
Abu Ghraib incident, 163n29
Alford, C. Fred, 146n19
Allen, Michael Thad, 144n87
Allied Forces: propaganda of, *95*;
    reeducation program of, 104;
    war crimes by, 95, 154n13. *See also*
    confrontation visits
Aly, Götz, 19, 70; critics of, 55–56,
    58–59; on economy of genocide,
    45, 55–56, 60–61, 141n52; on
    Germanization, 139n31; on ghettos,
    52, 53; on Nazi administrators,
    61–62; on Nazi ideology, 143n74;
    on overpopulation problem, 43–44;
    on population management, 49, 50,
    63; reading of documents, 56, 59;
    on resettlement, 46, 52; on self-
    determination, 47
Americans: effect of genocide myths
    on, 123–24; familiarity with
    Nazi atrocity, 96, 132n16, 147n20;
    political complacency of, 65
anti-Semitism, Nazi: American
    familiarity with, 17; eliminationist,
    48, 66, 68; in population transfers,
    47; role in genocide, 55, 60, 66, 119,
    138n15, 140n34
Arendt, Hannah: on the absolute,
    3; on Anton Schmidt, 81–82;
    assessment of Eichmann, 23,
    25–27, 38, 65, 70–74, 80–85, 88,
    91, 115, 120, 122; assessment of evil,
    16–19, 21–22, 25, 26, 66, 67, 115–17,
    120–21, 148n29; on compassion,

73–74; on conscience, 75, 149n54;
    on crimes against humanity, 35–38;
    critics of, 26, 30–34, 39–40, 64–67,
    133nn25,29; on Eichmann trial, 20,
    25, 37, 59, 90, 135n42, 136n55; on
    emotions, 74, 149n48; on empathy,
    82–83; on extermination camps,
    130n46; on Final Solution, 136n48;
    on Hausner's indictment, 18–19; on
    imagination, 80; on imperialism,
    127n29; on Jewish complicity,
    26–27, 30, 136n48; on judgment
    process, 64; on justice, 137n60;
    on moral collapse, 34; on Nazi
    guilt, 38–40, 111; on Nuremberg
    International Military Tribunal,
    39–40; on pan-movements, 138n12;
    on population management, 16;
    response to critics, 39–40; on self-
    examination, 74–77; on Stalinism,
    138n10; on state power, 138n11; on
    subject formation, 122; on thinking,
    74–77, 114–15, 149n51, 161nnn2,4;
    on thoughtlessness, 19–20, 26, 114,
    130n57; on totalitarianism, 7, 41–43,
    56, 118–20, 123, 127n29; use of Kant,
    122. Works: *Eichmann in Jerusalem*,
    1–2, 65; *On Revolution*, 73; *The
    Origins of Totalitarianism*, 35, 41, 43,
    56, 116, 117–18, 127n29, 129n38
Aryans: legal identification of, 112;
    racial policy on, 144n77
atrocities, claim to legality, 137n60
atrocities, Nazi: as aberration, 10;
    Americans' familiarity with, 96,

132n16, 147n20; as benchmark,
10; German's witnessing of,
103–4, *104*, *105*, 107, 158nn46,48;
popular discourse on, 1; prewar, 12;
rationalization of, 13; visual texts
of, 105. *See also* genocide, Nazi;
Holocaust

*The Atrocities Committed by the
German-Fascists in the USSR* (film,
1946), 99, 100

atrocity images, Nazi, 13–14;
configuration of narrative field,
113; defendants' viewing of, 108,
110, 159n59; at Eichmann trial, 25,
86–88, 106, 108; Eisenhower on,
158n47; and genocide myths, 21–22;
indescribable character of, 106,
158n52; interpretation of, 40; at
Nuremberg International Military
Tribunal, 95–100, 103–8, 110; in
popular imaginary, 40; prejudicial
impact of, 100, 102; semiotic context
of, 113; soldiers' photographs of,
129n39; use in teaching, 151n85. *See
also* concentration camps, liberation
footage of

Augustine, Saint, 148n29

Auschwitz, 142n53; crematorium of,
50; escapes from, 135n41; German
plans for, 144nn76,79; role in
industrial revolution, 63; Soviet
liberation of, 100, 157n38

authority, obedience to, 65–66, 67–68,
146n9, 147n19

Baehr, Peter, 116

Bamm, Peter, 150n76

banality of evil, 1, 17, 21, 161n10;
disruption of genocide myths,
22; Eichmann's embodiment
of, 18, 23, 25, 70, 115–16, 122;
global interpretation of, 116;

self-abandonment in, 119–20;
thoughtlessness in, 77. *See also* evil

Bartov, Omer, 55, 56, 59

Bass, Gary Jonathan, 92–93, 96,
134n33, 152n3

Bauer, Yehuda, 143n74

Bauman, Zygmunt, 68–69, 70, 124

Bay, Christian, 65, 114

Belgian Congo, violence in, 137n57

Belzec (extermination camp), 142n53;
prisoner uprising at, 144n79

Ben-Gurion, David: and Eichmann
trial, 27, 29, 36, 152n5; establishment
of historical record, 33; wartime
priorities of, 32

Bennett, William, 5

Bergen-Belsen concentration camp,
69, *109*

Bernstein, Richard, 116–17, 136n48,
148n28, 162n11

Biagioli, Mario, 15, 160n66

Biddle, Francis, 100

Bitburg (Germany) cemetery, Reagan's
visit to, 69–70

Borman, Martin, 140n32

Bradley, Omar, 103

Brand, Roy, 134n38

Brandt, Edmund, 141n51

Brauman, Rony, 20, 85. See also *The
Specialist: Portrait of a Modern
Criminal*

Browning, Christopher, 54, 55, 140n32;
on German occupation policy,
141n46; *Ordinary Men*, 146n9

bureaucrats, Nazi, popular conception
of, 66–67

Burgdörfer, Friedrich, 51

Bush administration (George W.
Bush): creation of political reality,
5–7; policy in Sudan, 126n23;
torture during, 128n34, 163n29

Bushnell, Prudence, 8, 9

Canovan, Margaret, 116–17, 119–20,
127n29
capitalism: effect on genocide,
12; global, 124; liberal, 11, 114;
role in state power, 138n11; role
in totalitarianism, 41, 127n29;
subjectivity of, 114
Caroll, David, 13
Carr, David, 60
Carter, Jimmy, 37
Cesarani, David, 142n60
Chelmno (extermination camp), 53, 79,
142n53; prisoner uprising at, 144n79
chosenness, Jewish concept of, 138n12
Churchill, Winston, 94, 156n29; on
castration for Nazis, 134n33
classification systems: banality of, 19;
Western, 63
classification systems, Nazi, 44, 45, 56;
continuation of, 112, 124, 160n69;
homosexuals in, 160n69
Cole, Tim, 147n20
colonialism, role in genocide, 13
compassion, Arendt on, 73–74
complacency, individual, 67–68
concentration camps: of Boer
War, 119; Eisenhower at, *101*;
experimentation at, 16, 42, 130n45;
forced labor at, 50; in Israeli fiction,
134n38; liberation footage of, 20, 21,
26, 40, 86–88, 95–100, 103–8, 110,
155n16, 157n38; remaking of human
nature, 42; Soviet liberation of,
100, 157n38. *See also* extermination
camps
confrontation visits, 103–4, *104, 105,*
107, 158nn46,48
conscience, Arendt on, 75, 149n54
criminality, Nazi, 21; collective, 94,
153n11, 154n12; comprehension of,
38–39; the demonic in, 39, 41, 66,
117, 162n11; groups charged with, 94,

153n11, 154n12; at Nuremberg trials,
92–93, 106; visual evidence of, 98

Darfur, genocide in, 8, 37, 126n23
Davenport, Charles, 130n54
denazification, 20, 103. *See also*
confrontation visits
Des Pres, Terrence, 13
destruction, agents of, 65–66, 67–68
Didion, Joan, 4
Diner, Dan, 55–56, 58–59
documentary films: of concentration
camp liberation, 20, 21, 26, 40,
86–88, 95–100, 103–8, 110, 155n16,
157n38; at Eichmann trial, 84–90;
knowledge-producing strategies
of, 102, 152n90; of New Deal, 102,
157n45; at Nuremberg trials, 21,
95–100, 103–8, 110; role in crisis
management, 102–3
Dodd, Thomas, 97
Doenitz, Karl, 110
Doherty, Thomas, 155n15
Donovan, James, 96
Douglas, Lawrence, 26, 132n7, 136n55

Eichmann, Adolf: appearance of, 71,
134n36; Arendt's assessment of,
23, 25–27, 38, 65, 70–74, 80–85,
88, 91, 115, 120, 122; banality of
evil embodied in, 18, 23, 25, 70,
115–16, 122; character of, 26, 65,
66–67, 71, 83; commonplaceness
of, 79, 71, 72, 114; in court, 24, 35,
78, 87, 89–90; demythologized
account of, 83; on genocide, 78–79,
143n66; inability to think, 72–73,
74, 77–78, 82; Israeli capture of,
23; and Jewish identity, 142n60;
on Jewish resistance, 62; and
Judenräte, 73; and Kasztner, 29–30;
knowledge of right and wrong,

78–79; meaning of, 25; persons included in, 142n60; political economy of, 55–56; versus territorial solution, 50, 78

Fish, Stanley, 3, 4

Ford, John, 99, 159n54

Foucault, Michel, 56; on Nazi regime, 61, 144n78

Frank, Anne, 67, 72, 147n20

Frank, Hans, 32, 51, 110; resettlement responsibilities of, 47

Fraser, David, 112, 113, 137n60; on classification schemes, 160n69

freedom, techniques of control in, 124

Friedländer, Saul, 55

Funk, Walther, 110

gender: in Holocaust literature, 133n32; in Nuremberg trials, 31–32; in reception of Arendt's works, 31

genocide: as aberration, 14–15, 128n33; effect of capitalism on, 12; emergence of, 13; geopolitical framework for, 11; international penalties for, 37, 137n60; of late twentieth century, 8–9, 37, 128n33, 130n57; and modernity, 2, 15; outside first world, 11; and postmodernism, 2, 7; role of colonialism in, 13; role of imperialism in, 13–14, 127n29; role of nation-states in, 11, 19; role of Western liberalism in, 11, 128nn32–33; role of Western socio-politics in, 10–12; Rwandan, 8–9, 128n33; Serbian, 8, 130n57; standards of judgment for, 2, 7; unacknowledged, 7–9, 12, 37, 124

genocide, Nazi, 19; and anti-Bolshevism, 142n57; assenting community of, 146n12; comprehension of, 38–39; as crime against humanity, 35–38;

economic factors in, 45, 48–49, 55–56, 60–61, 141n52, 143n70; Eichmann's role in, 23–24, 34; following population transfers, 46, 47; following Wannsee Conference, 54; formulation of policy, 53–55; formulative conditions of, 59, 61, 70, 122; ignoring of, 69; infrastructure of, 19; international responsibility for, 36–37; myths of, 21–22, 70, 123–24; planned extent of, 138n15; in popular imagery, 40; rationalization of, 38, 43; resistance to, 62, 82, 133n25; role of anti-Semitism in, 55, 60, 66, 119, 138n15, 140n34; role of ideology in, 36–37, 45; simplification of, 34; social modernization and, 19; visual rhetoric of, 22, 131n61; witnesses' assent to, 150n76. *See also* atrocities, Nazi; Final Solution; Holocaust

Germanization, 47; qualifications for, 139n31

Germans: housing shortages for, 51; resettlement of, 45–46, 139n27; as victimized people, 100, 156n35; witnessing of extermination camps, 103–4, *104*, *105*, 107, 158nn46,48

Germany, overpopulation problem of, 43–44

Germany, postwar: Allied configuration of, 156n29; destruction in, 93; reconciliation with, 69; visual landscape of, 103

ghettos: establishment of, 47, 51; exterminations from, 53; German debate over, 52–53; number of, 141n47; productivity of, 53, 141n51; slave labor from, 143n70

Gilbert, Gustave, 107, 108, 110, 159n53

Goldhagen, Daniel: *Hitler's Willing Executioners*, 66, 146n12

the good, Arendt on, 39

Göring, Hermann, 110, 134n35, 156n34; prosecution's depiction of, 32; psychological testing of, 159n53
Gouri, Haim, 33, 136n46
Great Britain, manipulation of markets, 128n35
Greece, classical: culture of discourse, 6
guilt, Nazi: Arendt on, 38–40, 111; by association, 154n12; grandeur in, 39; images of, 41; limiting of, 93
Guttenplan, D. D., 125n4
Gypsies, Nazi classification of, 160n69

Halevi, Judge, 121
Hasian, Marouf, 155n19
Hausner, Gideon, 18, 28, 93; on Holocaust images, 86, 151n85; on Israeli national identity, 29; on Jewish collaboration, 30; on nation-building, 132n15; prosecution of Eichmann, 18, 24–25, 27, 66, 70, 88; and The Specialist, 86, 88
Heim, Susanne, 143n70; on Nazi economics, 60; on population management, 49. See also Aly, Götz
Heydrich, Reinhard, 46, 51, 139n27; on Final Solution, 54
Hilberg, Raul, 15, 133n25, 160n70; on definition of Jews, 112; The Destruction of the European Jews, 30
Himmler, Heinrich, 46, 141n42; on Russian campaign, 141n42
Hollywood, work with War Department, 156n34
Holocaust: as administrative massacre, 36; Americans' knowledge of, 96, 132n16, 151n80; challenges to legal systems, 113; children's knowledge of, 147n20; consciousness of, 37; contemporary discourse on, 1, 9; deniers of, 125n4; discourse of evil in, 13; events

preceding, 47; Jewish complicity in, 26–27, 29–30, 31, 33–34, 133nn24–25, 136n48; knowledge regimes of, 14; memorials to, 37; in popular culture, 13, 122–23; in postmodernism, 126n21; reductive discourse of, 34; sacralization of, 34, 70, 123; teaching of, 151n85; visual evidence for, 26, 40; Western culpability in, 27. See also atrocities, Nazi; Final Solution; genocide, Nazi
homosexuality, Nazi view of, 32, 134n35, 160n69
Höss, Rudolf, 79, 80
human beings, economic value of, 53, 139n22
humanity: crimes against, 35–38, 94, 96, 137n57, 152n3; as guarantor against danger, 136n52
Hurwitz, Leo, 84, 85, 131n58

ideology: Nazi, 36–37, 45, 143n74; in totalitarianism, 42, 43, 117–18
imagination, Arendt on, 80; Eichmann's lack of, 80, 82
imperialism: in Africa, 41; Athenian, 6; as prototype for totalitarianism, 118–19; role in genocide, 13–14, 127n29
indigenous peoples, extermination of, 119
Inquiry (research group), 130n54
International Federation of Eugenic Organizations, 160n70
Iraq war, relationship to September 11 attacks, 5
Israel: culture of remembrance, 33; generation gap in, 132n15; national identity in, 27–29, 36 132n15

Jackson, Robert, 12, 128n34; on film footage, 99; on German

people, 156n35; on indictment of
organizations, 153n11; opening
address of, 98–99, 111; on resistance
movements, 155n25; strategy of,
97–98; on witness testimony, 17,
155n26
Jaspers, Karl, 39, 43, 110, 111, 117, 122; on
German guilt, 38
Jewish question: Eichmann's view of,
23; Heydrich's responsibility for,
139n27; physical solutions for, 23;
territorial solution for, 50, 78; in
Western Europe, 143n70
Jews, European: cooperation with
Nazi regime, 26–27, 29–30, 31,
33–34; deportation of, 55, 140n33;
forced labor by, 54, 143n70;
ghettoization of, 47, 51; legal
identification of, 54, 112, 142n60,
160n70; and pan-nationalism, 41,
138n12; productive capacity of, 53;
rescue efforts for, 132n17; versus
Sabras, 135n39
Jews, German: deportation of, 53
Jews, Polish: deportation of, 46, 47,
50, 51, 141n45; living conditions of,
141n46; resettlement plans for, 48,
51–52
Jim Crow laws, influence on
Nuremberg laws, 111–12
Jones, Edgar L., 163n29
Judenräte: complicity with Nazis, 27,
30, 33–34, 133n25; Eichmann and, 73
judgment: Arendt on, 64;
indeterminacy of, 7; Jewish
leadership's, 30
Judt, Tony, 93, 104, 113; on genocide
myths, 123; on population transfer,
152n7
justice, Arendt on, 137n60

Kant, Immanuel: Arendt's use of, 122;
categorical imperative of, 73

Kasztner, Rezsö, 29–30
Katyn, Soviet action at, 154n13
Kellogg-Briand Pact, 153n10
Kelly, Douglas, 107, 108
Kértesz, Imre, 148n36
Kessel, Joseph, 110
knowledge production: by
documentary films, 102, 152n90;
historical, 58; in modernity, 15
knowledge production, Nazi, 44,
57; continuation of, 124; role in
genocide, 19
Koonz, Claudia, 144n77
Kristof, Nicholas D., 137n61

Landau, Judge, 131n2
Landsman, Stephen, 94, 100
Lange, Dorothea: Migrant Mother, 102
law, Nazi: racial inferiority in, 160n69;
versus "real" law, 14, 112–13
Lemkin, Raphael, 154n12
Levine, Mark, 124, 127n29; Genocide in
the Age of the Nation State, 10–11, 12
Linn, Ruth, 135n41
Lippman, Walter, 130n54
Lódz ghetto, shutting down of, 50
London Charter, 106, 153n11;
determination of criminal charges
in, 94
Lozowick, Yaacov: Hitler's Bureaucrats,
66

MacDonogh, Giles, 156n29
Madagascar, proposed resettlement at,
48, 51–52, 141n49
Majandanek concentration camp,
Soviet liberation of, 100, 157n38
Mapai (Socialist Zionist Party), 32
markets, British manipulation of,
128n35
Marty, Martin, 69, 70
masculinity, in Nuremberg trials,
31–32

Matthäus, Jürgen, 53–54
Maxwell-Fyfe, Sir David, 153n11
Mayer, Arno, 54, 142n57
McCarthy, Mary, 35
meaning: culturally shaped, 2;
    destabilization of, 6, 125n4;
    indeterminate, 7
media: Eisenhower's use of, 40;
    prioritizing of sentiment, 131n63
medicine, Nazi, 14
mentally ill persons: cost of, 139n22;
    extermination of, 139nn29–30;
    Nazi treatment of, 44
Milgram, Stanley: experiments of,
    65–66, 67, 146nn9–10,19; Obedience
    to Authority, 66
Mill, John Stuart, 67
Mladic, Ratko, 130n57
modernity: genocide and, 2, 15;
    knowledge production in, 15; social
    failures in, 19; technologies of, 15, 19
Mombert, Paul, 48–49
Montesquieu, Baron de, 42
morality: role of empathy in, 20;
    rupture under Nazi regime, 96, 98,
    111, 112, 113, 122–23
Morgenthau, Henry J., Jr., 156n29
Mulisch, Harry, 71, 72, 148n32
My Lai massacre, 163n29

national identity, Israeli: gendered,
    135n39; role in Eichmann trial,
    27–29, 36, 132n15
nation-states: capitalism in, 127n29;
    disruptive effects of, 10; ethnic
    consolidation in, 10–11; role in
    genocide, 11, 19; tribal nationalism
    of, 13–14
Nazi Collaboration Law (Israel, 1950),
    29
Nazi Concentration Camps (film,
    1945), 99, 132n7, 156n33; defendants'
    reactions to, 108, 110

The Nazi Plan (film, 1945), 99–100,
    156nn33–34, 159n54; defendants'
    viewing of, 159n59
Nazi regime: administrative apparatus
    of, 36, 45, 61–62; censuses under,
    57, 63; collective life under, 57–58;
    compromises made by, 45, 46, 60;
    conditions favoring, 41; continuation
    of structures, 112; databases of,
    14, 57, 129n42; economics of, 45,
    48–49, 55–56, 61, 129n35; ethnic
    redistribution under, 45–52;
    exclusion policies of, 45; failures
    of, 45, 60; homosexuality and, 32,
    134n35, 160n69; ideology of, 36–37,
    45, 143n74; Jewish complicity with,
    26–27, 29–30, 31, 33–34, 133nn24–25,
    136n48; logicality of, 49; modes of
    relations, 62; moral collapse under,
    26, 34, 115; as moral rupture, 96, 98,
    111, 112, 113, 122–23; mythology of,
    21–22, 39–40, 43, 70, 117, 123–24;
    population policies of, 43–52; power
    techniques, 62; propaganda films of,
    99; rationality of, 62; registration
    practices of, 63; regulatory
    mechanisms of, 56, 63; resistance to,
    62, 82, 133n25, 155n25; rise of, 128n35;
    Russian campaign, 45, 141n42;
    societal goals of, 15, 16; statistical
    techniques of, 57; technologies
    of, 14–15, 56, 129n42; and world
    conquest, 153n9
Nazis: feminization of, 32, 134nn35–36;
    self-understanding of, 16
New Deal, documentaries of, 102,
    157n45
New Yorker, Arendt's reporting in, 25
Norman, Montague, 129n35
Novick, Peter, 33, 34, 132n17, 135n42; on
    teaching of Holocaust, 151n85
Nuremberg (Germany), symbolism of,
    14, 129n41

Preparata, Guido Giacomo, 128n35
propaganda: American military, 95;
    Nazi, 99, 118
Pryor, William C., 102
psychiatric patients, Nazi murder of,
    51
Pulitzer, Joseph, 156n29
punch card machines, Nazi use of,
    14–15, 129n42

racism: role in totalitarianism, 41, 42;
    scientific, 42, 45, 61, 111; state, 19
Reagan, Ronald: Bitburg cemetery
    visit, 69–70; support for Israel,
    147n26
reality: in historic scholarship, 59–60;
    in law, 14; political creation of, 5–7;
    relationship of totalitarianism to, 7
relativism, September 11 attacks and,
    2–3, 4
Reserve Police Battalion 101, 146n9
responsibility, individual, 68; Arendt
    on, 25
Reveh, Judge, 120, 121
Riefenstahl, Leni, 159n54
Rieff, David, 37
Ring, Jennifer, 31, 32, 133n25
Robinson, Jacob, 33, 133n29
Roosevelt, Eleanor, 147n20
Roosevelt, Franklin D., 102, 156n29;
    on castration for Nazis, 134n33; on
    postwar Germany, 156n29
Roseman, Mark, 54
Rosenblatt, Roger, 3
Rosenfeld, Alvin H., 147n20
Roth, Karl Heinz, 62
Rothstein, Edward, 3
Rwanda: genocide in, 8–9, 128n33;
    post-colonial conditions in, 128n33

Sabras, versus Diaspora Jews, 135n39
sadism, in institutional settings,
    147n19

Schirach, Baulder von, 134n35
Schmidt, Anton, 81–82
Scholem, Gershom, 116, 136n48;
    Arendt's response to, 39–40
Schulberg, Bud, 99, 159n54
science: cultural assumptions
    concerning, 160n66; Nazi, 14. See
    also racism, scientific
Security Police (SD), exterminations
    by, 53
seeing: at Nuremberg trials, 22;
    technologies of, 124
self-examination: Arendt on, 74–77;
    Socrates on, 75–76
September 11 attacks: and discourse of
    relativism, 2–3, 4; effect on political
    life, 1; moral clarity concerning, 5;
    public discourse on, 3–5
Sereny, Gitta, 149n60, 150n76
Shandler, Jeffrey, 17, 132n16, 151n90
Simon Wiesenthal Center, 147n26
Sivan, Eyal, 20, 85. See also The
    Specialist: Portrait of a Modern
    Criminal
Sobibor (extermination camp),
    142n53, 150n76; prisoner uprising
    at, 144n79
Socrates, 149n54, 161n4; on self-
    examination, 75–76
Soviet Russia: on causes of war, 156n35;
    concentration camp footage from,
    99, 100, 157n38; German invasion of,
    45, 141n42; German nonaggression
    pact with, 45, 47; overpopulation
    in, 140n37; starvation in, 49
The Specialist: Portrait of a Modern
    Criminal (Sivan and Brauman), 20,
    84–90; critics of, 152n90; editing
    of, 84–85, 151n83; raw footage of,
    131n58; sound track of, 151n83;
    special effects of, 151n83
Sprecher, Drexel A., 156n34
Srebenica massacre (1995), 130n57

The Stalags (pulp fiction series), 134n38

Stalin, Joseph: overpopulation policy of, 140n37; on postwar Germany, 156n29

Stalinism, Arendt on, 138n10

statecraft, modern: management tools of, 63

state power: Arendt on, 138n11; illegitimate use of, 67; role of capital accumulation in, 138n11

Steinberg, Jules, 133n29

Stevens, George, 99

Steven Spielberg Jewish Film Archive, 20, 84

Storfer, Bernard, 79–80

Strangl, Franz, 150n76

Streicher, Julius, 110, 134n35

Struk, Janina, 152n85

subject formation, Arendt on, 122

suffering, production of, 11, 127n31

survivors, Holocaust: at Eichmann trial, 24, 40, 81–82, 131n2; at Nuremberg International Military Tribunal, 17–18, 100; vigilantism of, 29

Suskind, Ron, 5, 6

Svendsen, Lars, 137n57

Szondi, Leopold, 148n36

Tagg, John, 102

Taylor, Telford, 14, 97; on Nuremberg documentaries, 100; on Nuremberg ethos, 96

Ten Commandments, 16

The Tenth Level (movie), 146n10

terror, 138n12; Arendt on, 138n13; complicity with, 30; ethical perspectives on, 3; rationality in, 4; reductive discourse of, 4; resistance to, 82; role in totalitarianism, 42, 43

thinking: and acting, 64; Arendt on, 74–77, 114–15, 149n51, 161nnn2,4;

critical, 75–77; dangerous, 76–77; Eichmann's inability in, 72–73, 74, 77–78, 82; humanity through, 76; maieutic function of, 161n4; non-cognitive, 77; political consequences of, 114; in problem of evil, 161n6; solitude in, 149n51; uses of, 114–15

Thor, Rebecka, 131n58

thoughtlessness: apathy of, 20; Arendt on, 19–20, 26, 114, 130n57; in banality of evil, 77; and capacity for evil, 17, 19–20, 26; dangers of, 161n2; Eichmann's, 25–26, 77–78, 80–81, 90–91, 115; and intelligence, 82–83; Mladic's, 130n57; of radical evil, 120

Thucydides, 6

Tocqueville, Alexis de, 67

totalitarianism: Arendt on, 7, 41–43, 56, 118–20, 123, 127n29; authentic, 119–20; constitutive principles of, 41–43; demonic dimensions of, 120; emergence of, 41–42; empathy and, 74; as historical rupture, 119; ideology in, 42, 43, 117–18; legacy of, 7; logicality of, 42, 44, 56; pan-nationalist movements and, 41, 42, 127n29; population management in, 42; radical evil of, 162n11; relationship to reality, 7; role of capitalism in, 41, 127n29; role of imperialism in, 118–19; role of racism in, 41, 42; role of terror in, 42, 43; and self-interest, 118; survival, 16, 123–24; techniques of, 7, 119, 123

Treblinka (extermination camp), 142n53, 150n76; prisoner uprising at, 144n79

Tryster, Hillel, 151n83

Umwandererzentralstelle (UWZ), 139n27

About the Author

Valerie Hartouni is Professor of Communication at the University of California, San Diego, and author of *Cultural Conceptions: On Reproductive Technologies and the Remaking of Life* (1997).